Best wishes!

Don't Just Stand There – Sell Something

by

Stu Schlackman
with
T.C. Hayes

authorHOUSE

1663 LIBERTY DRIVE, SUITE 200
BLOOMINGTON, INDIANA 47403
(800) 839-8640
www.authorhouse.com

First published by AuthorHouse 06/13/05

ISBN: 1-4184-9663-4 (sc)

Printed in the United States of America
Bloomington, Indiana

This book is printed on acid-free paper.

Don't Just Stand There – Sell Something

by

Stu Schlackman
with
T.C. Hayes

authorHOUSE

1663 Liberty Drive, Suite 200
Bloomington, Indiana 47403
(800) 839-8640
www.authorhouse.com

First published by AuthorHouse 06/01/05

ISBN: 1-4184-9663-4 (sc)
ISBN: 1-4184-9662-6 (dj)

Printed in the United States of America
Bloomington, Indiana

This book is printed on acid-free paper.

Don't Just Stand There – Sell Something

Contents

This book is dedicated to my wonderful wife Betty, who has been a constant source of support and encouragement.

And thanks to my good friend Trevor Hayes for working with me to put this book together.

Stu Schlackman

Introduction

I remember a time in the not-too-distant past when many sales managers in high-tech industries had an easy job just tracking sales, updating forecasts and giving out awards to their overachieving sales reps. Many technology markets were new and the demand was much greater than the supply. Those were times when sales people could earn a living picking up purchase orders every week without really having to *sell*.

Perhaps times like those will roll around again – but don't bank on it. In most industries today, competition is fiercer than ever, and customers are more knowledgeable and more demanding. Sales people need to be credible, convincing and capable. Sales managers need to be effective coaches, strong leaders, and competent managers. They need to understand the challenges faced by their sales teams and be there to help them succeed. There is no room for passengers, or for klinks.

A klink is an inept manager with limited management skills, no leadership talent, and the ability to get almost everything exactly wrong. Klinks have always been with us, but in today's highly competitive environment they are more of a liability than ever before.

No one has to be a klink. Sales managers and team leaders can choose to be SMART instead. People can choose to do better – but only if they know that there is a better way, and if they know the traps to avoid. In this book I try to help corporate sales managers who want to lead successful teams, sales reps who aspire to be sales managers, and executives who are responsible for recruiting sales managers.

Everything in this book is based on my years of experience as a sales rep, as a sales team leader, and as a sales trainer in the world of telecommunications and computer software, hardware and services. But the messages are relevant to anyone who is involved in business-to-business technology or solution sales at any level and in any industry. I started out as an engineer, not as a sales person, and I admit that at first I didn't really appreciate how vital a role sales people played. As a sales person, I soon found out that being in sales was more challenging and frustrating than I had imagined. But I also learned that sales can be exciting, interesting and worthwhile.

To be successful, businesses need effective sales people. To be effective, sales people must have good leaders. What qualities does a good sales team leader need today? Having toiled over twenty years as a sales professional, I believe I have some answers to that question. And that's why I wrote this book.

Stu Schlackman, July, 2004

x

Chapter 1
Sales Management is Important

Companies often seem to undervalue the role of sales managers and sales team leaders. Yet businesses can't succeed without selling their goods and services; and selling needs talented and effective sales professionals.

Sales management is important because it is impossible to attract and retain the right quality of sales person without having the right quality of sales management.

Is that so difficult?

Why Bosses Still Matter

Some years ago when I was new to the sales profession, I had a boss who was a great example of how *not* to be a sales manager.

What I needed as a sales neophyte was advice and practical support. I needed to learn – and learn fast, because in sales, then as today, if you don't sell, you eat in roadside diners, not in upscale restaurants.

What I needed was an introduction to the tools of the trade, some advice on how to make good contacts, get appointments, structure proposals and close deals. I needed to know how to work out which prospects might lead to something and which were more likely to lead to dead ends. I needed to understand how to quickly and accurately assess the competition and come up with a proposition that would lead to a successful deal.

Instead of help and support, what I got from my boss was: "Don't just stand there – sell something."

I also got lectures on how important it was to submit my weekly list of calls, list of prospects, and forecasts of closing dates and projected revenues.

I soon found that my boss was pretty much like quite a few other sales managers. They belong to the "klink" school of clueless management.[1] Klinks are managers who range in capability from inept to dangerous. They are often insensitive to the disruption they cause, and invariably have no idea how clueless they really are. Like too many new sales reps, I had to decide not to rely on my boss for any help, and worked out my own path forward. I read some books and went to some helpful seminars. I spent time with more experienced sales people and they helped me learn the profession. They helped me understand that the most successful sales people combine the right attitude to the job with skills in building relationships. They taught me a host of other tricks of the trade that otherwise I would have had to learn by making mistakes.

> *Klinks are managers who range in capability from inept to dangerous.*

Along the way I encountered one or two bosses who showed me that things could be different. They actively coached the less experienced people in their teams. They were valuable partners in the

---

[1] Why "klink"? It just sounds right. I was possibly subliminally influenced by the character of Colonel Klink in the sixties TV series *Hogan's Heroes*.

sales effort, working closely with beginners and veterans alike. Two people trading ideas and working out tactics will always come out with something more effective than one person working alone.[2] The way these enlightened bosses participated in the sales process was the exact opposite of the clueless klink I encountered on my first day in sales.

My experience has left me smarter in many ways. But I am still not smart enough to answer this question: "Why do so many large companies recruit and retain sales managers who are clearly incompetent?"

My fear is that things are getting worse. I see more klinks entering sales at the management level with only shallow sales experience, no idea of leadership and no clue how to create a successful sales team. Often these people appear to succeed because they are lucky enough to have a few experienced people around them who continue to deliver despite the obstacles put in their way.

In today's business world, especially in my world of technology solutions, having good products and services is important, but it's never enough. Every company has to compete for the attention of customers and for their dollars. Every company has to *sell*. Sales success drives business success – everyone claims to recognize that. But sales success ultimately needs much more than a simplistic package of incentives and penalties, wielded by a klink who adds no value to the business.

Companies must sell to survive. The success of sales people is profoundly influenced by the way their teams are managed. If sales people are successful, it's because they have bright, enthusiastic and totally supportive management around them; or else they have worked out how to counteract the worst efforts of a short-sighted and dim-witted management "sales prevention expert".

Poor sales management costs companies money and can undermine any strategic plan no matter how smart top executives think they are.

> *Poor sales management costs companies money and can undermine any strategic plan...*

Sales management matters, and sales leadership matters.

Leadership is not the same as management. Strong leadership is essential for the health of any enterprise that wants to improve and

---

[2] To avoid misunderstanding let me say that a team of one can be OK, but two in a team is always better. Three is good too. Eighteen extremely smart people all working on a single sales strategy could bring disaster.

evolve to meet new challenges in a changing environment. Sound management is essential for the effective day-to-day running of any business operation.

While leadership and management may be different things, leaders and managers aren't necessarily different people. The best leaders have good management skills too: they are not just visionaries, but can also turn that vision into a pragmatic plan for change and make it happen. The best managers have some leadership skills: they manage the day-to-day operations with care and professionalism, and achieve good business results. But at the same time they are always tuned in to opportunities to make things run better, and have the strength of character to change things when needed.

Leadership involves questioning the status quo. Management means understanding the current or planned way that things should be done, and executing according to the plan.

Leaders focus on the longer term and create positive and possibly original visions for the future. The timeframe for management priorities is generally shorter, and so managers concentrate on more immediate operational challenges. Leaders answer the question "What is the right thing to do next?" Managers answer the question "How should we do this thing right – right now?"

Managers make sure people are equipped, trained and empowered to do their jobs, repeatedly, day after day, and achieve the results the business expects. Leaders inspire people to rise to challenges, to persist against adversity and to achieve things they ordinarily would not have thought possible.

Managers drive for consistent performance and predictability. This results in a stable environment that delivers good results for the business. The role of the leader is to push for change, which causes short-term uncertainty and perhaps some disruption, but leads to a new stable environment that delivers even better results for the business.

In most organizations, everyone recognizes the "leaders". Others are clearly in "manager" roles. But despite the labels, everyone will, or should, display forward-looking leadership and sound management together, to some degree. The most valuable people in the management structure of a company are people who know how to lead, and know how to manage, and have the wisdom to know which approach is better in each and every situation. This is especially true in the sales organization.

Selling is not a mechanistic predictable process. Taking a prospect from cold call to closure is one of the most complex and least predictable processes in business. Selling is essentially a human activity. Humans make decisions based on information supplied by other humans (at least for the foreseeable future). Innovation in sales is not simply about automating the process or gathering numbers more efficiently. Competence in sales is not just about working a well-defined methodology. It should be about understanding what makes people buy a product from one person rather from another. This is a science *and* an art, involving understanding of psychology and motivation. Managing sales involves making subjective judgments based on an understanding of the true nature of this complex process.

Any sales manager who does not have some essential leadership skills cannot cope with the unpredictability of the sales process, and the richly human nature of the activity. Mere administration and supervision cannot cope with the variety and unpredictability of the sales activity. Equally, someone who tries to lead a sales team purely by exhortation and charisma will stumble, because some honest-to-goodness management qualities are needed too. This applies to everyone at every level in the business hierarchy, from first line team manager to the board executive.

Every sales manager must be a leader too. I prefer to call these people "sales leader-managers". (It's a bit clumsy, but I'll use it until someone comes up with a more satisfactory title.)

The best sales leader-managers blend leadership talent and management skills in a way that makes their sales team bounce with enthusiasm and energy, but in a controlled way, so that energy is not wasted on no-hope opportunities.

Leader-managers create environments that encourage their team members to express their views, and to give feedback to management and colleagues. They are creative themselves and they welcome new ideas from their

> *Leader-managers*
> *…want their team to*
> *be around for the*
> *long haul…*

team members. They encourage growth and development of their people. They want their team to be around for the long haul, not just a year or two.

Leader-managers use their talents to motivate in two ways: to help people rise to the immediate challenge of achieving the best possible results in whatever situation they find themselves; and also to encourage people to find new and better ways of doing things, to create even more success in the longer term. Leader-managers view their people as highly valuable company assets. They take their stewardship of those company assets very seriously, and nurture them.

Leader-managers are ready to make the right decisions, even unpopular ones. Their decisions carefully balance longer-term opportunities and short-term imperatives. They think through the impact of their decisions, but they don't agonize unnecessarily. When a decision has to be made, they make it.

Sometimes that leads to other people getting upset. Most of us don't *like* to upset other people. That's what makes some decisions tough to make. But sometimes a leader has to make a tough decision, and a good leader will know exactly when to do that, without hesitation. Sometimes the welfare of the team must take precedence over the feelings of an individual. Sometimes the future of the company must take precedence over the preferences of your team. If you're really doing your job as a sales team leader then now and again you'll upset someone.

I've seen too many managers dither over important decisions because they rate being liked higher than being effective. The result is they end up making people angry anyway, because the smart, creative and enthusiastic people in the team get frustrated at the inaction and ineptitude of their klinkish manager. If you try all the time to make the sort of decisions that will make everyone like you, then you're guaranteed to be unpopular.

> *If you try to make the sort of decisions that will make everyone like you, then you're guaranteed to be unpopular.*

The Rise of the Klinks

I've known a few sales leaders who actually played on the same team as their sales professionals. They jumped in there with you, understood the obstacles you faced and sat on the same side of the desk with you. They knew you and they knew your customers. They knew how to help and when to give you space. They helped you find your way around company politics, and managed the team firmly but fairly. Above all they respected who you were and appreciated what good sales people brought to the company.

Is this type of leader getting to be a rare species? It seems that increased pressure to perform, more intense competition, rapidly changing markets, accelerated innovation in products and services – all these things have rolled a sense of urgency down the organization. Yet – it seems to me – in this more demanding environment, the quality and effectiveness of sales management (and therefore sales) has somehow got worse, not better.

Today, success in sales often happens in spite of the quality of sales management and leadership - not because of it.

I know we can't hold on to all the old ways of doing things – some of the old ways of doing things just don't work any more. But – and this is important – some tried and tested principles that are critical for success are being abandoned, because managers and sales people believe that in these competitive times, there just isn't time for old stuff like: building relationships, thinking ahead, being trustworthy, showing trust, respecting others.

I have observed the evolution of the sales profession from four perspectives: as a front-line sales person; as a sales trainer; as a sales manager; and (just like every one else) as a customer experiencing the subtle and not-so-subtle attempts of other sales people to sell me things: houses, cars, timeshares, stock investments and other benefits of twenty-first century civilization.

My bookshelves (and the shelves of airport bookshops) are stacked with books about how to be more successful in sales. I know lots of people who buy them and read them. And many of them are very good. Many of the ideas included in this book will already be familiar to some readers. And sure, we have some new toys to play with in the form of contact manager software and customer relationship management applications.

But most people I talk to in sales agree with my basic thesis: in too many companies the general level of competence and capability in sales management is declining, not improving.

The underlying reason for this malaise is simple: too many klinks in sales management at all levels; too many inept, clueless executives with C-level responsibility for sales, who in turn recruit inept clueless sales managers.

Bright, enthusiastic, capable people like to work for bright, enthusiastic, capable people and they will always try to avoid the klinks. In some companies it seems that a spiral of decline in sales talent has been going on, inexorably, for twenty years or more. All of the capable sales people I have talked to while

> *Bright, enthusiastic, capable people like to work for bright, enthusiastic, capable people.*

preparing this book agree with me: the rise of the klinks is real, and in many companies there's no sign of it going away, and sometimes no sign that the company knows they have a problem.

However, one company's problem is another company's opportunity. Some companies, even some giant corporations, have highly effective sales teams. Some people know how to do it right. When you look at companies that succeed best in sales, the common characteristics leap out: relatively low turnover of sales people, an emphasis on professional standards – and an absence of klinks in the sales management hierarchy.

Klinks are special people. In this section I am going to describe the species in more detail and I'll expand on some of their more notable characteristics later on in the book.

In the previous section we just looked at managers and leaders. Sales management needs elements of strong leadership and sound management to be successful. Klinks are a special type of leader-manager: they are weak leaders and they are inept managers.

Almost everyone I have discussed this with immediately recognizes klink-like behavior. Most people in business have come across someone, who, more or less, is a klink. (Warning: if you're sure you've never met a klink, you might be one.)

It is possible for klinks to have a certain amount of modest success in undemanding roles, for a time. A barely competent person can sometimes be lucky enough to land as leader of a team that benefits from a continuing stream of repeat business from established clients. If the klink inherits a team of energetic and capable reps, no one higher up will notice that the new manager is adding no value, at least for a while.

In the interests of fairness and balance, I should point out that very few people are complete klinks. It's usually possible to find some worth in almost everyone. Someone may be a charismatic presenter even if their ideas are nonsense. Even if someone is not capable of developing a business plan, they can always buy the team a fine meal to celebrate its completion.

The complete klink may be a rarity, but klink-like behavior is very common. Here are the main features of klinkness that I have identified:

- Some klinks believe that only wimps think things through, plan ahead, weigh options, and try to understand the potential impact of their actions.

- Other klinks do the opposite – they over-plan. They spend so much time gathering data and weighing options that they never make decisions. The planning process never actually ends in a usable plan of action.

- Klinks display a lack of understanding of the real reasons why forecasts and budgets are important to a business, and cannot apply the fine balance of objective measures and subjective judgments needed to run a sales team.

- Klinks have no ability to tell the difference between useful improvement and unnecessary change. Some klinks combine this with an arrogance that prevents them learning from the experience of others.

- Klinks are impatient for good results, but don't have a clue how to help their team succeed. Klinks always are quick to complain about poor results without any interest in *why* results might not be good or what to do about it. Klinks don't like to visit customers to find out what's really going on out there.

- Klinks have a one-dimensional approach to employee motivation, mainly along the lines of: "If you don't deliver, you're gone." Klinks berate, rather than encourage, support and coach. Klinks focus on weaknesses not on strengths.

- Klinks do not trust their subordinates, so they feel a need to control and direct everything in minute detail.

- Klinks often ignore valuable suggestions from their team.

- Klinks constantly worry about what upper management thinks of them. They do everything they can to avoid taking responsibility for problems, and somehow manage to claim responsibility for every success. They will shift blame anywhere else, even onto their own team, rather than face it themselves.

Of course, klinks pop up everywhere, not just in sales. Throughout industry they provide competent managers with lots of opportunities to shine by fixing the problems caused by klinkish cluelessness.

Klinks provide worker bees[3] with a continuous source of amusement. Talk to field engineers, sales reps and customer service representatives for a while and you'll eventually uncover a rich seam of jokes and anecdotes concerning the favorite klinks in their organization. Worker bees always give klinks a witty nickname.

Klinkish management ineptitude causes a problem for everyone in their team and costs the business money: lower productivity, high staff turnover, lost revenue opportunities. Sometimes a good team can work around the defects of the klink-in-command and succeed in spite of everything – but at a cost. Having klinks in the company may be good for the humor mill, but it's bad for the health of the business.

Here is a quote from Peter Drucker that really rings true for me: "By and large, executives make poor promotions and staffing decisions. By all accounts, their batting average is no better than 0.333. At most, one-third of such decisions turn out right, one-third are minimally effective, and one-third are outright failures. In no other area would we put up with such miserable performance; indeed, we need not and should not. Managers making people decisions will never be perfect, of course, but they should come pretty close to batting 1.000". [4]

When it comes to recruitment of sales managers my experience completely confirms Drucker's assertion.

Some companies repeatedly employ klinks, who are at best ineffective, and at worst get in the way of people trying to do a good job. On the other hand, some companies seem to do OK, recruiting sound professionals into sales management jobs. What makes the difference?

There's no single answer and there's no simple answer. Over the years I have observed a number of phenomena that may help to explain it.

Sometimes, in the search for a fresh idea, companies will recruit people into sales management who have minimal sales experience - no feel for sales, no idea of the challenges and inspiration involved in selling successfully, no inkling of how to win a customer. Or they may bring people in who know nothing about the needs and aspirations of

---

[3] This term is a compliment. People who do real productive work of value to customers are still of immense value even in this age of automation. Worker bees make the honey.
[4] Originally in Harvard Business Review, quoted in *The Essential Drucker*, Peter Drucker (Harper Business, 2001).

the customers in that industry. It's easy to think up a fresh idea if you know nothing.

If you're a company executive responsible for recruiting sales managers, you should think objectively about this, and weigh the advantages of freshness against those of appropriate experience. If you are thinking about recruiting a sales neophyte to a sales management position, my instant advice is: "Don't do it."

> *If you are thinking about recruiting a sales neophyte to a sales management position, my instant advice is: "Don't do it."*

But, the executive might claim, maybe this is a special case – you've found someone with great management skills and solid industry experience, who wants to make a move into sales. Still, you really should make sure that every sales manager has experience in an active selling role before placing him or her in charge of one of your valuable sales teams. Arrange for at least a couple of months on the road with a sales veteran to make sure the new person has some grasp of the basics of selling.

The investment will pay off: either the insights will make them more capable managers, less likely to be constantly mocked by their subordinates; or else they will decide to choose a different career path, thus relieving you of the need to fire them later.

Problems also arise when executives fall into the trap of equating good performance in one job with the potential to handle a job one level up in the hierarchy. Too many sales managers turn out to be people who have been promoted to their "level of incompetence".[5] Just because someone is a competent sales rep, that doesn't mean he or she can become a competent sales manager. It's a good start, necessary, but not sufficient.

Another way in which the wrong people can find their way into sales management roles is because the people who do the selection have very limited ability to probe beneath the surface so they can find out what a person is really capable of achieving. Either they have never been trained in interview techniques, or they simply aren't any good at it.

The solution? Every executive who is expected to make recruitment or promotion decisions should receive formal training in the tools and techniques of interviewing and selection. This training should not be reserved just for people in HR. Executives ought to participate in recruitment and promotion decisions, but only if they

---

[5] Described in much greater detail by Dr. Laurence J. Peter and Raymond Hull in *The Peter Principle* (William Morrow 1969).

understand the basics of how to do it so as to obtain good results. Recruitment is not as easy as it looks, and this is one area where most companies could benefit from an investment in skills training. The best training courses have practical sessions and a rigorous assessment. (Yes - it's possible to *fail* these courses.) If companies could insist that every recruitment and promotion decision could be made by people who have learned some of the tools and techniques of evaluation, perhaps we'd see fewer klinks in sales management roles.

Finally, we have a persistent problem that even training might not cure: klinks recruit klinks. Some executives look for people who are just like them, and if they happen to be a klink, then another klink can appear in the business, even if this person is not right for the job. This tendency is reinforced by another

> *...we have a persistent problem that even training might not cure: klinks recruit klinks.*

klinkish trait: distrust of talent. Some executives don't like the idea that someone who works for them might be brighter, more experienced or more talented than they are. The easiest thing for them is to recruit someone dull.

This sets in motion the downward spiral towards a company dominated by klinks: a klinkdom.

The downward spiral is a phenomenon that is interesting to observe from a distance, but it's frightening when you get too close. Sometimes it just takes one big mistake - for example, the recruitment of one new VP of Sales, who has had modest success in a previous role, thanks to a supportive team living on repeat business.

Imagine this new VP, tackling the new role with gusto, starting off by importing some of the people recently left behind in his old company. This is astonishingly common. People know what worked for them before and they strive to recreate the old environment in which they were warm and comfortable. Some of those imports may be capable people, others less so, and one or two may be klinks. The klinks recruit more klinks. To make room, some established sales veterans are let go. A proliferation of klinkish behavior creates rising uncertainty and tension. The team loses its sense of direction and focus. At this point, the downward spiral is well under way. Good people leave. The klinks recruit more klinks. I don't have to fill in further details - you've probably seen something like this yourself.

Senior executives need to remember that it is so much easier to demolish a productive culture than to build one. Inserting just one klink near the top of the sales management hierarchy can start the

13

downward spiral towards klinkdom. So if you are an executive with responsibility for recruiting sales managers in your company, then please take this responsibility seriously. If your normal list of evaluation criteria includes only the usual things like: skilled with spreadsheets; expert user of a PDA; belongs to the CEO's golf club; and so on, then you maybe need some more stringent standards. Reading the rest of this book will give you some clues what to look for.

Being SMART in Sales Management

Not all managers are klinks. Some are *SMART*. I use the acronym 'SMART' for the five areas in which people need to excel to become outstanding sales team leaders:

- Skills: being expert in the skills that your team needs to sell successfully, and being able to coach your team in those skills.

- Motivational Management: directing and controlling day-to-day activities of the team, and motivating them to perform their best.

- Attitude: bringing a positive, supportive and success-oriented leadership approach that stimulates and motivates team members.

- Relationships: building sustainable, trust-based relationships with team members, customers and business partners.

- Thinking: applying brain cells to the planning and organizing the team and its work.

Skills, Motivational Management, Attitude, Relationships, Thinking: get all five right, and you've got what it takes to become a SMART sales manager or sales team leader.

Each one of these topics is discussed in a separate chapter later in this book. Naturally, life is not always as convenient and nicely packaged as we sometimes hope, and I've chosen to present the chapters in a more logical order: Attitude, Skills, Relationships, Thinking and Management. This spells ASRTM. Please don't look it up. It's not a word.

Attitude and Skills provide the foundation for all sales activities. Those need to be in place to provide a foundation for building Relationships, which lies at the heart of the business. Thinking and Managing go together – broadly this is about planning, then doing, preferably in that order.

Sales is not an easy profession to succeed in. Being a sales manager is every bit as challenging and demanding as being a sales person in the field. (Sales managers have one big advantage over sales reps: a sales manager finds it easier to blame other people when things go wrong.)

But as in so many other walks of life, when you make it as a SMART sales manager, it's exhilarating, rewarding, and worth the struggle. In this book I aim to give you insights into SMART behavior and attitudes, so you and your team can do more things better. At the same time I'd like to warn you against the sort of behaviors and attitudes that characterize the klinks among us.

Becoming SMART in Sales Management is what the rest of this book is all about.

Being SMART is not just the absence of klinkishness. Effective sales management needs a whole array of positive attributes.

I learned a lot about SMART leadership from my former boss Don Jones. I worked in his team back in the eighties, and his lead-from-the-front approach was what made our team the most committed, energetic and successful in the company. His leadership skills provided a great role model for me and for other team members. He's now one of my best friends but even so I still have to admit he was an outstanding sales team leader.

Not all sales managers know much about selling. Don had been in field sales long enough to understand the tools and techniques of selling, and he was an accomplished sales person in his own right. He was a natural coach and was always keen to pass on his knowledge and understanding to team members.

He never stopped reading, experimenting and learning, so that he could continue to grow and adapt his skills as the business grew and evolved.

As a motivational manager, Don was a natural. He respected every team member, encouraged people to accept responsibility and to be accountable to the others for their actions or decisions.

He generated a positive team spirit, which created success, which increased our enthusiasm even more. In 1986 Don's sales team was number one in the region at 286% of forecast. This was previously unheard of in the company. At the same time Don made sure we played by the rules. All the business was solidly and cleanly earned. No playing games with the numbers, and no playing games with the customers.

Don's commitment was to his customers and to his team. This made him outstandingly successful. But he wasn't always popular with top management in the company. His goal was to break down the corporate barriers that stopped us doing our very best for our customers. In doing this he occasionally bent the rules and got into confrontational positions with company executives, but he usually got his way. He took his customers' requests to the top of the company to get them what they needed. He created a "try it and buy it" program – an innovative demo development system – and persuaded the company to support it, against some skepticism. He managed to arrange a four-day training and celebration session on Cape Cod for us, when all the other sales teams had a token one-day session back at home base. On one memorable occasion, he laid his job on the line to get his team the rewards he felt we deserved.

He always told his team that he was "here to help and support you", but unlike many sales managers, he actually did it, often and with enthusiasm.

Don was always interested in meeting with customers, and loved to talk with them. Although he lived in Memphis, about 250 miles away, he visited me and my customers in Birmingham at least three times a month, and spent face-to-face time with customers at every opportunity. He was always asking them questions, showing his interest in their business, building personal relationships, and looking for ways to help them with their issues.

He worked with us to plan campaigns, and worked with us to initiate, negotiate and close deals. Our sales drives set the standard and the pace for the entire company, and it was a great experience to be on his team and to share in the success.

I have seen Don operating in different locations and different companies over the last fifteen years – always with the same, successful results.

Reading this, you might think that Don was close to perfection as a sales manager. Well, mostly he did things that worked, and he hardly ever did things that didn't work. Above all, Don was ideally suited for the role: he had the right personality and attitude, and the whole business of selling fascinated and energized him. The combination could be described as nearly perfect, but I'd prefer to describe him as just really, really good at his job.

This brings us back to a basic and very important principle. Not everyone is cut out to be in sales, just like not everyone is ideally suited to being a brain surgeon, a navy seal, a gardener or a hypnotist.

Not everyone is cut out to be in sales, just like not everyone is ideally suited to being a brain surgeon, a navy seal, a gardener or a hypnotist.

Yet many people seem to be unaware that sales is a profession that needs very special skills and aptitudes. Maybe this is because everyone seems to know someone who is in sales, and everyone interacts with sales people from time to time – everyone buys stuff. So people think they know how the sales process works. But just because I went to a clinic to get my back fixed doesn't qualify me to be an orthopedic surgeon. And just because someone has bought a car or a house doesn't give them the insights or knowledge needed to sell a complex technical solution to a multinational corporation.

17

Don chose to enter a profession for which his way of thinking and his attitude to life fitted perfectly, and so he became an outstanding sales manager. If he had somehow ended up as, for example, a tree surgeon, it might not have worked out so well.

People who find themselves in the sales profession without any clear idea how they got there, who don't understand what it takes to succeed, and have no real enthusiasm for the art of selling, are destined to be mediocre performers, or worse.

Companies should never recruit people into sales management unless there is good reason to believe that they understand what they are getting into, have demonstrable selling skills, know how to manage and motivate people, have a positive attitude towards the business and its customers, and have ample capability of thinking things through.

If you are a sales manager, or aspire to be one, and you think you have what it takes, then Chapters 2 to 6 will fill in more of the details of what it really takes to become a SMART sales team leader, leading a successful team.

Chapter 2
Attitude

If you want to be successful in sales and in sales management then you and your team need the sort of attitude to business and life that will create success, not an attitude that gets in the way.

You and your team need: Optimism, Persistence, Enthusiasm, Resilience and a certain amount of Affability.

Attitude is not just an optional extra. Having the right attitude lays the foundation for building relationships, acquiring skills, and everything else that's important in a sales career.

The Right Attitude

How can a sales manager train someone to 'have the right attitude'? My experience tells me that the most successful approach is to set a good example. If the sales manager has the right attitude, chances are the team will come to have the right attitude too.

Simply *talking about* 'attitude' usually has only a slight effect, if any. Unless accompanied by a good example, berating and preaching often makes attitudes more cynical and negative instead of filling people with optimism and enthusiasm.

In my experience the best way to encourage people to be positive and upbeat is – to be positive and upbeat yourself. It is difficult to instruct people on 'attitude' but people can certainly learn it by example

As a sales team manager, you are always on show for your team. Even if you try to hide away in your office, that behavior tells them something about you – and your attitude.

> *The best way to encourage people to be positive and upbeat is to be positive and upbeat yourself...*
> *As a sales manager, you are always on show for your team. Even if you try to hide away in your office, that behavior tells them something about you – and your attitude.*

Have you ever met a sales person with an attitude problem? Of course you have. Ever met a *really good* sales person with an attitude problem? Nope. Every successful sales person I've known has shown above-average levels of optimism, persistence, enthusiasm, resilience and affability. This is where it really does help to be a 'natural'. Let's face it, whether it's upbringing, or in the genes or some mixture of the two, some people just have the right combination of these attributes to be successful in sales.

Do you have the right attitude? Are you able to convey the right attitude to your team?

Let's think about the arena of high-tech products and services. A few years ago, it was *easy* for a high-tech sales person to have a positive attitude. Back in the eighties and early nineties during the computer boom and Internet explosion, just about everyone was successful in high-tech sales – the vast majority of sales professionals made or exceeded their sales targets for several years in a row. There was great demand for computer hardware, communications services, software solutions and services. Technology was hot and everyone wanted it. I can remember the days when a customer would have to order a system nine months in advance and they were willing to wait! Under these circumstances it was easy to have a positive attitude.

Today it's a different story. Companies have already invested heavily in technology products and services, and are reluctant to spend more until they have squeezed as much value as possible from those investments. Clients have much more knowledge of technology than ever before and are more sophisticated and skeptical when selecting technology (which is undoubtedly a good thing for their businesses).

Negotiations are tougher, decision delays are longer, competition is more intense, margins are slimmer. Altogether, life as a sales person in the world of high tech complex sales is much less fun than it used to be. Looking around the industry, I see so many people who used to be up-beat now looking beat-up instead. Companies are turning over their sales professionals much faster, with some people having to find new positions every couple of years.

One of the attributes that a good sales person must have is to retain a positive attitude, even in the midst of all this adversity. And one of the attributes that a good sales manager must have is the ability to motivate and inspire the team so that they maintain their enthusiasm.

For sales professionals to succeed, the right attitude is essential. The way a sales person behaves is influenced by his or her attitude to the job and the customer, and this behavior is discerned directly by the customer. If a sales person says one thing and does another, then customers notice.

When the sales person has a positive attitude, the customer's attitude to the sales person becomes positive too. The customer perceives someone who will work to deliver, and will cajole and influence others in the customer's interest. They see someone who will get excited about their company and strive energetically to meet their goals and solve their problems. Having a positive attitude engenders customer confidence. Customers want to do business with people who have a can-do attitude, are flexible, come across concerned to help them achieve their goals and are always looking for the win-win solution.

> *When the sales person has a positive attitude, the customer's attitude to the sales person becomes positive too.*

What are the key characteristics of someone with the 'right' attitude? They are the OPERA characteristics:

- Optimism
- Persistence
- Enthusiasm
- Resilience
- Affability.

Put all these together in one sales person and we undoubtedly have someone with a positive approach towards the job and the customer.

It is the job of the sales manager to encourage a positive attitude in every member of the team, including the unsung heroes who provide support and sustenance to the front-line sales reps. And the first step in creating a team with a positive go-for-it attitude, is for the sales manager to have one too. A positive attitude is contagious, just like a smile.

The starting point for a positive attitude to the world is a positive attitude to yourself. Having a positive attitude starts with who you think you are and how you feel about yourself. Think about it. Someone who has low self-esteem will find it really hard work to be (or to appear to be) consistently optimistic, persistent, enthusiastic, resilient and affable. Solid self-esteem is the platform on which positive attitudes must be built.

People are mostly likely to have strong self-esteem if they know that they are valued by colleagues and by customers; if they work in an environment in which commitment and strong ethical values are seen as assets; and if the work environment allows some room for enjoyment and self-expression.

It is important for a sales manager to provide regular self-esteem boosts to team members. If someone has done a good job, he or she should be told so: this will help to engender a positive attitude more than a commission check (even). If they've somehow messed up, that should not be ignored, because if you ignore it, you're sending the message that it doesn't matter. But the conversation should be mainly positive: what can we do to make sure we have a more successful outcome next time? Contrary to popular belief, working through the reasons behind failure usually makes people feel better, not worse, especially if they realize they have learned something, so they will not make the same mistake again.

People work best when there are sensible rules governing behavior. Every sales person should understand what the rules of behavior are. Some people are surprised when I point out that clear statements of value and ethical behavior can generate a more positive attitude. But they do. I believe the reason is that clarity in this area removes a degree of uncertainty, and so allows people to make faster and more assured decisions about what to do next.[6]

At the same time managers need to allow people some room to direct the course of their everyday lives. The sort of minute-by-minute micromanagement exercised by some klink-style managers can be profoundly de-motivating.

A good sales team leader will show a reasonable amount of trust, and will also encourage people in the team to help each other. It is remarkable how contagious and useful that can be. By helping each other, and by helping customers, people can get a psychological boost that is worth much more than a bonus or a lecture from a motivational speaker. (Not that they aren't useful sometimes too.)

We really can't afford to take ourselves too seriously all the time. I always find it interesting how much better I can play a round of golf if I'm with friends who have a positive attitude and like to have fun. You don't hear many complaints about the shots, there's some laughter and kidding around and the atmosphere is relaxed. But at the end of the round my score is often quite respectable and I come to believe I have what it takes to become a good golfer one day. Yet when I work at my golf game as one of a deadly serious foursome, I never score so well, and I always feel a little dejected at the end of the game. (Not for long – I have a built-in ability to bounce-back despite these setbacks, which is why I continue to be a golf addict, I suppose.)

I almost always have a positive attitude. I am aware that not everyone is like me, and as a manager I have to try to understand what makes other people less resilient and more susceptible to gloominess.

How will you know if someone in your team has self-esteem problems? What should you do if someone in your team has self-esteem problems?

This book does not set out to make you into a trained psychologist. Sometimes meddling in people's innermost emotional processes can produce unexpected and unwanted consequences. But you should be aware that if one of your people continues to display a 'bad' attitude to the job and to customers, despite encouragement and coaching, then the underlying cause could be related to emotional problems elsewhere in that person's life. In such a case, no amount of

---

[6] Some people seem to react negatively to too much choice, and I guess that applies to ethical choices too. See Barry Schwartz, 'The Tyranny of Choice', *Scientific American*, April 2004.

cajoling, encouragement, training or acting lessons will make a long-term difference to the attitude portrayed to customers and colleagues.

You may think that people with depressive problems and low self-esteem are pretty unlikely to become sales people. But depression seems to strike all sorts of people in all walks of life. People who are bouncing with enthusiasm one week, can find themselves listless and with a feeling of hopelessness the next.

Everyone has down periods. An occasional 'down' is nothing to get too concerned about, as long as there are plenty of 'ups': after all, you're dealing with people not robots. But you should take note if one of your team seems to be persistently low in spirits. Or if someone shifts rapidly between high levels of nervous energy and periods of deep gloom. Persistent negativity and lack of commitment are signs of a problem.

The first responsibility of a manager is to take note of what is happening, and offer help. A quiet conversation sometimes reveals something in the work environment that has become an issue inflated out of all proportion: perhaps a work colleague whose behavior is becoming unacceptable or oppressive; or

> *The first responsibility ... is to take note of what is happening and offer help.*

a backlog of work that is becoming a real burden. As a manager, if there is a problem in the work environment, you should do your best to fix it.

In some cases the underlying problem may be more serious – a family issue, or mental illness. If you think this is likely to be the case, then you should encourage the person to seek help. Help can come from a variety of sources and you should not assume that only one way is best. Most large companies have access to professionals who specialize in the area of depression and mental problems and you should access those specialist resources as early as possible.

The best most of us can do is to be reasonably sympathetic, and to share whatever wisdom we think we possess.

Self-esteem and self-confidence are good things, leading as they do to a positive attitude and good sales performance.

However an *over-inflated ego* is not a good thing, at least not in sales.

Where is the boundary, and what difference does it make?

Most sales professionals have pretty good size egos, and so do company executives. When someone is successful they always feel good about who they are and what they've accomplished. This is usually all to the good.

From my perspective, someone crosses the line from mature self-esteem to over-inflated ego, when they ...

- are unwilling to listen to the advice of others;
- believe the most important opinions are their own;
- can't recognize mistakes they have made, and therefore are unable to learn from mistakes;
- blame the customer when the decision doesn't go in his or her favor;
- are convinced that the relationships they have with customers and co-workers are deeper and more substantial than they really are.

Sometimes – probably mostly – people like this were pretty good at their jobs at one time. But for them, success acted to do more than bolster self-esteem: it destroyed their ability to be self-critical.

In some jobs, a degree of megalomania seems to be a positive advantage. (I recognize this fact without liking it particularly.) But in most sales jobs, the arrogance that accompanies too much ego is not helpful, and can cause deals to fall apart. I remember one occasion in which a customer chose to go with a competitor purely to try to puncture a particular sales person's exasperating ego. This case involved a VP of sales who was not only arrogant, he was so sure of himself that he didn't realize that having a couple of drinks right before a customer meeting might not be an appropriate thing to do.

Natural selection means that extreme and persistent cases of too much ego are somewhat rare in active sales roles. People whose ego gets in the way of success in sales, are likely to voluntarily move to jobs in which performance of measurement is less direct, or in which their self-absorption is less of a hindrance. Or else they get fired.

Now and again a sales manager has to handle an egomaniac in their sales team. But more often sales managers are faced by situations caused by sales people who forget for a few minutes to keep their egos under control. This can happen to any of us if we're not careful.

The traditional saying, "The customer is always right," is founded in an understanding of a certain reality. Argue with the customer, or make the customer look foolish, or contradict the customer's understanding of their own needs, and you're likely to lose that customer.

> *Argue with the customer, or make the customer look foolish… and you're likely to lose that customer.*

Customers value objective advice, but they don't like being told how to run their business. Customers like to be given alternative options to consider, but they don't like being contradicted.

Whenever there is a difficult message to communicate to a customer, there is usually a right way which the customer will welcome and appreciate. And there's a wrong way which tends to be confrontational, and turns the customer off. In my experience, too much ego gets in the way of empathy, which results in the wrong type of communication.

When making a customer visit, you and your team should reflect on what is driving your attitudes to that customer. And if it's going to get in the way, check any excess ego at the front door before you go in.

Optimism

I think of optimism in sales primarily as an *active* optimism: the ability to consistently expect a favorable outcome from one's actions. I contrast this with passive optimism in which someone might "expect a favorable outcome" without actually doing anything to make it happen. Someone could do this sitting on a sofa watching cartoons on TV, which seldom results in closing sales deals.

Active optimism is an essential component of a "positive attitude". A sackful of optimism is one of the most valuable assets a sales person can have. Optimism enables people to make a sales call when there's no very good reason to suppose it will lead anywhere. Optimism makes the sales person ask for a chance to bid when a competitor is already well-positioned to close the deal. Optimism can rescue an apparently hopeless situation by injecting renewed energy into the effort: "OK let's just go through these numbers one more time – there must be a way to make this work."

Optimism is the engine that enables a sales team to give 100% on every deal and not despair when they don't win 100% of deals.

> *Optimism is the engine that enables a sales team to give 100% on every deal and not despair when they don't win 100% of deals.*

Some people under-rate optimism, thinking that optimists are foolish or deluded. Statistically, the cynics have a point, but it's an empty point. In some sales jobs, people count themselves fortunate to close one deal in five. It seems to follow that four times out of five, the effort doesn't pay off, and optimism is misplaced. So if some smart analyst can tell me for sure in advance which deals will work out, then I can save my energy, right? The problem is, looking back over the many, many deals I have closed, I find it difficult to come up with a way of working out what I might have looked for at the outset to help me decide for sure which ones would come good, and which would not. In many cases, the only thing that made the difference between winning and losing was the presence of the energy generated by optimism. Once a deal has been won, it is of academic interest whether the optimism that got you there was based on reality or just on wishful thinking.

The important thing is to keep going, even when you get a 'no'. Optimism is the fuel that keeps you going. Zig Ziglar – a great optimist – told me he used to close about one out of every twenty-five deals. Every time he got a 'no' he said thank you and accepted it graciously.

He reckoned that every 'no' brought him one step closer to the one in twenty-five that was going to be a 'yes'. Optimism increases activity levels. Optimism generates persistence. Optimism leads to closed deals.

Actions driven by optimism don't always pay off, but often enough they do. Actions *prevented* by pessimism never pay off.

My friends think I am an eternal optimist. In fact, like most other people, I worry at times, and can sometimes feel gloomy. But mostly when I am faced with a troubling or challenging situation, whether in work or in my personal life, I feel compelled to make a choice: do I focus on a hoped-for upside, or on the feared downside? Just as a matter of practicality, I focus on the positive. In sales, no one ever won a deal by choosing not to compete.

There is another benefit derived by people who cultivate an optimistic attitude: it makes you, and others around you, feel so much better. I often get teased on the golf course for my unbounded optimism (not to mention my unbounded shots). When someone plays a bad shot I say something like: "Good shot – you missed the lake. Those bushes aren't too thick, I'm sure you'll have a playable shot." Even if the shot was pretty bad, they feel better about it. And laughing instead of griping really does seem to make people play better, because it dissipates tension.

Does optimism require people to become detached from reality? Some people might think so. Optimism is not about ignoring reality, or denying it. In fact the most useful type of optimism is rooted in reality. The sales optimist recognizes that where the outcome is probabilistic, any probability of success significantly greater than zero is worth thinking about.

Suppose you're working in an industry where the company you are selling for is one of five equally matched competitors. Suppose for the sake of argument that every competitor competes for every opportunity, and so (other things being equal) the chance of winning any particular job is around one fifth (20%). Looking at a specific opportunity, a pessimist might argue that with a 20% probability of success, it's not worth the effort.

On the other hand, an optimist would look at the bigger picture: "It looks like the odds are pretty much the same for everyone. OK, if we bid on the next ten jobs like this the odds of winning at least one job are… (quick flurry of calculator activity) …wow! Almost 90%.[7] I can live with those odds. In fact, chances are we'll get two out of those ten jobs. How much revenue does that give us? Sounds good to

---

[7] $P = (1 - (0.8)^{10})$

me. Now, what can we do to change those odds even more in our favor?"

The numbers are the same whoever does the math. Pessimists – not optimists – are often those who are guilty of ignoring the underlying realities.

Another important perspective on 'realism' relates to the relationship between the first line sales manager, the sales team and the executives of the company.

For the sales team and the team leader, optimism is the useful fuel that generates energy, commitment and success. It can also lead to misconceptions in the minds of upper management. I admit that upper management often only wants to hear good news and never the bad. That is a symptom of denial, not of optimism.

> *...upper management often only wants to hear good news and never the bad. That's denial, not optimism.*

Just because they want to hear the glossy version, doesn't mean that is all they should get. When reporting on sales prospects and probabilities of success, do not allow your optimism and enthusiasm to get in the way of the facts. Reality and optimism need not be in conflict.

Many times, sales reps have come to me with the news that a deal is "in the bag". They tell me "it's ours to lose". They put the probability of success at "better than ninety per cent". Closer examination reveals that the competition is strong, there's an incumbent supplier and we've only had one meeting with the customer so far. Full marks to the sales rep for enthusiasm, but zero out of ten for realism. When reps always come with good news and ignore realities, they suffer from "happy ears", which is not a good thing.

There is no benefit to be gained from hiding from the reality. In fact, it can be positively bad. It's much better for the sales rep to say something like this: "We've managed to talk to some of the decision makers, but we're behind and there's a long way to go. Still, I really believe we can pull this one off. It would really help if our CEO could pay a visit and get across some of our key messages at that level." That's optimism, but it's also realistic.

Does being an optimistic sales person mean that there are no 'bad' opportunities? Should optimism drive you to go after everything? Probably not. I suppose if the choice is between sitting with your feet on a desk doing nothing, or going after a 'no-hope' opportunity, then go for the no-hoper. But for most people life is not like that. There is a minimum amount of effort required to close any deal. If you can do justice to every opportunity, fair enough: go for them all. Usually you have to prioritize and that means saying 'no' to some opportunities.

Pessimists find it easy to say 'no' and so end up going after too few opportunities to achieve a successful flow of deals. Over-optimistic people find it difficult to say 'no' and so end up spreading their efforts across too many prospects, so that very few of their bids are successful.

Oh no, it's that balance thing again! No one said this was supposed to be easy. Even optimists have to use judgment.

How is it that optimists stay up-beat all the time? I'm generally optimistic – but always realistic. I don't expect everyone in my sales team to be bright and cheerful all the time, especially if they've listened to the early morning news on the radio on the way in to the office. A certain amount of gloom is inevitable from time to time. People who are optimistic about everything every day are rare.

While I can't expect everyone to be bouncily optimistic all day, every day, I *do* expect everyone in my team not to be *negative…*

"No can do! No Way! Impossible!" My eyes start to roll in my head. I really find it hard to be patient with persistent negativity. "My customers are all going away, and the company is going to have layoffs next week. Next, I hear the sky is going to fall on us."

It's not just me that finds negative attitudes a turn off. Customers do not have much time for sales people who claim to be victims of circumstance. Decision-makers in corporations have plenty of problems of their own, and the last thing they need is negative vibes from someone who should be there to help them. When a customer has a problem to solve, they want a sales person to give an optimistic response – "Sure we can do something for you here. Let's work on some ideas." They don't want to hear some downbeat response like: "Well, we can probably sell you a solution, but it looks like you guys are toast anyway."

A general atmosphere of negativity can poison a sales team and even an entire company. Perhaps you have observed (or even been part of) a situation where several of the sales team would go out to lunch and the entire conversation goes something like this…

…negativity can poison a sales team and even an entire company.

"Have you heard the latest? The pressure is coming down from the top. Everyone has to be out of the office on sales calls from 10 till 4 and every day at 5 there will be a status meeting. What is management's problem? Just look at the economy. No one's buying right now. They're waiting until first quarter when new budgets come out. What do they think we will accomplish? Do you think they'll start laying off? I think it's time to polish up the résumé. They say there's going to be another reorganization. It's a waste of time calling on the accounts they gave me, when I'll be handed a whole new set of accounts I never heard of and they'll probably never buy from us anyway. Why can't the company get their act together? I have a friend at XYZ Company who is pulling down tons of business this year. We should check out to see if they have any openings. This place couldn't care less about us, just look at the turnover in the last year."

People sometimes spend so much energy complaining, they just can't be productive. Let's face it, most corporations have agendas that generally don't have "make the sales force sublimely happy" at the top of the priority list. So it's not news to me, or anyone else, that most of us are relatively unimportant to CEOs who are concerned with keeping shareholders happy and the company afloat (and, in some cases, stashing some spare cash in an offshore account). "The truth will set you free, but first it will make you miserable."[8] So please stop going on and on about it.

Some people are unhappy in every sales job they take. Some people take six or more different sales positions in two years. Sometimes they chose to move on, sometimes they were encouraged to go. This is a symptom of someone who is in the wrong job. What many people complain about is just the reality of being in sales.

I admire the persistence and optimism of farmers around the world, particularly in third-world countries. The world may be in political turmoil around them, markets in chaos, and drought a real possibility. Those farmers don't sit back and say "It's too hopeless, it's not worth the effort". No, they plant, and they tend the crops.

People in sales with chronic feelings of negativity need to consider a career change. Or else they should divert a chunk of the time and energy they spend complaining into selling more stuff, then send a few of their commission bucks to support a self-help irrigation project in the third world.

We all have a choice about how we respond to any situation. We can face up to a challenge and look at it as an opportunity to shine; or we can choose to turn away, believing the future holds no promise, so it's not worth trying.

Our choices do make a difference. When we choose wisely we help to make the future *what we want it to be*. When we choose not to choose, the future gives us what we deserve.

---

[8] James A. Garfield, twentieth President of the United States.

32

I really enjoyed *The Rookie*[9], a feel-good movie from 2002. This is the real-life story of Jim Morris, who eventually gets to fulfill his childhood dream of becoming a major league baseball pitcher despite injury and other adversity. Central to the story – for me, anyway – is the power of optimism to "make the future what we want it to be".

As a young man Jim Morris had tried out for the majors but had to quit playing the game because he injured his throwing arm at the age of twenty. As the movie opens, Jim is a thirty-five-year-old high school science teacher and baseball coach in a small West Texas town. The Big Lake baseball team doesn't have a great record of wins.

One day at practice, Jim decides to pitch for the catcher after batting practice. The catcher asks him to throw the heat. Jim does just that – and everyone in the team is amazed at how fast this thirty-five year old can still throw the baseball. The guys in the team propose a deal with Jim – if the team can win the district championship, then Jim will try out for the majors.

Jim has doubts. He says he doesn't have it anymore. Nobody in their right mind would think someone his age can try out for major league baseball and make the cut. But eventually he agrees – at least that will give the team something to aim for.

Against all the odds the team wins the district, and Jim has to fulfill his side of the deal.

At a try-out, to the amazement of all the assembled coaches, and to the delight of his son, Jim pitches at ninety-eight miles per hour. Phone calls and offers follow, and in due course, Jim – with the constant support of his wife and eight-year old son – eventually succeeds in making the major league. But there are hard times and difficulties all along the way. This is no overnight success.

The message of the movie is simple – this is Disney after all. But simple messages can still be important. For most of us, life piles up difficulties and problems. When the going gets tough, giving up always seems like an option. But optimism – and support and encouragement – can create success, against seemingly impossible odds.

Optimism can be undermined by a very normal human emotion: fear. Fear is extreme anxiety or distress caused by real or possible (or even imagined) danger or pain. There has always been a certain amount of fear around: the words "fear not" appear 366 times in the Bible.

---

[9] *The Rookie* (Walt Disney Pictures 2002). Cast included Dennis Quaid, Rachel Griffiths, Angus T. Jones.

So in what ways does the activity of selling make people fearful, or even just uncomfortably anxious? Does selling generate actual or possible danger? Not often. Can it generate pain? Certainly: losing a deal, failing to meet budget, and losing a job can cause emotional pain and hardship.

Perhaps the biggest fear for sales people lies in the fear of being rejected by their customers. Sales people need to be able to feel that they are valued by at least some customers. Maybe some sales people need to be liked, and they interpret rejection by the customer as a personal criticism. The reality is of course that sometimes customers just have to say 'no' because they really have found a better deal somewhere else. We all become anxious when we are in a situation that can lead to rejection and might hurt our self-esteem. But for some people, the anxiety felt at the prospect of rejection is close to fear.

Sales managers need to help their team face the possibility of rejection by ensuring they retain a realistic and balanced attitude towards not winning, because losing some deals is an inevitable part of the system in a competitive environment in which customers have choice. It helps to think of losing a deal as no more than that – losing a deal. Someone once told me that 'failure' is not an event; it's a judgment on an event. Sales managers need to encourage and support their teams by pointing this out sometimes.

Managers also need to ensure that when they offer criticism, it is both constructive and fair. Many sales reps have told me that persistently unfair criticism from their team leader is one of the main reasons why they became anxious, lost optimism, lost enthusiasm – and left the company.

> *Managers must ensure that when they offer criticism it is both constructive and fair.*

Managers can do a lot to maintain optimism, and a lot to destroy it. Stupid management decisions can make sales people more anxious and fearful. Unfair compensation plans, or plans that frequently change, make people worried that no matter what they do they won't make enough money. When they're anxious, they can't be optimistic about their future in the company, and so they won't have a positive attitude to customer engagements.

Managers can destroy optimism by neglecting to tell their team what is going on in the company, so they imagine things are a whole lot worse than they really are.

When we let fear take control, we can't be proactive or optimistic with the opportunities that lie before us. Fear makes us reluctant to take any risks – not just big risks but even mundane everyday risks.

Fear is the enemy of purposeful action, because if we don't take risks, we'll never do anything new.

Underlying all this is the notion that making mistakes is something always to be avoided. If fear of making mistakes is holding you back, you need to think about the reason you feel that way. What's more, if you are a sales manager and the people in your team seem to be unwilling to take any action that might be slightly risky, you need to ask yourself why that is.

People in sales, their managers, and company executives need to be very clear that in business, mistakes happen. If the attitude of management is that even a single mistake is unacceptable, then people will never make progress or try anything new. Is that what management really wants? I can understand managers wanting to fire someone who makes mistakes all the time. But I can't understand managers who are aggressively critical of people who make the occasional slip - especially when those slips are the result of honest endeavor to make progress.

In some companies, top executives are highly critical of mistakes made at lower levels: they see every mistake as a symptom of incompetence or stupidity. (Executives view their own mistakes quite differently, as examples of creativity and 'pushing the envelope'.)

Companies need to create an environment that lets their sales professionals lead the charge to more sales and not live in fear. I've seen too many examples of management beating up sales people, leading to higher turnover, not better performance. Sales people are mostly very optimistic, but in the last several years I have found it amazing how down and pessimistic sales teams have become because their managers simply don't care about them, their concerns, or their ambitions. If the number one concern of the sales team is survival and not success, then how creative, tenacious and effective will that sales team be?

Ultimately, it doesn't much matter if fear of action is caused by a rational assessment that a mistake will cause management displeasure, or by an unrealistic assessment of other possible consequences - such as embarrassment, suffering barbed criticism, or worse. The fact is that fear prevents people taking effective actions, and then people and companies are deprived of the benefits that might accrue from those actions.

It's a truism that people who feel no fear don't need a whole lot of courage to be able to do things; there are some people who go through life oblivious of the adverse consequences of their actions. Some of these achieve success in their professions despite making a few mistakes along the way. Conversely there are some talented people in the world who don't achieve even a fraction of their true potential because their fear of the consequences of action becomes inflated.

Most of us lie somewhere in between these extremes, and it is possible for most of us to push ourselves to take a few more risks without becoming reckless megalomaniacs.

Managers need to understand what makes their team anxious and tentative. Sometimes managers can help dispel fear by removing the underlying cause. But more often the manager's role is to help people combat their fear so they can get on with the job.

How can people combat fear, particularly those fears that are rooted in strongly held beliefs that are not justified by the reality of the situation? It's easy enough for a manager to point out that courage is all about overcoming fear. But your sales people want to know exactly how to do it.

I tell them that it all gets back to building confidence in who you are and what you are capable of doing. Look back at the times where you did something special so you stood out above your competition and won a significant deal. What made the difference?

Courage is about pushing forward when we are hesitant and doubtful. It's about just doing it: taking a risk that moves things forward, drawing a deep breath and accepting that what needs to be done must be done. Recognize that once you've thought things through, too much more thought just gets in the way of action. Think, but don't agonize.

Often the difference between action and inaction is just a matter of attitude. Sometimes you have to ask yourself "What's the worst that can happen?" Usually the answer is "Not much that's going to change my world." In my experience people who take some risks don't actually make any more blunders than those people who always avoid risks. Inaction can cause problems too. In general people who take risks, up to a point, probably get more done. And they certainly have more fun.

A few years ago, our sales district team went to Larry Wilson's Pecos River Training Center for a team-building event. An objective of the course was to generate creativity and innovation by making breakthroughs in team behavior. A key component of this was that individuals needed to overcome fears in a team environment, and these lessons were made strikingly clear because the challenges were physical and – for most of us – tough.

One of the exercises in the ropes course required us all to jump off of a 176-foot cliff on a zip line across the Pecos River. We knew that no one had ever been injured doing this exercise, but for some of us that wasn't all that reassuring. I've always been uncomfortable with heights. Uncomfortable? Actually some heights scare me, and a 176-feet drop falls into the scary category. I knew that it would be OK not to do it. But, despite my fear, I didn't want not to do it either.

The night before, I admit I slept like a baby… I woke up every two hours crying. Early on a cold morning, our team of eleven climbed to the top where the instructor explained to us the procedure and the safety rules.

For some of the team members this was actually going to be exciting and fun. Several on the team went right away. You could hear them shout with glee as they zipped across the Pecos River.

I was sitting all the way in the back of the large rock, behind all the others. I had a death grip on a branch hanging next to the rock. I was sweating pretty well at this point although it was still pretty cold. Then it came down to the final few of us who had the same fear I had. At that point I was convinced that I was not going to go through with it.

Pam – back at the office she was my admin support person – was now next in line and trying to muster the courage to leap. Once she had the zip line locked on she stood there for a full twenty minutes while the rest of the team encouraged her. Then she plunged, screaming all the way. Success!

At last it was down to good ol' me in the back. Would I say 'pass' which I know would have been OK with my support group? Or would the encouragement I had been receiving for the past hour be enough to make me make this jump? Even at that point I couldn't be sure which way I was going to go. I had analyzed every step of what I needed to do – if I could bring myself to do it. I realized that the free fall lasted one second and then the zip line would carry me across the river. No one had died. No one was injured. I was getting cold. I took a deep breath of the cold air and decided to go.

As the instructor locked me onto the line, he started to give me the same instruction everyone else received, which I'd now heard ten times. He ended up talking to himself because as soon as I was locked in I jumped. For one long second I was terrified. The next two or three seconds were wild. The last five seconds or so were exhilarating and really fun. I'd never had so much fun. What a rush!

I felt so good, not just because I enjoyed the ride. I had made a huge breakthrough by overcoming, for the first time, a fear that had been with me my whole life. This was a transforming experience. Now don't go asking me to sky dive like my son Greg. Not yet. But I'd learned in a dramatic and direct way that working through and overcoming fears can bring a whole new perspective on the opportunities and challenges that face us.

Fear keeps us from taking risk and stretching our ability to learn and grow. As Larry Wilson[10] might have said, "It's tough to learn from mistakes we never made".

Imagination is a wonderful thing. But often our imagination inflates our fears and makes challenges seem bigger and worse than they really are. This is probably a preservation mechanism for the human race – playing safe is natural. But once we realize that for many of us, most fears are based on inaccurate expectations, then we have the starting point for personal growth.

On a more mundane level, knowing that things never turn out to be as bad as we fear they might be helps us be optimistic enough, every day, to lift the phone, follow up that contact, make that deal.

> *...knowing that things never turn out to be as bad as we fear they might be helps us be optimistic enough, every day, to lift the phone, follow up that contact, make that deal .*

Optimism fuels endeavor, enables us to overcome fears, and keeps us going when things are tough. Optimism gives us the courage to confront realities and tackle problems. Optimism helps us drive forward when 'the only way out is through'. Optimism generates purposeful activity and is an essential factor for success.

Optimism is great stuff. Get some.

---

[10] Larry Wilson is the founder of Pecos River Learning Centers.

Persistence, persistence, persistence

Every SMART sales executive knows how important persistence is. There are many sales people out there who know pretty much all there is to know about the theory of selling, but they are less successful than others. One of the characteristics that can make the difference is the ability to *persist* against apparently overwhelming competition and lack of customer interest.

Persistence and tenacity are wonderful qualities. Everyone knows the proverb: If at first you don't succeed, try, try, try again. Persist, and if that doesn't work persist some more. However productive persistence and futile repetition are not the same thing.

> *...productive persistence and futile repetition are not the same thing.*

Futile repetition is when you come across a brick wall and you try to get by it by banging your head against it. It seemed a good idea at first, but it didn't work, so what you do is bang some more, longer and harder.

Futile repetition is painful and... well, futile.

Productive persistence is when you come across a brick wall and try to get by it, first of all by looking for a door. There's no door, how about climbing over it? Let's see if any bricks are loose enough to kick out? Can I dig under it? Perhaps I can borrow a ladder? I'll get some friends and form a human pyramid... and so on. Eventually you get by the wall, and useful, tenacious persistence has paid off.

Futile repetition is also likely to be annoying to a customer. (Note that it's generally counter-productive to annoy customers.) If you repeatedly offer the customer the same thing and make no adjustments to meet the customer's needs, then you will indubitably irritate the customer. This is being a pest. On the other hand, if you listen, if you show a real willingness to work with the customer to create a solution that works for them as well as for you, then you will be seen as responsive and cooperative, and not annoying. People actually appreciate the right type of persistence: persistence without being a pest.

I once talked with a sales executive (let's call him James) who was still flushed with success after winning a multi-million dollar contract, against all the odds. At the start, no one in his company gave James much of a chance of success when he paid his first sales call to the customer. This was a new account, not just for him, but for his company.

Nothing seemed to be in his favor. There was a deeply rooted incumbent who had been supplying software and technical services for years. Most decision-makers in the company were happy with their existing supplier, who had a solid reputation in the industry for providing good quality products at sensible prices. This one needed a huge sales effort, with little chance of success. Clearly this was a no-hoper – to everyone except James.

James had this notion that the executive-level decision makers in a large public corporation would have no choice but to buy the best value-for-money solution. All he had to do was make sure his solution was the best, talk to the right people, and the deal would be his.

James spent almost a year building relationships with his customer: making regular visits, being available, being helpful. He learned their business. He kept digging to find out how to close the gap so he could close the deal.

He was persistent inside his own company too. He insisted that senior executives from his company should visit the customer and create valuable personal relationships at the top level. He negotiated with his own company on behalf of the customer to ensure that on every point of quality, competence and price, he had an edge over the competition. On several occasions he was told to give up by his own boss, who felt James should be spending time on more productive accounts. James time and again persuaded his boss that he should keep going.

James put together a package that he felt was convincing in every respect. His company put a 'valid until' date on the offer, which was their usual practice. But it turned out that the customer's board meeting was going to be held one day too late. Taking a deep breath, James went to the top of his own company to get an extension. Then the customer changed a key requirement at the last moment. James worked all night to revise the offer.

Eventually the customer signed the deal. James attributes his success to three things: building close personal relationships and a high level of trust throughout the customer's organization; tenaciously working to make the offer such good value that it would have been difficult for the customer to turn it down; and persistence, tough-minded persistence.

There's a game played by some people who lack persistence... I call it the *When...then* game. It goes something like this:

- "When the market picks up, then I'll make my budget."

- "When the customer shows some interest, then I'll make a call."
- "When my sales manager is supportive, then I'll give 100%."
- "When the company gets its act together, then I can sell."
- "When our customer service improves, then I can get add on business."
- "When we come out with some new products, then I'll try to get some new customers."

See how the *When...then* game is played? The game is an excuse for inaction.

It's possible to apply the *When...then* approach to everything in life, if you choose to (and some people do). "When I find the perfect partner, then I'll settle down." "When I settle down, I'll have time to start going to the gym" "When I have time to go to the gym, I'll get in better shape." "When I'm in good shape, then I'll find the perfect partner."

Every sales manager should be aware of the insidious and debilitating nature of the *When...then* game. Everyone plays it to some extent, because of course there is never a perfect time for anything. There is never a perfect time to change careers, to invest in the stock market, to buy a new car, to learn to sky-dive. People can always find an excuse for not doing something *right now*.

Sometimes it's possible for the sales manager to turn the *When...then* discussion right around. For example, a rep says: "When we come out with some new products, then I'll try to get some new customers." One response might be: "Tell you what, go and talk to three prospects on the list, and find out what sort of products they need and will buy. Then we'll talk again." Chances are, the discussion will not only produce intelligence that will be useful for future product development – it will also raise possibilities for selling existing products and services to the customer.

Sometimes this works. Sometimes, however, *When...then* is played by people who are just played out. And then the sales team leader's response has to shift gear into a different game: *Unless...then...*

A good sales person always feels that every opportunity is worth some effort. Excellent sales people see real prospects where others see only futile effort, and have the tenaciousness to turn those opportunities into deals.

Many sales people are too willing to give up early.

Should you give up if the customer sounds unenthusiastic? No. Customers can sound unenthusiastic right up to the point of saying 'Yes' especially if they want to negotiate a discount.

Should you give up when the customer says they prefer the opposition? Certainly not, because now you have something to work on. Their statement tells you two things: first, they plan to buy from someone; second, if they prefer the competition, they have some reasons for saying that: it's your job to find out why and eliminate the competitive gap.

Should you give up when the customer says 'No'? No, you shouldn't. NO stands for 'Never Over'. If the customer hasn't yet signed with a competitor, they can still sign with you. I recently won a deal when the customer had not only said 'No', but also told us that their rules didn't allow us to make a new offer. We did anyway, and this time we convinced them that our services offered the best value for money. What were they going to do? Stick to the rules and buy something of lower value that they didn't really want? They signed with us.

Should you give up when the customer signs with a competitor? No. I've experienced more than one situation when a deal fell apart on the details of contract terms, or the supplier found they couldn't honor their offer after all. Keep in touch and be prepared to submit a fresh offer if the opportunity arises.

Should you give up when the competitor has started work on the contract? No. With some suppliers there is a big gap between their offer and the reality of delivery. Suppliers can fail, and then there is an opportunity to step in and be a hero by rescuing the situation. Even if the competitor finishes the job, look out for mopping up opportunities. I have won business before by being able to send in troubleshooting teams to fix the problems caused by other suppliers!

Above all, by being persistent, by always being there for the customer, you are positioning yourself for the next deal.

Enthusiasm

Enthusiasm – a lively, energetic and absorbing interest – is essential for a sales person. A good sales team manager creates enthusiasm just by being enthusiastic, because enthusiasm can be contagious. (Unfortunately, so can apathy, which is the exact opposite.)

Optimism and enthusiasm go hand in hand. Optimism makes it easy to be enthusiastic about a project. Enthusiasm creates the sort of positive vibes that allow optimism to flourish.

Michael Jordan was one of the greatest basketball players ever. He led the Chicago Bulls when they won six NBA Championships in the nineties. After a career in which he dominated the basketball court, he retired from the game. Encouraged by his father, he decided to give baseball a try. But his enthusiasm for basketball was paramount: he came back to basketball. He played for the Chicago Bulls a second time and brought them to another Championship. He then retired from playing basketball for the second time.

Being a team manager was the natural next step. He took over the Washington Wizards, but his enthusiasm for playing the game took over, yet again. He made another come back as a player, and the Wizards sold out every home game for two seasons, which probably had a greater financial benefit for the team than anything he did as manager.[11]

Jordan's enthusiasm and love for the game made him successful as a player, and no doubt his consistent playing success helped to further boost his enthusiasm. Jordan approaches his sport with total commitment: "I don't do things half-heartedly. Because I know if I do, then I can expect half-hearted results."[12]

Some baseball experts will always argue about who was the best pitcher ever. Everyone else will vote for Nolan Ryan, who pitched for the Texas Rangers until he was 46 years old, and became well-known to people who normally weren't baseball fans. His fame wasn't due just to his technical skill on the field. He came across to fans as decent and disciplined, but above all as someone who had unlimited enthusiasm for the game. He gave the game his total commitment until he retired, which was many years after the usual retirement age. He had a no hitter the season before he retired. Ryan played baseball as

[11] The exuberant enthusiasm that made Jordan excel as a basketball player was just not evident in his time as a baseball player, and then as a basketball manager. Doing what you really love doing is more likely to lead to success than just doing a job.
[12] Michael Jordan, quoted on houseofquotes.com.

long as he did because he loved the game and he loved giving fans enjoyment. Was he successful because he was enthusiastic, or was he enthusiastic because he was successful? Both.

Like athletes, sales people have to love their work. Sales people must enjoy selling, must love their products and must get delight out of delighting their customers. Otherwise selling is just hard work and no fun.

> *Sales people must enjoy selling, must love their products and must get delight out of delighting their customers.*

A few years ago, Tom Peters quoted a company executive as justifying his company's approach to customer service as follows: "We're no worse than anyone else..."[13] Can you imagine working for a company like that? No enthusiasm, energy or commitment. Excellent sales people will never be happy with being no worse than anyone else. Excellent sales people want to be among the best, even though they know there will be setbacks and upsets along the way.

Can you remember back when you were a kid? Can you recall the energy and enthusiasm you would have when going on a trip with your family – to the beach, to the movies, to an amusement park? You probably could not sleep the night before out of excitement.

If you ask a class of fifth-graders "Does anyone wants to run a marathon?" pretty much the whole class will raise their hands in excitement saying "I do! I do! Pick me!" The next question from the class would be: "What's a marathon?"

As we get older, fear of losing, fear of rejection, fear of not conforming, and fear of not living up to expectations all set in. All the excitement and enthusiasm that we had when we were kids gets dampened by other people – our bosses, our colleagues, our friends – telling us what we can and cannot do. We lose faith in our innate ability to do just about anything, and so we lose the enjoyment of trying. We start to think of failure as merely failure, instead of part of the learning process.

Enthusiasm engenders a positive attitude. A positive attitude is essential if we are to try our best 100% of the time and make the most of our God-given talents. If we merely play not to lose, our effort will be minimal. And our level of success will be minimal too.

Children are natural enthusiasts. But there's nothing childish about enthusiasm. In the adult world, enthusiasm is what stimulates people to learn, to discover and to act purposefully. Enthusiasm makes the

---

[13] *In Search of Excellence*, Tom Peters and Robert Waterman (HarperCollins, 1982).

difference between mediocrity and excellence. Ask Jordan, ask Ryan. Ask any successful sales person.

Since sales is really a competitive sport[14], lets look at another lesson from the world of sport.

You can tell the difference between a team that is "playing to win" and another team that is simply "playing not to lose". The first team will be more tenacious, more challenging, more persistently aggressive. Playing to win is an attitude of mind that ensures every team member takes nothing for granted and keeps playing to the end.

A sales team that plays to win will never assume that the deal is done until after everything is signed and sealed. Even then, they will work with the customer to avoid buyers' remorse, they will keep going through delivery, and they'll be around to make sure they understand what else the customer needs.

Merely playing not to lose means missing opportunities and maybe even losing a whole deal to a competitor at the last minute. In other words, playing not to lose will increase your likelihood of losing.

> *Merely playing 'not to lose' means missing opportunities and maybe even losing a whole deal to a competitor at the last minute..*

In Super Bowl XXXVII in January, 2003 we saw the Tampa Bay Buccaneers against the Oakland Raiders. Oakland was favored to win with the number one offensive team in football at the time.

It's the end of the first half, Oakland has the ball on their own 12-yard line with just thirteen seconds to go. Oakland is down 20 to 3. Everyone assumed Oakland would run the clock out and regroup in the locker room for the second half. Most teams in Tampa's position – up 17 points with just thirteen seconds left in the half - would have gone along with that. Instead, Tampa Bay called a time out! They figured there was a chance they could get a turnover, get the ball back and score again. On that occasion they were certainly playing to win. No let up, no opportunity allowed to be missed, nothing taken for granted. Tampa went on to win the game 48 to 21 with 5 interceptions.

I once had an interesting conversation with a sales rep from a large company. Dennis told me he had just closed one of the biggest deals his account team had ever won. That success exemplified the benefits of playing to win...

---

[14] More on this in Chapter 3.

- **Taking nothing for granted.** His company was the leader in the sector, so Dennis might have been forgiven for putting in a boilerplate bid, because he could still have had a reasonable chance of success. Instead Dennis took the time to look under the surface. He found out about some special requirements, and so made the effort to create a proposal that was exactly tuned to the customer's needs.

- **No opportunity missed.** At first the deal looked like it would not be very big – when Dennis told his boss about it he thought at first that it might not be worth any special effort. But the opportunity grew and grew.

- **No giving up.** On several occasions, it looked as if the deal would fall through. Competitors came up with more and more aggressive pricing; the customer's requirements changed and changed again; the customer's budget went down as the requirements increased. Dennis managed to creatively massage the deal to give the customer what they wanted while maintaining decent margins to keep his own company happy.

I asked Dennis whether he ever thought about letting the deal go, and moving on to something more obviously productive. He really didn't understand the question. He knew from the start that this deal was winnable, and so he could think of no reason why he shouldn't play whole-heartedly for the win. I'd like everyone on my team to be like Dennis.

Enthusiasm and passion can create success against all the odds. Equally, *apathy* will guarantee failure, even when the situation is favorable.

Apathy requires no effort and generates no effort. Apathy is not caring. Apathy is not answering phone calls, not checking voicemail, not answering e-mail messages. Apathy is forgetting to make routine calls to check how your customers are doing.

People who are apathetic seem to have no goals to aim for, no drive to succeed. I've always thought it strange that people who can't be enthusiastic about selling end up in sales, but it happens. I have worked alongside people like that in the past, and I sometimes couldn't believe some of the things they would say. They would get a call from a customer and not return it. Why not? They would say "Oh, I know what they want and I can't get it for them, so I'm not going to waste time just giving them bad news. There's nothing in it for me."

Such indifference is really difficult to address. As a manager, you can always find some way to work with someone who has some commitment and needs more encouragement or direction to become really enthusiastic. But a truly apathetic person presents a more severe challenge. You need to recognize what's happening and help the truly apathetic person to face the reality that with this sort of attitude he or she should be in a different job. Very few people are apathetic about everything, unless they're seriously depressed, and that's another issue. Most people who are unenthusiastic about being in sales actually do have something else in their lives that they find interesting and compelling. My career advice isn't limited to people in sales: when looking for a job, the single biggest factor influencing your future success is how much you love it. It is possible to get the best of both worlds: success and in a job that you enjoy. If you're not enjoying most of every day, find something else to do.

I remember someone I came across who was consistently bored with his job, which was in technical sales support. No energy, no commitment. Eventually he figured out what was wrong and made a complete change of career. He became a farmer, worked all day every day of the year, and loved every moment. He made money, and above all, he was happy. Boundless energy, total commitment, lots of passion.

When I was a kid, my friend Glen and I decided to try out for ninth grade junior varsity football. We were both about the same height, both about the same weight, both quite fit. It appeared that we both had the potential to be good football players.

One morning Glen came by my house ready to go running and told me it was time to start training for the try-outs. Training? I just wanted to play some football. I couldn't care less about training.

The season started and training was brutal. Glen loved it, he worked his weight down to about 130 and I stayed up there at 150. When the team ran a mile, the coach would start me a lap early so I could finish at the same time as the others. I ended up on the third string. The only one on the third string.

Glen, meantime moved up from the second string and ended the season in starting linebacker position. That was a great accomplishment for someone only 5' 4" in height. The difference between me and Glen was obvious at the time, and remains obvious now: Glen was passionate about playing football. I really couldn't care if I became a great football player or not.

We aren't all natural enthusiasts for everything. Some people get thrills playing football. Some people are passionate about opera. Others love forensic accounting. People are so different it's wrong to expect that everyone will be enthused by the same thing, and we should celebrate that diversity. Which is why everyone has a responsibility to at least try to track down a career path that plays to one of their areas of enthusiasm, not to one of their areas of indifference. And if you or someone in your team is not having fun in sales, my advice is to consider moving on and finding something that makes you happier.

I found that I had much more passion for swimming and tennis and played my last football game in ninth grade, the year I started.

Glen grew to all of 5'7" and continued to play football with a passion. For three years in high school he lived and breathed football and during the spring he played lacrosse to stay in shape. Looking at him, you would never have thought Glen would have the size or the speed to start in the backfield defensive positions, but he was equally able to play linebacker or free safety, and he had heart. He seemed to be able to be everywhere on the field, and no one wanted to be tackled by Glen. One time, Glen flattened a player named Chuck who was around 6'3" and was the best running back on Long Island. (He went on to play in the NFL) On the sideline after the tackle, Chuck's coach grabbed Glen and pulled him over to his sideline. He yelled: "Chuck, you let *this* guy tackle you?"

Passion and enthusiasm make the difference in sales as in any other career. If you have the passion, the sky's the limit. If you're apathetic, you've already reached your limit, the floor.

> *Passion and enthusiasm make the difference in sales as in any other career. If you have the passion, the sky's the limit. If you're apathetic, you've already reached your limit, the floor.*

It's sometimes said that a good sales person can sell anything. Up to a point this is true. But the best sales people have - or are able to develop - a real enthusiasm for whatever it is they are selling. I tell my team that the best sales people *love* their products.

Suppose you land a sales position selling specialty equipment to restaurants. But you've never made even an omelet and don't care to try, and anyway rich food gives you heartburn. Even if you know every sales trick in the book, your credibility will plummet the first time the all-important small talk gets round to topics like kitchen management, and the rigors of managing the flow of work and coping with kitchen crises. This is all about *connecting* with your customers. But not on the superficial level of *pretending* to be one of them, but by actually *being* one of them. If you don't have enthusiasm for your product and really know how it is used in the real world that your customers work in, every conversation is an opportunity to make a fool of yourself, instead of an opportunity to impress, relate, and *sell*.

Of course, this doesn't mean that you need to have a life-long love affair with a product before you can sell it. It seems to work the other way round. Good sales people have such an urge to be good at selling, that they naturally become attached to their products, whatever they are.

Good sales people have such an urge to be good at selling, that they naturally become attached to their products...

Does your sales team have that capability for enthusiasm? (Do you?)

We all come across sales people in stores who are marking time in the job. They are not *involved*, and they cannot involve their customers. In retail stores, people often end up buying anyway, because they know what they want. I admit that as a sales professional, I like to spend my money in stores where I see evidence of that enthusiasm shining through. Why should my money go to pay commission to someone who doesn't care?

I have my own favorites. There's my special clothes store where they know my name when I walk in, and remember what I like and don't like. There's the sports store where they really know about running shoes and how shoes can make a difference to performance and the health of my knees. There's my local health club where they really want to help me get fit and enjoy doing it. Everyone has favorites, whether it's a music store where they keep the oddball music you like, or a food store with an outrageously wide range of real cheeses.

The thing to note here is that we all have these preferences, in those areas where what we buy is important to us. Sales people who do not enthuse about their products turn us off, and we go elsewhere.

Now think about that in the context of corporate sales. Are the buyers strongly interested in buying the right solution? Are they likely to value intelligent and expert advice from a sales person? Do the buyers care what type of company they buy from? The answers are yes, yes and yes.

Frank Visgalio is a good friend who was on my team back in 1996 when I ran sales for a company that produced specialist software for laboratories and hospitals. Frank's enthusiasm was continuous, contagious and convincing. He clearly loved his product, and loved to help his customers solve their technical and business problems. When he talked about our solutions I would sit back and listen and watch the customer's reactions. We had the best solution on the market at that time, and Frank's commitment and energetic enthusiasm convinced just about everyone. He never had a problem arranging a follow-up call, and his enthusiasm helped him close deal after deal.

I tell my sales people: *you* are the company as far as the customer is concerned. If you are enthusiastic and knowledgeable, your customer will draw the conclusion that your company is enthusiastic and knowledgeable.

> *I tell my sales people: you are the company as far as the customer is concerned.*

If it's important for some people to buy their vegetables from a store that knows about – and is enthusiastic about – vegetables, it seems sort of obvious that corporate decision makers are going to feel that it's important to buy complex solutions from people who know and deeply care about complex solutions, and who have professional enthusiasm for the products they offer.

Love your products and solutions with enthusiasm, and maybe your customers will love you.

50

Resilience

The R in OPERA stands for Resilience. How do you feel when a customer says 'no' to you? How do you feel when a member of your sales team assertively disagrees with you? Bursting into tears is not helpful, and if that's how you're likely to react, you're going to have a hard time in a sales role or in a sales management role.

On the other hand, do you automatically shrug it off, knowing you are right, assuming that you're dealing with an idiot? That's not helpful either, because being able to learn from failure is really important.

Resilience is a multi-dimensional attribute. In general, people who are resilient are able to learn from mistakes and welcome change. If someone fears change and avoids risks, then they are probably people who get very gloomy every time an obstacle to progress appears.

Other attitudes of mind that seem to be correlated with resilience are having a sense of values, an eagerness to learn new things, ambition to make progress coupled with a sense of proportion about the importance of work when set alongside family, friends and non-work activities.

I'm no psychologist, just an observer of people and their behavior as I encounter them in the workplace. It seems to me that people who rapidly plummet into despondency when there's a setback may be lacking in self-esteem. Even so, they somewhat contradictorily place themselves at the center of the situation, blaming themselves for the failure, when there are many contributing factors, not just their personal performance.

Resilient people are able to bounce back from failure. This doesn't mean that having resilience involves not caring about failure. Instead it means:

- understanding that **failure is a necessary part of trying to do better**
- putting failures in perspective, and realizing that **failure is a normal part of the sales process**
- realizing that failures have an upside too – **failures provide an opportunity to learn**.

We have already talked about fear of failure as something that undermines optimism and breeds apathy. Let's look at some more perspectives on failure, because sales managers need to strike a balance: failures should not be ignored, but we have to understand the difference between failures caused by persistent lack of care and attention, and failures caused by trying hard to make progress and grow.

If someone is regularly careless in preparing customer proposals, or routinely drops the ball in a customer negotiation, or neglects the necessary routine contacts with customers needed to build a relationship, or tells lies to customers, then that sales person is failing to do the job properly and needs to be improved or removed. These are failures that should not be ignored or forgiven.

But suppose in an effort to build a relationship a sales rep bends some company rules or offends some protocol in an attempt to get attention?

I've been known to bend the rules myself, so it's difficult for me to say that the rules are always sacrosanct. Sometimes it's easier (and better) to ask for forgiveness than for permission.

I've approved the shipping of equipment early in order to get a signature. I knew I should wait for final credit approval, but I also knew the customer had a genuine need for quick delivery (and they had plenty of cash.). This was a calculated risk, and it paid off.

Many of us have introduced a customer to new prices a couple of days before the official release date. This is almost always against the rules, but we all know how customers react if they sign up one day, and the prices drop the next. They trust us to keep them in the picture on these things…

The question the sales manager has to ask is: "If it had worked would I have been happy or furious?" If the answer is "happy" then you need to moderate your wrath when it goes wrong.

Sales professionals all need to cultivate a balanced perspective on failure. The attitude of the sales manager can help greatly; and so can open discussion of failures among the team members.

Failure is a necessary part of trying to do better. An occasional failure is the price of entry to growth as a person and out-of-the ordinary success for the business.

"The man who makes no mistakes does not usually make anything."[15]

How many self-improvement books been written pointing out that failing is part of growth; that if you don't fail sometimes you can't be trying hard enough; that all great leaders have some failures in their past? The trouble with self-help books is that mostly the people who buy them need less 'help' than the people who don't.

---

[15] Edward Phelps

The way a company can show that it believes all it says about the learning value of failure, is not by getting its managers to make platitudinous speeches, nor by handing out self-improvement books at seminars, but to *act as if the company believes it.* In other words, managers shouldn't beat people up when they err trying to do better, or do something different, or because they are really trying to learn. If you do that, you'll find that they'll become too cautious and risk-averse to make it in sales (until they move on from your team).

Making some mistakes really is at the heart of stretching and growing. Some trial and error is at the heart of every creative, imaginative and ground-breaking process. So the freedom to make mistakes – and learn from them – must exist everywhere in the company, not just at CEO level.

> *…the freedom to make mistakes – and learn from them – must exist everywhere in the company, not just at CEO level.*

"Creativity is allowing yourself to make mistakes. Art is knowing which ones to keep."[16]

Failure is a normal part of the sales process. From a sales perspective, it seems that the word "no" is the most-used word in the customers' vocabulary list. If we're really lucky, sometimes you'll get a more extended response: "No thank you."

Learning to live with "no" needs to happen early in a sales career. Sales people need to develop a sense of proportion about rejection. This is why sales is a profession for people who are pragmatic and don't always expect perfection. Striving for perfection is a good thing, up to a point. But for perfectionists, a proposal document is never quite good enough, a sales brochure is always lacking, and a sales pitch never quite hits the mark. As a result, innate perfectionists are always discontented – but in the sales profession they could become suicidal.

Good sales people know how to prioritize their efforts and spend their energies wisely. Which is usually not about making sure every interaction with the customer is perfectly judged. It's about creating the right relationship with the customer so your offering gets a fair hearing.

And good sales people know that when they hear the word "no" from a customer, they need to interpret it as "not right now – keep trying".

---

[16] Scott Adams

Failures are an opportunity to learn. The thing we call experience is mostly based on working out what we did wrong and avoiding it in future.

"Once we realize that imperfect understanding is the human condition there is no shame in being wrong, only in failing to correct our mistakes."[17]

Sales people can only get better at assessing customer situations through successive learning experiences – and just as much learning comes from losses as from wins. Perhaps more.

> *Just as much learning comes from losses as from wins. Perhaps more.*

Sales managers should encourage and lead discussion of losses and failures whenever there is a reasonable opportunity to do so. (One way people don't learn anything from a failure is by pretending it didn't happen, or by forgetting it as soon as possible.) In leading such discussions the emphasis should not exclusively be on "What did we do wrong?" The aim should be to discover "What can we do better next time?"

A clear sign of a lack of resilience in a sales person is being a sore loser.

Playing to win is important. Simply playing not to lose is not good enough. But for some people, total commitment to winning has an unfortunate side-effect: they become sore losers.

Different people react to losing in different ways. One person might express anger and disappointment to everyone within hearing distance, while another finds an empty room where no one will hear the stomping and table thumbing and whining. Some people just bottle it up until they can have a gentle weep in private. Others wail out loud.

It is normal to have some sort of reaction. It is normal to be upset and disappointed. This is a natural consequence of high levels of commitment. I'll never condemn anyone for a genuine display of emotion.

But there is one reaction that I will never sympathize with: the reaction of blaming the customer. Good sales people usually know where things went wrong: maybe our price was too high, or the product specification wasn't a great fit, or our proposal wasn't as compelling as it should have been or perhaps we just didn't do a good pitch on the day.

---

[17] George Soros

On the other hand, an inexpert or inexperienced sales person may automatically blame the customer: "How could they? That's such a *stupid* decision!" I admit it, I've been close to saying that myself, and it can be a fairly natural reaction.

But I've got three good reasons for advising you to work really hard against having that reaction, no matter how you feel at first:

- Blaming the customer gets in the way of learning.

- Blaming the customer sours your future relationship with the customer.

- Blaming the customer is being a sore loser, and no one likes a sore loser.

Every failure is an opportunity to learn. Michael Jordan, indubitably a great basketball player said: "I've missed more than 9,000 shots in my career. I've lost more than 300 games. Twenty-six times I've been trusted to take the game-winning shot and missed. I've failed over and over and over again in my life... And that is why I succeed."

Simply dismissing a lost deal as due to the stupidity of the customer is missing a big opportunity to learn. Certainly, some corporate decisions might not be very bright, but every decision is made for some sort of reason. By understanding those reasons you stand more chance of getting them to decide in your favor next time. And if they decide to go with your company, then maybe that won't be such a stupid decision after all, even if the underlying reasons for making that decision are still irrational.

You also have to make sure there is a 'next time'. So no matter how disappointed you are, you need to keep close to the customer, show them you can handle the disappointment and make sure they know you're ready and willing to do business. You have to stay available on their list of good people to work with. If you view a single lost deal as signifying the end of your relationship with a customer, you could rapidly run out of potential customers.

When you contact the customer, it's OK to tell them you're disappointed. But it's not OK to tell them they're crazy, or to ask them if they were under the influence of some illegal substance, or to ask them what Caribbean island they're headed to with the bribe money. That would be indelicate. Worse, it would be counterproductive. You would be a sore loser. You'll find it difficult to get appointments. They'll stop returning your calls. Selling is hard enough anyway – you don't need to build additional barriers for yourself.

Many times in sales, we can expect to lose at first before being successful with a customer. Customers can learn a lot about our character by how we take a loss. By asking for a review with the customer, you show that you are willing to learn, and you'll uncover valuable information on how to do better next time. By accepting a loss gracefully, you will help to make sure that you are offered a chance next time.

On one occasion a small professional services company I know well lost a deal with a giant multi-national manufacturer. My friends were dismayed that the manufacturer had followed a weird and eccentric path to making a buying decision. First of all, the customer decided to use a bidding process designed for buying hardware components instead of a process more suited to services. Then they used selection criteria that attached more weight to the size of the discount rather than the actual price. And they defined the scope of the project in such a way that it was inevitably going to be an inefficient and unproductive piece of work, so any conscientious bidder had to make a bid that listed multiple exceptions to the scope of work. To add to the frustration, the operational managers who needed the work were told that they couldn't participate in deciding which supplier to use.

When the 'no' decision arrived the immediate reaction was predictable: "How can they be so *stupid?*" The work had gone to a large consulting company with a relationship at the top. Their price was higher, they were not the first choice of the users, they had a track record of not delivering and of charging much more than the contracted price through smart use of extras and contingencies.

To their credit, the sales team overcame their disappointment very quickly so they could start to recover and to learn. They immediately reconnected with the client to let them know they were still interested in doing business, and that they were not despondent. They realized that they had completely underestimated the importance of executive-level personal relationships in the decision-making process. They had assumed that because they had won over the people who needed the work, the people who paid the bills would fall into line. And they had assumed that the big company's understanding of value was the same as theirs. Now, that sales team has a different sense of priorities driving what opportunities to bid for, and what makes the difference when bidding.

Being a good sport is healthy. Being a sore loser is unproductive, distracting and wastes energy. No one likes the pain or irritation of dealing with a sore loser, so don't be one.

In today's selling environment, it's certainly not over - even if the "fat lady sings". If your competitor is not really paying attention to the customer, even a "done deal" can be reversed. And if you lost gracefully, you could be in with another chance.

Resilience, like every other OPERA attribute is a type of behavior that flows from a certain positive attitude of mind. People who lack resilience can still sell. But people who have high levels of resilience sell better, and bounce back when others droop in despair.

Affability

When you, as a sales manager, recruit a new sales person, chances are one of the things that you look for, consciously or unconsciously, is a degree of *affability*.

Affability is not just about being pleasant and courteous. Being conventionally polite can even get in the way of the real communication that springs from genuine affability. Most people can be outwardly friendly some of the time to some people. However, the affable person cultivates an open-minded attitude to new contacts so that from the start, there is warmth in the relationship.

Affable people make few assumptions about others, and like to find out what really makes people tick. Affable people place others at the center of the discussion, not themselves. Affable people are not just friendly, they're *helpful*.

> *Affable people are not just friendly, they're helpful.*

Affability is not all that easy to pin down in words, but you know it when you come across it, don't you?

People find it easy to open up to an affable person, and seem to be willing to share their thoughts and opinions more readily than with others.

Think about that: how useful is it for a sales person to be the sort of individual that people are willing to talk to? I write elsewhere about the importance of really understanding a customer's, needs, preferences and enthusiasms in order to sell successfully. In my experience, affable sales people find out all these things faster, more accurately, and in more depth than sales people who are not genial and warm by nature. Affable people seem to be able to quickly come to an understanding of customers' needs, and identify with them. Affable people are therefore well equipped to pitch just the right solution in just the right way.

To some readers, this may sound somewhat cynical and manipulative. This is a danger that I recognize. But please note: I do not propose that people go out there and simulate affability just to get sales. False affability is pretty obvious to most humans, so don't try.

I encourage my team to think about their attitudes, and to try hard to cultivate in themselves a perspective on their dealings with others that will generate that warmth of relationship that is so useful in the sales profession.

The source of affability seems to be rooted in a genuine interest in other people, and a real desire to help others. (Does this sound too saintly? It isn't intended to be: to the extent that saintliness exists in this world, I suppose that saints tend to be affable. But being affable certainly doesn't make you a saint.)

I have always benefited in my sales career from deriving genuine pleasure in the company of a wide range of people, and also getting kicks from helping others out. This drives a lot of what I do in my personal life, and I can't suppress this when I'm doing business. And I won't try to suppress it.

Some sales managers reading the above will say "Sounds great, where are the affability exercises so I can build up my team's affability muscles?" Unfortunately, as with all the OPERA attributes, there's no easy path. Some people are naturally affable and will find that being warm and approachable for customers is something that just happens. Some are the exact opposite: customers never ask them for advice, and seldom share their real thoughts with them.

Most people are somewhere in between, what I would describe as selectively affable. They don't always feel like it. People who fall into that category can develop this aspect of their personality positively.

When sales people ask me how to do this, I don't have a one-size-fits-all fitness program. But I do suggest this exercise: think back on the occasions when with a customer (or anyone else), you have realized they are exceptionally willing to open up and share experiences and opinions. What did you do (or not do) that triggered that? Can you recall what sort of things contributed to the relaxed attitude? Chances are that the things you did can be summarized as: you were being affable. Try to do more of those things.

Furthermore when you review each customer meeting (as you should always do) think about the extent to which the customer was prepared to open up. What was the context, what stimulated that openness? Were there any moments when the customer seemed to withdraw or clam up? What caused that? Learn from these reflections.

If some affability is good, does that mean more affability is even better? Perhaps not. I need to insert some words of caution.

As with all of the OPERA attributes, balance is essential. Not everyone can be affable all the time, and no one should aspire to that. You need to be able to switch off your affability whenever it looks like being too sociable is going to get in the way of necessary direct speaking. The need to be generally affable should not prevent candor with your customer when that's needed. Affability need not mean that you hide your true opinions and feelings. But when it's appropriate to speak your mind, you should be able to do it in a way that's constructive not destructive.

Nor should you allow the warmth generated to ·eliminate all skepticism. In business today there are plenty of people who are well practiced in the art of cynical manipulation, and (I regret to say) there are some practical limits to trust. Never totally abandon all skepticism Always use your rationality and experience to make reality checks on what you're being told.

Another concern that people sometimes express about the notion of affability, is that while it is more than friendliness, it is not the same as genuine *friendship*. So is affability really hypocritical? If this is the sort of philosophical issue that troubles you, then consider this: affability is something in itself, it is an attitude of mind that you can adopt in all sincerity with many people who are not friends: a new customer, the person you find yourself next to at a party, the agent who always books your travel tickets for you. Affability is not a pretend type of friendship. Affability can establish a foundation of communication that could eventually grow into friendship. I have lots of personal friends that I met for the first time in a business context. But mostly business contacts remain business contacts, and that's OK. As long as *you* don't confuse affability with friendship, your customers won't either.

A Final Word on Attitude

Being in sales, and being good at it, can be a lot of fun. The converse is true also: people who enjoy selling make good sales people, usually.

Enjoyment is linked to a positive attitude. If you and your team are positive about what you believe you can achieve, and positive in the way you endeavor to achieve it, you will enjoy being part of the sales profession. And if you enjoy it, you will be good at it.

When we build a positive attitude in a team, each and every team member works better. Newcomers fit into the team more easily and become productive more quickly. Team spirit develops from the positive attitudes of all the individuals in the team.

Other people think well of positive people – they can't help it. Everyone makes mistakes, but if you are generally an understanding person, people will overlook your occasional lapses. People find less fault with people who don't find fault with others. People don't complain much about people who are not complainers. It's much harder to criticize and blame someone who is positive and encouraging every day than it is to criticize and blame someone who is negative and whining all the time.

Given the choice, people would rather be around someone who is positive, up-beat, and enthusiastic. Make sure you and your team give them that choice.

There are many different ways of looking at this thing we call Attitude. I have chosen to focus on five perspectives that seem to me to be most important in a selling environment. They are the OPERA characteristics:

- **Optimism** – the ability to consistently expect a favorable outcome from one's actions.

- **Persistence** – the ability to work hard, consistently and determinedly to achieve results.

- **Enthusiasm** – the ability to approach the business of selling with energy and commitment.

- **Resilience** – the ability to bounce back from setbacks and disappointments, and to learn from failures and keep going.

- **Affability** – the ability to be sociable, outgoing and open to communication.

In putting down my thoughts on the five important components of Attitude, I find myself repeatedly coming back to the realization that none of these components is independent.

I have found that people who display one of the OPERA attributes inevitably show positive signs in all these dimensions. People who are optimistic tend also to be persistent, enthusiastic, resilient and affable.

I stated the reason for this up front in this section: the common factor is a "Positive Attitude" which in turn is rooted in strong self-esteem. I should also add that in sales, strong self-esteem needs to be moderated by realism, a sense of proportion and a sense of humor!

So the crunch question for a sales manager who is responsible for the performance of a sales team is this: "If attitude is so important to performance, do I work on attitude directly, or on self-esteem, or on each of the OPERA items individually?"

The answer, as you probably worked out already, is: "Work on all of them, all the time."

If someone is feeling pessimistic about the prospects for winning a particular opportunity, that person is also likely to lack energy and enthusiasm for the case, and is unlikely to bring to the task the level of persistence which is really needed to close the deal.

The sales team manager can help by emphasizing the reasons why the opportunity is worth going for, by highlighting the payback and also by quoting examples from experience in which deals were won in similar situations. But above all, the sales manager can help most to build enthusiasm by *being enthusiastic*! Enthusiasm is contagious, so spread some around.

Then, guess what? An enthusiasm boost makes everyone's attitude a little more positive and that spills over into everything else: people become more optimistic and more persistent. They become more resilient when things go wrong along the way, which they are bound to do. And they (without trying too hard) become more relaxed and affable when dealing with the customer. The pay-off is immediate, and all-round.

We need to avoid the big mistake of trying to make people be more positive simply by exhorting them to be more positive. That approach doesn't work, any more than telling people to shape up and be smarter, or less scared. ("Just pull yourself together, won't you?")

But we really *can* help people become more positive (and for that matter we can help them become smarter and less scared too.)

We can do it by setting a good example and by helping people with specific things they need to do. We can do it by helping people to be successful in what they are trying to do, allowing them to share the credit, and reminding them of the good things they have achieved.

As a sales manager, your attitude is critical. I have never come across a sales team with a great spirit if the team leader was morose and unsupportive.

Sales team managers must lead the charge. You cannot lead by being a klink: being negative, not being where the action is, constantly complaining and criticizing. No matter how justified you might think your grousing is it simply doesn't work, if your objective is to build a successful team.

People can be enormously influenced by role models, for good and bad. If you demonstrate the right sort of attitude and behaviors, your team will pick up on that and follow your good example. If you are complacent, apathetic, and careless, you give your team members license to behave like that too.

Chapter 3
Skills Development

In sales, just as in sports, natural talent is very useful. But there are no sports stars so talented that they don't need to train and practice.

In the same way sales people need to understand the array of skills that are needed to be successful in sales. They need to learn those skills, and practice them.

Good sales managers know how to build skills in their teams, by formal training, coaching and encouragement.

Sales is a Competitive Sport

The S in SMART stands for Skills. The development of selling skills is fundamental to anyone's success as a salesperson. Ensuring that sales team members acquire and continue to develop skills is a primary duty of every sales manager. I've found that many sales people underestimate the importance of building basic skills, and so do not invest anything like the time and effort in learning that they ought to.

Have you noticed that at sales conferences and dinners, it's often athletes who make keynote speeches and give presentations on everything from teamwork to motivation?[18] It's not just because conference organizers want to get cool gear for themselves and their kids, although that may be part of it.

The parallels between selling and sports are so many and so obvious that perhaps everyone in sales takes it for granted. But for those people reading this who are not in sales, or are new to sales, it's worth laying out the similarities just to make sure the point is not missed.[19]

Sales *is* competitive. Sure, people compete in every area of business. But sales is the place that attracts competitive people because it's *officially part of the job*.

In some business areas, competition can be a mixed blessing. People allow their competitive instincts to surface inside the company. They compete directly with their colleagues, and this can get in the way of communication and collaboration. It can generate mistrust. It drives internal company politics, power plays and personal agendas.

A lot of that dysfunctional behavior happens in sales too, of course. But sales people have a healthy outlet for their competitive instincts, and it's called, naturally enough, *the competition*. Some people go so far as to call it the *enemy*.

The enemy is anyone who can *beat* you to the deal, anyone who can stop you *winning*, anyone who's not clearly on your *team*. To win, you must have a *game plan*. You perform better if you *train*. Good managers are also good at *coaching*. Sales *is* a competitive sport,

---

[18] Here are just a few athletes who have impressed me with their motivational presentations: Tommy Heinsohn, coach of Boston Celtics; Jim Tunney, former NFL Referee; Emmitt Smith of the Dallas Cowboys; Bart Starr of the Green Bay Packers.

[19] Being willing to state the obvious is a much under-valued characteristic. Being prepared to ask questions about 'obvious' things is another.

with stars, rules and trophies. Sales, like professional sports, can be a risky career, but with big rewards for the successful.

With this in mind, it should be obvious why I've devoted a whole section in this book to the skills needed to be successful in sales. Can you imagine a football player, or a distance runner, or a downhill skier or a chess player, or any other competitive athlete who does not spend significant time on understanding and developing the skills needed to win? Nope. But there are some sales people who stopped trying to learn after they received their first commission check. And there are some sales managers who never notice when this happens.

Good sales people do pretty much what competitive athletes do to improve. They are always trading ideas and tips with other people on their team. They are always on the lookout for new approaches and new angles – anything to increase their chances of winning. They are constantly trying to improve their understanding of the process, the tricks of the trade, what works and doesn't work. *All* the successful sales people I've worked with or met are constant learners. And once they've learned new skills they actually use them so they get better and better. (This is what athletes call *practicing*.)

Clearly being successful in sales needs an understanding of the basic techniques of the sport. Here's the sort of thing I tell sales people on my team. As a sales manager, you will need to develop your own version of this pitch. It should go something like this...

You need to acquire the basic skills to do the job. That means spending time, effort and maybe some money in learning. If you stay in sales long enough you'll acquire a whole bundle of skills as you make mistakes, do things right, and work with other sales people. Left to chance, you'll maybe learn your last important lesson the week before you retire, and then how will you feel?

Think of skills training – through courses, discussion and reading – simply as a fast track approach to learning all the things you'd work out for yourself in due course anyway. There's no disgrace in being a neophyte, but there is a disgrace in being a neophyte and not doing something purposeful to accelerate learning.

You've heard of athletes that have "natural ability". We all have natural ability to some extent, but it's what we do with it that counts. Natural ability goes wasted if not trained and improved upon. It's the same in sales as in any other sport.

People tend to gravitate towards those 'natural' personalities who enjoy company and take a real and unassumed interest in others, seeking to understand what stimulates and drives them. These naturals are personalities who always seem to be in a good mood, are tirelessly upbeat, and unquenchably sociable.

Lots of potentially good salespeople like to think that they will succeed because they are 'naturals'. Because they are naturally engaging and persuasive people, they think that selling is going to be easy. And sometimes that works out just fine, up to a point. But anyone, even the most scintillating personality, can become much more effective by tapping into the accumulated wisdom that sales people have acquired over the years.

In other words, continuous learning, training and practice should be a big part of any sales person's life, just like it is for any athlete.

Terry Noble is a close friend of mine. He is an outstanding golfer, and he played as a pro golfer on the mini tour a few years ago.

When we played golf together, Terry would be on just about every green in regulation, hitting every ball straight, right down the fairway, and every wedge shot would get him right up to the pin. By contrast I would consistently duff the ball or attract applause from by-standers by hitting my own special slice into the woods. Terry is such a patient friend, he even played with me more than once.

I guess I assumed that we played so differently simply because Terry was a naturally great golfer, and I just wasn't.

But Terry took the time to explain to me that there was more to it than that. He told me that golf had been his passion ever since he was a kid. He spent thousand of hours hitting golf balls at the range; thousands of hours practicing sand shots; thousands of hours on chip shots and even more hours putting. For Terry, it became second nature to swing the golf club and to know, or feel, exactly what to do on every shot. In other words, according to Terry, his natural athleticism was just a starting point. It took time and effort in learning from others and practicing over and over that made him a top-ranking golfer and raised him to the ranks of golfing professionals.

This was one of my early lessons on the importance of continuous learning and serious practice. As a sales person, it convinced me that having an outgoing personality would never be enough to hit the top ranks: it would always be necessary, even for a 'natural', to learn and practice the skills of the trade. As a golfer, it encouraged me to seek out advice on how to improve my game, and to practice and practice. As a result my golf game is much less embarrassing than it used to be, and I get much more enjoyment out of the game. I accept I am never going to be a professional golfer. But I do have some natural talent for selling, and, here I am, a professional sales person. I think I made the right career decision.

The Sales Skills Toolkit

What are the essential skills a sales person needs to be successful? Here is my list of the most important skills areas for sales people, and for sales team managers.

- Listening and Questioning
- Presenting
- The ability to work comfortably with numbers – forecasts, quotas, prices, discounts etc.
- Writing clearly and concisely
- Keeping track
- Developing sales strategies
- Negotiating
- Building relationships and getting along with people
- Understanding the sales process and techniques, from identifying opportunities to closing deals.

Most of these are covered in later chapters in this section. Building relationships is so important I've written an entire additional chapter about it (Chapter 4 of this book.) Understanding the sales process and applying sales tools and techniques is a big enough topic to justify another book.[20]

I have taught classes in all of these areas, but in this book, I'm not going to try to communicate everything there is to know about all these topics. My approach is to explain why it's important for you to build skills in all these areas, to encourage your team to do the same, and point you in the right direction to find out more.

---

[20] *Don't Just Stand There, Sell Something – Volume 2.* To be published sometime.

Building Your Team's Skills

One of the most important aspects of the role of a sales manager is to ensure that every member of the team has the basic skills needed to be successful. A sales manager builds a successful team in a number of ways:

- By recruiting people who are already skilled and experienced.
- By being a role model for team members: demonstrating the application of key skills every day.
- By taking opportunities to coach team members as they do their work.
- By taking skills development seriously: formulating training programs for team members, and making it possible for them to attend training events when this is the best way for them to develop.

In all cases building your skills and the skills of your team fully will need a multi-faceted approach: reading, coaching, attending courses and practicing the skills.

Being coached is vital, but some people are not all that good at being coached, just as everyone is not good at coaching. As a sales manager you need to learn how to coach, and practice that skill. And as a good coach you will help your team to understand what they need to do to take advantage of the wisdom you possess. (If you don't think you have lots of wisdom substitute 'stuff you know'.[21])

You need to encourage your team to remember that the path to learning starts with questions. Here are the 'rules' and some of the advice I like to hand down to my own team...

> *...encourage your team to remember that the path to learning starts with questions.*

In my experience, most people are aware of their own deficiencies, but very few are prepared to admit it in public. But if you want to build knowledge just go ahead and start to ask questions. *Aggressive Learning* is the first step on the journey towards acquiring wisdom.

---

[21] Is there a difference between 'wisdom' and 'stuff you know'? Yes – wisdom is stuff you know reinforced, tuned, adapted and expanded by the twin forges of experience and thinking deeply about things. I credit many people who know stuff with also having chunks of wisdom, even if they are too modest themselves to describe it as such.

There are no guarantees you'll get there, but making the journey is better than staying in one place.

If you want to learn, remember these rules:

- Never be afraid to ask for help.
- Never be afraid to ask a dumb question.
- Never assume you're the only one who's confused.

Aggressive learning also applies to your selection of reading material. By all means buy the sales books you find on airport bookshelves (including this one). But don't stop there – be omnivorous. Read general management books too. Read business newspapers and magazines: I try to read The Wall Street Journal, Business Week and Forbes whenever I have time. If you're in international sales, The Economist and Financial Times can provide useful perspectives.

Look for insights into selling everywhere. Many novels explore relationships between people, attempt to uncover psychological foundations of behavior, and describe the transactions that go on when one person is trying to make someone else say 'yes'. If that isn't about selling I don't know what is. I found the movie Glengarry Glen Ross provoked as much thought about selling as any sales text book I've read.

Many people are reluctant to take time off to attend training seminars. In some cases, you may not have an option because certain companies mandate certain sales approaches and techniques. Fair enough: approach those events with a positive attitude, not as a chore. I admit, some sales training courses are rather dull. Make it your mission to enliven every event. Even if you don't learn from the presenter you might learn from the interactions with the other attendees, and it's more fun than snoozing.

Even if you think you've had all the training you need, it doesn't hurt to refresh your skills from time to time. A couple of years of front-line selling action can make you neglect good habits and acquire bad ones. Sometimes we have to get back to basic blocking and tackling to regain some simple disciplines.[22]

When you're an attendee at a training event don't be reluctant to be the first to ask a question. So many times, when I've been a participant in a seminar, one of the others has come up to me at the end and thanked me for asking a 'dumb' question. It's turned out that

---

[22] Good training sessions can be really useful. But there are many things that simply can't be learned in a classroom, so formal training is only a part of the picture – treat it as a launchpad for further learning. For further views on this topic, read *You Can't Teach a Kid to Ride a Bike at a Seminar*, David H. Sandler (Dutton, 1996).

everyone was lost, but everyone also assumed they were the only one who didn't understand. Be confident enough to assume that if you don't get it, you're probably not the only one: ask the question.

Once you've learned something new, get into the habit of rushing right out and using it. Rehearse in private if you think that will help. But don't just place your new knowledge in a dark box in the back of your mind. Bring it out, try it out and

> *Once you've learned something new, get into the habit of using it...*

find out how useful it is. You can always put it away again if it doesn't work for you.

And once you've tried a new skill, for real, just once, the next time will not be so hard. Whether it's a new format for writing a proposal, a new slant on an old presentation, a new source of sales prospects, or whatever: use it or lose it. I read somewhere that you need to do something every day for twenty-one days to make it a real habit. If you try out your new skill just one time, you'll probably lose it. You must do it often enough that it becomes ingrained as a habit.

If you take a golf lesson and learn a great new driving technique, it won't be much use unless you practice that technique at the driving range, many times until it becomes part of your game. To take a lesson and not practice is a waste of dollars. That applies to sales training, as well as to golf lessons.

At the same time, you need to be practical about selecting your areas of study. For example, in some types of sales job you will hardly ever have to give a formal presentation – all your sales pitches will be one-to-one. In another job, every deal may require you to give one or more presentations to groups of tired and cynical executives, and you will be lost unless you develop a professional and relaxed presentation style.

Select what is most important, and build your own toolkit. But keep your tools sharp by using, rehearsing and refreshing your skills often.

Every sales person should put together a personal growth plan and update it every year, or more often. Where do you want to improve? Where do you need to improve? What exactly are you going to do to improve, and when? How will you measure success?

Don't rely on your own personal introspection to come up with this plan. As your manager, I am always ready to work this through with you. (When you move on to a new job, encourage your new manager to the same thing, even if he or she doesn't like to do that sort of thing). Gently elicit opinions from other business contacts and even friendly customers. This needn't be as embarrassing as it sounds. Just tell them straight: "Hey, I'm reviewing my personal development plan. You know I'm not perfect. What do you think I should focus on improving for the next twelve months?" You can do this over lunch, on the golf course, or perhaps with a martini after work if that's your sort of thing. Personally, I find a good quality single malt Scotch often promotes camaraderie and open communication.

Good managers want their people to grow and become as skilled and knowledgeable as possible.

The success of a manager can *only* be measured by the success of the team he or she manages. To be a successful manager, you need a successful team. A team that is knowledgeable and skilled will always do better than a team that lacks skills and doesn't know much. As a sales team manager you must always

> *The success of a manager can only be measured by the success of the team he or she manages.*

have the continual development of team skills and capabilities high on your priority list. It can be hard work, and time consuming. But ultimately learning is much more cost-effective than ignorance.

Listening and Questioning

Sales people are almost always good talkers. The profession attracts people who are outgoing and communicative. This is good. But I always encourage my team to learn to listen and question too. The best sales people know how to use a conversation to find things out that will help the sales process. Here are some of the coaching notes I've used with my sales teams on the topic of Listening and Questioning.

Shut up and listen. To be a good listener, first learn not to talk. I believe that the person who talks most is least in control, especially in a sales context. Let the customer do most of the talking. While the customer is talking, the sales person must *concentrate*. Don't just sit there waiting for an opportunity to say something. "We never listen when we are eager to speak."[23]

We need to devote considerable brain power to keeping quiet, while striving to understand the customer's perspective, where they're coming from, how they feel and what direction they are leaning towards. The more you dominate the conversation the less you will learn about the customer, and the more frustrated the customer will become. Instead of building a relationship, you build a barrier to understanding. More than likely you will fail to understand their real needs, their attitudes and preferences.

The more you dominate the conversation, the less you will learn about the customer, and the more frustrated the customer will become.

If you ever want to reach a point when you can say something relevant, then follow the sequence: listen, learn, think, speak. Or as Stephen Covey puts it: "Seek to understand and then to be understood."[24]

Especially in the early phase of a relationship with a customer, listening well is fundamental to building a relationship. You should allow – and encourage – wide ranging conversation, across a range of business issues and personal issues too. If you restrict the conversation to too narrow an area of interest you might miss out on some useful information.

[23] *Maxims,* Francois, Duc de La Rochefoucald (First published 1665; Penguin Classics, 1982).
[24] *The 7 Habits of Highly Effective People*, Stephen R. Covey (Free Press, 1990).

Open-ended questioning can lead to unexpected areas, but that's not a problem. You will find out much more about what your contact needs, and just as important, what he or she wants and likes.

Always, when you're face to face with a customer, make the most of that opportunity. Make the customer the center of your attention. Listen, show appreciation, ask intelligent questions, be interested in the answers and show that you care. If you care, you should show it. If you don't care, you probably won't build the sort of trusting relationships that lead to big deals.

Listen for the reality. People use more than words to communicate. Make eye contact, listen for inflections of the voice, observe gestures and body movements that might help you figure out the speaker's real mood and intent. This is not always easy.

On a new sales call, everyone finds it tough to work out what's really going on under the surface. You need to establish as early as possible what the customer feels about doing business with you, and look for signs of change as the relationship develops. There are three possibilities: willing, unwilling and indifferent.

At the simplest level, people mislead you because they don't want a confrontation. This is why people say things like: "The doctor will be with you right away" or "Hold still, this won't hurt a bit."

At a more complex level, people sometimes mislead others unintentionally because their behavior doesn't match their real feelings. And people allow themselves to be misled because of unwarranted optimism or needless pessimism. If you don't concentrate on listening intelligently you may well read the wrong thing into the customer's behavior. The way people converse has a lot to do with their basic personality type. Their behavior may well obscure their underlying opinion.

For example if a customer is an amiable, outgoing, sociable type, the conversation can swing along quite happily. It is easy to fall into the trap of assuming that this amiability means that the customer is actually interested in doing business with you. It just doesn't follow automatically. Amiable people may eventually find a way of telling you they don't want to buy, but they tend to take their time doing it.

The opposite can also be true. Someone who asks you lots of searching and apparently critical questions may just be a highly analytic personality. Their questioning may not be driven by a search for reasons to say no; it could just as likely be their way of confirming their inner decision to say yes.

Dealing with customers who are willing to do business with you is pretty much what we all want. But don't expect customers to lay their position out clearly for you. You'll have to do some work, and use your understanding of people and what makes them tick to come to the correct conclusion.

You'll get nowhere if you assume someone is on board just because they have a friendly outgoing style, and they're always agreeing with you. A person's 'style' is not necessarily a true indication of their opinion and attitude. While you are working to reinforce what you think is an attitude of acceptance, they could be working out reasons to say no. You should be identifying objections and addressing those objections; but you don't even know those objections exist, because you're having the wrong conversation.

> *A person's 'style' is not necessarily a true indication of their opinion and attitude.*

It's almost as bad to make the opposite mistake. Your customer is actually feeling fairly favorably disposed towards you, but you've jumped to the conclusion that they have all sorts of problems with your solution. ("Oh dear, all these questions... why doesn't she smile? She must be really unhappy.") By focusing on addressing imagined objections, you'll just irritate people, and maybe even turn a good prospect into a poor one.

Hold a conversation not an interrogation. Some sales people try to fit a customer into a rigid questioning routine: a pre-determined roadmap for uncovering needs and closing the deal. They believe that they always must be "drilling down" to uncover more and more detail. That sounds to me like something a dentist would do.

The drill-down approach goes an inch wide and a mile deep – aiming to take each issue and address it to the nth degree until we know as much about it as the customer does.

This approach tries to drive the customer down a narrow path that ends in a decision to buy. But I believe that just doesn't work well these days, whether the product is a pair of shoes or a ten million dollar software package. There is just so much a customer will share with you, and in my experience a less structured, more conversational approach always seems to reveal more information than the deep mining approach.

Your interaction with the customer should be a stroll across a meadow, not a rush down a narrow path. You should be having a conversation, not conducting an interrogation.

Questioning techniques can be used to steer a conversation in the right direction. But how many questions can you ask without sounding as if you are interrogating the customer?

The customer ultimately has to feel comfortable about conveying the real information we need, and that gets back to trust. It's hard to build trust with a succession of blunt questions. Instead we need to ask very open questions that gently lead a conversation in the general direction we want. We need to ask questions in an empathetic way, to demonstrate that we truly are concerned with the customer's needs. We need to build rapport – and confirm understanding – by playing back the customer's comments.

Listen to what the customer says, and use the customer's comments to extend the conversation, by homing in on key words, phrases and topics. Suppose you are discussing the general direction of the business and your customer just happens to mention a concern about productivity. Use this as a cue to explore areas where they feel costs are maybe too high, or there is wasted effort. These could be areas in which your products and services might be able to help. And if so, you will understand the specific areas of concern that the customer has so you can build them into your value proposition at the right time.

Ask open questions. If you want to find out something new, ask open questions. Closed questions are conversation stoppers.

Have you ever had a conversation with a teenager who would rather be somewhere else? "Hi Donnie, how are things going at school?" "*OK*" "Good. What class do you enjoy the most?" "*Um. Math.*" "Math?" "*I guess so.*" "You're good at Math?" "*I guess so.*" "How about sports - you on any teams?" "*Nope.*" And so on. Hard work.

Sometimes talking to company executives is like that. Their mind is somewhere else, and they need a little encouragement to open up. One way of doing that is to use open questions, and to avoid closed questions.

A closed question is one that can be answered with one or two words. If the answer can be 'Yes' or 'No' or a simple noun, it's a closed question.

An open question cannot be comfortably answered with a single word. The answerer feels compelled to provide a more extended answer. Open questions require an answer which contains explanation and detail to be satisfactory. Open questions therefore help to elicit new information.

I've heard it said that you should only ask questions to which you already know the answers. This may be critical for trial lawyers, but in sales that approach is limiting and likely to lead to dead ends. If you are genuinely interested in the customer's needs, and genuinely interested in providing solutions that deliver business benefit, then you won't shy away from asking open questions that may lead into uncharted territory.

Hi Donnie, what's going on at school?" "*Um. Not much.*" Silence. You keep eye contact. You don't break the silence. You ask for more with your eyebrows. "*Um. I joined the Glee Club.*" "Wow! That's great - tell me more..." Thirty minutes later, you're still listening, and Donnie's still talking.

Are closed questions completely banned? No, not at all. You should use closed questions in two important situations.

First ask a closed question when it's really important to obtain or confirm specific facts. "Exactly how many employees in the company will use this new software package?" "*2000.*" "Thanks, that will help me to give you a final price.

The other situation in which a closed question can be useful is if you need to gain commitment, or alternatively to close down a dead-end discussion. You need to choose your timing very carefully for this! "All right, you've had our offer for three weeks. Am I right to think we've now discussed all the details and addressed all your concerns? "*Yes, we've covered everything I was worried about.*" "So will you tell your board that you want this deal and ask the CEO to sign the contract?" "*Yes Stu, of course.*"

Eventually there has to be a question that must be answered with a 'yes' or a 'no'.

Build rapport with mirror questions. It often helps to confirm understanding by using mirror questions. A mirror question bounces back something the customer has said, with an extra question tagged on the end. Intelligent mirror questions can also uncover things that might otherwise be missed.

For example, your customer mentions that they are highly frustrated with their inventory system. The main problem is that they are constantly running out of parts, so they can't fulfill customer orders.

A good mirror question might be: "So the inventory system is the main reason you can't deliver orders on time?" Customer nods. You go on: "What impact does that have on customer satisfaction and repeat orders?" This is a fairly open add-on that may elicit valuable new information.

The sensible use of mirror questions not only makes sure you stay on the same wavelength as your customer, it helps to build rapport. People like to be understood, and your questions let the customer know you're keeping up. People also like to know that someone is interested in what they are saying. When you bounce back key messages, the customer knows for sure that you are listening. When you ask intelligent follow-on questions, the customer is able to discern that you are interested.

Mirror questions help you move, psychologically, across the desk. You're on their side. Mirror questions help you connect.

Use questions to handle indifference. If your customer loves you and your solution, you have the pleasant task of moving them towards closing a deal. If the customer is totally antagonistic towards you, you have a different challenge, but it's still a challenge that's clear cut: you have to dig to understand the root cause of the objections and then address them, one by one.

In a way, customer indifference is even tougher than straight rejection. You have nothing to work with, and nothing substantial to fight against. You have nothing to build on. Personally I find it easier to handle the objections of a customer who disagrees openly for plainly stated reasons, than to work with a customer who is apathetic or indifferent to what I'm saying.

In judo, it's easier to flip someone who is moving, forward or backward, than someone who is rooted in one place. An indifferent customer is rooted, standing still, taking no sides.

To counter apparent indifference, you need to move the conversation forward, to generate momentum by finding common ground, or unearthing a real difference of opinion.

You can do this by listening and questioning.

Active listening provides you with opportunities to ask the sort of open questions that will move the conversation to new ground.

There is no standard formula for success here. Open questions will uncover new information. Intelligent assessment of that new information will create further topics for discussion.

Sometimes you have to accelerate the process by introducing a controversial topic, relevant (tangentially) to the service you are offering. Suppose you are selling a service management solution. You could say: "One of my customers says they're going to close one of their service offices and set everyone up at their homes with high-speed Internet and VPN access to the data center. They're going to save $20 million a year, they reckon. What do you think of that?" Now, this may be nothing directly to do with your service offering, but it allows an off-center opportunity to discuss lots of issues related to service management staffing, productivity, training, supervision – and software.

Keep at it. Eventually your open questioning, empathetic listening and provocative comments will uncover something that excites or upsets the customer.

Listen. I have used the expression 'empathetic listening' a few times. This deserves further explanation. Empathy is about identifying with the needs, attitudes and feelings of someone else. If you are empathetic, you are putting yourself mentally in the other person's place, and trying to view the world from their perspective.

When you are being truly empathetic, you are doing a whole lot more than gathering factual information. You are paying attention to body language, to tone of voice, and to the emotions behind the words that are being spoken. This is why face-to-face meetings are still very useful, and why you can miss some tricks if you rely only on phone calls (even video-phone calls). Empathetic listening has to be done naturally and we need to adapt our style to the way the customer responds to each question. We need to know when to ask and when not to ask. You are reaching an understanding of the person behind the message, their fears, concerns and enthusiasms. You must see their business through their eyes, with their prejudices and preferences.

To do this effectively, you must not artificially constrain the discussion. The to and fro of question and response must remain natural and unforced. You must let the customer move the conversation wherever he or she wants it to go. Nothing is off limits. And for most people this necessarily means going beyond discussion of 'business as usual' into family life, personal concerns and ambitions, and much more.

You can do this comfortably, without appearing to by prying, only if your comments and questions are rooted in genuine concern for and interest in that individual. It is really difficult to fake that.

In Chapter 4 of this book I will expand on this topic some more. This is all about much more than questioning technique – this is all about building relationships.

Mastering Sales Presentations

Presentation skills are important for sales managers and for sales reps. The advice and observations I make in this chapter are equally applicable to you, as a sales manager, and to your team members. They are relevant if you are preparing and delivering a presentation to a customer, to a group of company executives, to your local Chamber of Commerce, your golf club, ski club or church.

I know someone who would rather have a stomach ache than give a presentation to a large group of people. As a result he often gets stomachaches. He's not alone. Many surveys have shown that making a presentation is more feared than poisonous insects, snakes, flying, and even death. Those surveys tell us two important things: sure, presenting makes people anxious; and also, you should treat the results of popular surveys with some skepticism.[25]

Most sales people are nervous before making a big presentation. But in my experience, sales people tend to be less anxious than the typical executive. Sales types must be psychologically more robust than other business people. (Or perhaps they are movie star wannabees. Or maybe they just don't know enough to be scared.[26])

Nervousness can certainly be a problem. But it's too easy to blame nervousness for poor performance. Everyone can learn to deliver more impressive presentations by investing time and effort in learning the basic skills. And some nervousness is good: it's energy that can be channeled to raise your level of performance. In this chapter, my aim is to share my experience to help you not just reduce tension and anxiety, but to set you on the road to delivering high-impact, persuasive and enjoyable presentations.

Preparation. It takes a lot of work to make your presentation appear fresh and spontaneous. Spontaneity can't be left to chance! If you are presenting a new divisional sales strategy to your company's board, and you want to make a great impression, you'd better spend a lot of time making sure your message is clear and compelling. If your presentation is to launch an important new product at a big

---

[25] If you know anyone who would really rather walk over a cliff than give a presentation, they need more help than this book can give them. A study quoted by Mike Klepper in his useful book *I'd Rather Die Than Give a Speech* (Irwin, 1993) found that 20% of executives would rather do taxes, 20% would rather try to lose 10lbs in a month, and 45% would rather have a cavity filled. None (0%) said they would rather die. That's a relief.

[26] "If you can keep your head when all around are losing theirs, you clearly don't have a clue what's going on." Apologies to Rudyard Kipling for the misquote, by Anon.

international trade show, with fancy lights and music, it becomes a major production, and should be treated as seriously as anything in showbiz. If you are presenting a small proposal to a group of two or three people who you know well, then most of your effort will be in getting the proposal itself right: but you will still have to spend a few hours working out how best to pitch it. Although the investment of time and effort will vary, no presentation is so unimportant you can skip the preparation stage.

First, decide what you want to achieve with the presentation. Why are you doing this? How will you measure the success of the presentation? (Don't think kind words will be enough.)

There are, broadly, three types of presentation. Presentations that aim to inform and educate; presentations that aim to inspire and motivate; presentations that aim to persuade – or sell. Your presentation will almost always contain some of each, but one will dominate.

Think about the type of people who will be in the audience, and what you are trying to achieve with them. Your measurement of success will depend on what you are trying to get across to your audience. Did the participants learn something? Will they be inspired to go off and do great new things? How will you know?

The success of a persuasive or selling presentation is the easiest to measure objectively. Did the board accept the plan? Did the team agree to act? Did the customer sign the deal? When you're selling, at least you get feedback.

Write down one sentence to describe who it is you'll be presenting to, what it is you are trying to achieve, and how you will know if you have been successful. For example: "This presentation will persuade the board of Bigcompany Inc. to buy my solution, and I'll know that the presentation has been successful if they sign a letter of intent in one week." Or: "This presentation will help everyone in the sales division to understand the new product better, and I'll count myself as successful if they give me a score of better than eight out of ten in the post-session evaluation survey."

The importance of deciding up front what you want to achieve, is that you will use that objective to assess the value of everything you might think about including in the presentation. Will this comment help or hinder? Will this picture move the audience in the right direction? Is this joke really going to work? By having a clearly defined aim, you have a mechanism to answer all these questions. Make sure you ask yourself those questions as you prepare, and make sure you throw out anything that is unhelpful. Be ruthless.

Once you have your key points, emphasize them with stories, allegories and relevant examples. Repeat the most important points.

Use statistics to prove and drive home your points, but keep your comments at a high level.

Jokes are sometimes good, sometimes they crash. If you're not comfortable telling jokes in social situations, you probably shouldn't try to tell funny stories in a presentation. Even if everyone tells you you're a great comedian you need to be disciplined about jokes: if a joke doesn't have sharp relevance to the topic, and doesn't illuminate a point, keep it out. (If it's really funny, save it for another time. I have a lot of hilarious material that I've never used, waiting for that *appropriate* event to come along.) And remember that telling jokes – that is, funny stories – is not the only way to make your audience warm to you.

You can be witty without telling jokes. You can make people smile by touching the nerve of shared experience. You can make people happy by giving them insights, or something new to think about – in other words by being interesting. And enthusiasm is infectious. Spread some around. Purposefully build all of those good things into your presentation.

When you are developing your presentation material, build it in three main parts: an introduction, the main presentation, and the conclusion. In these parts you tell them what you're going to tell them, then you tell them, and finally tell them what you just told them![27]

If your presentation is long and complicated, break it into subsections, with one theme and one key message per subsection. Each subsection can have its own few words of introduction, and a conclusion to drive home your point.

Above all, keep it simple. In presentations, people can't go back and re-read things. If they do, they're missing the new stuff you're trying to get across. Less is more.

In most business presentations, your audience will have an opportunity to ask questions. Part of your planning and preparation should be to think about possible questions in advance, and work out how you can use the answers as an opportunity to drive home the message that you're trying to get across.

What about those slide packs? So far I haven't said much about presentation slides, or charts. They seem to be pretty nearly compulsory these days.

It is essential that you should think through your presentation outline and structure first, and then, and only then, think about the charts.

---

[27] An old chestnut that's been around for years. It's still true.

Charts can be really helpful in conveying and reinforcing a message. I've read that people only retain about 20% of what they hear. On average, they retain about 30% of what they see. The good thing is, if they see and hear something simultaneously, they might retain about 50% of the information.[28] My experience bears this out. Especially in an instructional environment, good graphics and headlines that reinforce the spoken message work really well.

The important point here is that the slides need to be good and relevant. By working out your outline first, and even drafting a script, you can start to think about slides that will have real impact. Good slides illustrate your spoken points, and reinforce them. Poor slides repeat your spoken words without adding emphasis, color, or additional insights.

Simply putting the words of your script in bullet points on a slide is not particularly effective. Most people do just that, which is why most presentations are boring. Pictures on screen, plus words from you, are the most powerful combination. It allows the audience to receive the message with two different parts of their brain at one time and this reinforces the message. Add to this an effective presentation style - energetic, varying intonation, some audience interaction - and you have the ingredients for a great event.

Examples of good use of words and pictures together are all around you. A good TV documentary has an engaging 'voice over' and interesting pictures on the screen. Notice - they don't fill your TV screen with bullet pointed text. The same is true for magazines and textbooks. In all cases the words are important, the pictures are important, the style of presentation is important, and together they are really powerful.

In a newspaper, what attracts your attention? Possibly a strong picture - or an interesting headline. You can use headlines - bullet points on slides - in exactly the same way, to attract and hold the audience. But if instead of headlines, you make the mistake of actually putting the full text up there, you'd might as well sit down and let the audience read it by themselves. Slides ought to be like billboards - you can pass them at 60mph and still get the message.

But before you fire up PowerPoint™[29], just check whether you really need slides at all.

Think for a moment of the some of the most effective speakers you have heard - and don't restrict this to your everyday business

---

[28] I can't remember where those numbers came from. Probably I heard them in a presentation. I remembered half the story (the numbers) but not how they were established or who said so. See - the 50% rule must be true after all.

[29] *Microsoft PowerPoint* is a trademark of Microsoft Corp.

environment. My list of memorable speakers is very mixed. I can think of several motivational speakers who made a big impact on me. I can clearly remember a number of after-dinner speakers who held my attention. Then there are some preachers, stand-up comics and a few politicians: people who can paint a picture in speech, all memorable, all great communicators. All highly effective, and mostly talking without benefit of a projector. Slides can be useful, but they're not always necessary.

In a business setting, especially if your message is complex, you'll probably decide to prepare a few slides. Not too many: start out with just one for every fifteen minutes of the presentation. Add more if you think it's going to be essential to get the message across. If you end up with more than eight slides for a half hour presentation you probably have too many. Just remember that slides are there to enhance the show, not to be the show. Too many, or the wrong type, can distract or bore the audience.

Rehearse, rehearse. You should 'dry run' every presentation with a friendly audience. *Practice* helps you to store the presentation in your memory so it can be recalled when you need it, even if you're stressed and nervous. Repetition is essential. When you were at school, this used to be called rote learning, and educationalists used to argue about whether it was good for you. Don't worry about it. Committing things to memory is actually good for your brain cells, enhances your performance, and boosts your career.

For a short informal presentation to a group of two or three, it will probably be enough to run it through a few times with one person, to make sure it flows logically and doesn't contain any obvious mistakes. Check the timing carefully and be prepared to cut text and slides. It's better for you to decide what to drop ahead of time, than to be forced to lose everything in the last ten minutes.

For a big, important presentation, you should go even further. Ask two or three people you trust to sit through it, and present it pretty much as you plan to do it on the day. Take careful note of the feedback and change things if necessary. Sometimes the hardest thing is to throw away a favorite joke or story. But listen to the advice, ask for reasons why, and remember that things sound different on the other side of the microphone.

If your presentation will have multiple presenters, you must have a full rehearsal so that there are no surprises. One time, I was a reluctant participant in a team presentation where two of the presenters chose to fly in just two hours before the event. They never rehearsed with the rest of us. Guess what? The presentation was a total flop.

In a team presentation, everyone must understand the points the other presenters are going to make and the way the presentation is supposed to flow. Handovers should be planned in detail: every speaker should know exactly what words to say to introduce the next person. Don't let people make that up on the day. You should check the timing carefully and be ruthless enough to cut stuff out if the presentation is too long. Otherwise the poor person who is on last will have to drop all their good stuff. Also, agree how the team will handle the audience's questions. Usually it's best to let one presenter take the lead, receive the questions and then hand them to the other presenters to respond. Team presentations can be powerful and highly effective – but only if they are carefully prepared. Most team presentations fall short of excellence, and that can always be blamed on lack of preparation and rehearsal.

Should presenters use a script? There is no hard and fast rule here. At one extreme, some people love the extra adrenaline they get from speaking without any notes at all. Please note, most people who speak fluently and confidently without notes actually do a lot of preparation and rehearsing before hand; or else they've been giving the same presentation for years.

Some people cannot stand up in front of an audience without a complete script in their hand. Simply reading a script out loud is highly unlikely to be stimulating to the audience. The biggest mistake most people make in writing scripts is to forget that spoken English is quite a different language from written English. That's why so many scripted presentations sound stilted. But it is possible to write a script with more life. (After all, it works in the movies.) If you need a full script, read it out loud and rehearse in front of others several times, and change anything that sounds awkward or unnatural.

Most people like something in between. They have notes or cue cards so they can follow the planned flow, with timing notes. Sometimes the slideshow provides sufficient prompts. (But please don't just stand there and read from the slides.)

Ultimately, this comes down to personal preference. As you become more comfortable presenting, you will make do with fewer notes.[30]

Whatever else you do, make sure you know exactly how you're going to start and finish. Getting your opening and closing words fixed in your head is a great confidence booster. We all have nervous energy when we start, and knowing the first few sentences really well

---

[30] If you have a specific legal point or contractual point that your company attorneys insist that you make in a particular way, then write it down, no matter how confident you are in the power of your memory. Your attorney will be hiding somewhere in the room listening. That's what they do.

gets a speaker off to a good beginning and allows him or her to settle down quickly into the rhythm of the presentation.

And when you're coming to an end, there is nothing more embarrassing than just trailing to a weak and inconclusive close. You should know exactly how you're going to finish: it's the 'punch line' of your presentation after all. Your presentation aimed to inform, persuade or inspire: punch that home in your closing sentences. Rehearse your closing sentences several times, to make sure they have real impact.

Leave the audience in no doubt that you're finished, that you've said something valuable, and that it's about time they gave you a round of applause.

Presentation Style. "Just stand up and be yourself" is a piece of advice that novice presenters are often given. Is that good advice? It depends what it really means, and how it is taken.

I remember an after-dinner speaker giving that advice to one of my younger colleagues as we milled around after a particularly good dinner, and an excellent speech. "Honestly, I just stand up and be myself, and it seems to work OK for me. I suggest you just have to muster up enough confidence to do the same."

The problem was, the person giving the advice was a veteran TV presenter, whose entire life was about being the center of attention. Even in a noisy bar, his voice could easily be heard across the room. He was just being himself. My friend on the other hand, was fresh out of school, was keen to do well, but if he had "just been himself" when presenting, no one would have noticed he was actually speaking.

After a while this young man actually became a very good speaker. He did this by being someone slightly different from his normal self when presenting. He spoke more loudly, more slowly and more clearly than in normal conversation. His gestures were broader and more deliberate. He learned to smile, even when he was nervous. He remembered not to run his fingers through his hair all the time. None of this was "normal", at least not at first.

The thought of appearing in front of an audience as his normal self was even scarier than the thought of learning some new tricks. He went to presentation classes, absorbed the lessons, and practiced.

At the same time, he did stay "himself". He didn't change his basic character, he didn't try to imitate anyone else, he didn't try to adopt an alien style. He learned the basics of good presentation, and developed his own style, and it worked.

So: take note of what seems to work when other people give presentations, and try out new approaches. But retain the foundation of your own personality. Presenting is a bit like acting, but not totally. Actors are required to create a new personality. Presenters are expected to let their own personality ring true.

Once you have worked out that being just slightly "larger than life" is quite OK, you need to pay attention to other aspects of presentation style that make the difference between a stimulating event and a sleep-in.

Think about some of the best speakers you have ever heard and work out what made them so good. Here are some things that I've noticed in all good presenters:

- They show enthusiasm for their subject
- They have commitment to whatever it is they are communicating, and appear to be excited at having the opportunity to communicate it
- They use varying tone of voice and inflection to add interest and reinforce the messages
- They are consistently energetic
- They make intelligent use of pace, pauses
- They have the ability to appear to be making eye contact all the time
- They use movement and gestures to emphasize without distracting
- They are not afraid to display emotion and enthusiasm
- They manage to *connect* with the audience, every time
- They are totally in control, even when they are acting out of control.

Essentially, you must care or your audience won't care. If you care and are excited, and really want to get a message across, then your presentation will work. Almost everything else follows from this basic enthusiasm. The excitement will dissipate your nervousness. Your interest in the topic will add interest to your tone of voice. Your inner need to communicate effectively will help you become a more effective communicator.

Unfortunately the opposite is also true. People who are bored by the subject of their presentation cannot help but be boring presenters. It should be obvious how to avoid that trap.

Almost everyone gets anxious about making a presentation. But if you're genuinely fearful, it doesn't help much to know that everyone else is worried too. So if that doesn't help, what does? You can reduce (but not always eliminate) nervousness by preparing thoroughly before the event. Be genuinely interested in and excited by your presentation topic, because enthusiasm is also an antidote to fear and nervousness. Then, on the day, you need to somehow develop a "go for it" attitude. (It also helps to have done at least two hundred presentations already, but that takes time.) But where does the "go for it" attitude come from?

I know something about presentation fear. In my eighth-grade class I had to speak about one of my hobbies in front of my classmates for a whole three minutes. I stuttered and just about cried. Everyone laughed and someone actually shot paper clips at me. After that experience I managed to avoid presentations until my senior year in college, when I had to present to my engineering lab class of just six students and the professor. The presentation was to last twenty minutes, split between me and my lab partner. The topic was on creating the Mohr's circle on a cathode ray oscilloscope, which I suppose lets you know how old I am. (At least there were no personal computers around then, so I didn't have to struggle with Powerpoint at the same time.) Once again, I started stuttering and shaking in front of the class, even though I had a partner to help me and provide moral support. I finished my portion in just five minutes and let my partner take the next fifteen.

I suppose I decided that I just wasn't cut out to be a presenter because I never volunteered to present again for quite a few years. Then, when I was twenty-seven years old, I found myself forced to agree to do a big presentation. Eventually I just ran out of credible excuses. It was to be in front of twenty people who I didn't know. It was the first presentation in my new career, and only the third in my entire life. I lost sleep for a whole month thinking about that presentation. My brain just wanted to focus on my bad experiences in the past. I was afraid about being rejected or laughed at. What if I started stuttering again? It's true that FEAR is just False Expectations Appearing Real.

I made it through the presentation fine after losing my nervousness after about a minute. When I was done I had the best feeling I ever had. I made it through the fear and was actually quite appreciated by the group. That became a turning point for me, which led me into a career in sales and then sales training.

I made it, because eventually I was willing to confront my fear and "go for it" on the day. I was willing to take a risk and it paid off, and it always will for you too. If you never take the risk, you'll never live up to you're potential or realize all your God-given talents. "Going for it" needs just the same sort of mental attitude as taking your first ski-run down a steep slope, diving into a cold, cold swimming pool, doing your first parachute jump or a bungee jump[31]. Look ahead and envision a successful outcome. Breath deeply, decide you're going to do it, then just do it.

Looking back, I know now how I could have overcome my fear of presenting with less personal pain and anguish. On the ski slopes, you learn the basics from someone who is experienced. You try things out on the bunny slopes. You fall a few times, and learn how to minimize damage when you crash. You get a feel for what needs to be done by learning the skills in a relatively safe environment. When you get to the top of your first terrifyingly steep slope, you know what's expected of you. You also know that this is the only sensible way down, and people will eventually get tired bringing food up the mountain for you. You breath in, you let go, you do it.

I recommend you follow the same sort of regime to get yourself comfortable with presenting. Read up on the basic skills, and try them out in a friendly environment. At social gatherings, family events, your church or anywhere you're comfortable, look for chances to practice. Someone has to stand up and say thank you, make an announcement, propose a toast – make sure that you get to do it, at least sometimes. No one will mind if you fluff a few words, or pause too long, or trip over the punchline of a joke. Next time, you'll do it even better, I promise.

Presenting is one area in which practical training is really useful. Ask your friends and colleagues for recommendations of training courses they have enjoyed and benefited from. The great thing about a good presentation course is that it gives you a chance to practice the skills as you learn them. If you've only done a couple of presentations in your whole life, attend a three-day or four-day course, and by the end of it you will have upped your record to fifteen or more. Then you'll wonder why on earth you were so anxious before, and may even start to look forward to presenting.

And just like in skiing, if you do fall over, remember no one worth considering is going to laugh at you. No one is going to call you names. People will help you climb out of the snow and make sure you're not broken. People will help you on your way. We've all been there. We're all grown up now.

Stage Management. Remember Murphy's Law: "If anything can go wrong, it will." This is not a counsel of despair: what Murphy was trying to get across is that you shouldn't just assume that everything will go right; so if you want to be successful, plan for every possible

---

[31] OK, I admit I've never done a bungee jump, and don't want to. It's never kept me from closing a sale.

problem. When preparing to give a presentation, make sure everything is set up and working before you start. Do it personally, so you can't complain if it's not exactly the way you like it.

Get to the room early. Where do you want people to sit, especially decision makers? Assign reserved seats for VIPs. Check out the lighting in the room, and the sound settings.

Check the temperature settings. Slightly too cool is usually better than too hot. Is the heating or cooling system too noisy? It usually is in hotel conference rooms. Compensate with a good sound system. Or decide if the audience can survive without heating or cooling for the period while you are talking.

Check that your presentation equipment works and that the screen (or your flip charts) can be seen and read from everywhere in the room. Make sure you have a backup bulb for the projector. Make sure you have a buddy bring along another laptop with your presentation on it, just in case yours chooses to expire.

Check out how your voice carries in the room and rehearse there for if at all possible. This will give you a feel for the room, but remember it will sound different when it's full of people.

You must plant someone in the audience who will give you signals to let you know if you're ahead of time, or running out of time; if you are speaking loudly enough or if you are intimidating the audience by booming at them. Agree the signals ahead of time. And make sure you know where your friend has decided to sit!

Make sure there's some water for you to drink, if you need it. (Avoid sodas. The combination of sugar, caffeine, gas and adrenaline is likely to do more harm than good.)

What to wear? Dress roughly on the same level, but if in doubt aim for something slightly more formal than the audience is likely to be wearing. After all, you are the show.

Writing

Writing about *writing* is fraught with danger. In this section I risk attracting critical letters (and e-letters) from thousands of professors and other professionals who study writing for a living. Who am I to give advice when I've written a book that's full of ungrammatical constructions and slang? So be it. As long as the critics spend their money on this book, I can take any amount of criticism. For real in-depth advice on writing, you should buy some books written by those aforementioned professors and writing professionals. In this book, my aim is simply to convey the importance of clear written communication to your success as a sales professional, and point you in the direction of some steps you can take to make your writing a more effective sales tool. Those steps include:

- Buy some books
- Keep to the point.
- Don't get hung up on grammatical niceties.
- Get a second opinion.

You don't have to be a Shakespeare to be successful in sales management or as a sales professional. Your writing style doesn't need to be poetic, resonant and laden with concealed meaning. In fact, concealed meaning is the last thing you want in any of the documents you write, whether they are proposals, your résumé, or business letters and e-mail messages.

Here is a statement of the blindingly self-evident: your writing style must *illuminate* the message you want to convey, not *obscure* it. I know, I know: everyone knows this.[32] But if everyone knows it, why is so much business writing confused and rambling? Why do we sometimes have to read an e-mail message four or five times to uncover the simple notion hidden within? Why do teams of bid evaluators have to work so hard to extract the important nuggets from the dross of the typical proposal document?

People who write business documents have a responsibility to create a clear channel of communication. By shirking that responsibility, writers pass on a load of hard work to their readers. In every area of business this damages productivity. In sales it has an additional impact, because poor writing can lose you deals.

---

[32] Goethe observed, with commendable clarity: "If any man wish to write in a clear style, let him first be clear in his thoughts." He went on to observe "if any would write in a noble style, let him first possess a noble soul." Quite.

All sales people should aim to become effective at written communication. This requires some study, some objective self-criticism, and the ability to accept the criticism of others. But you're in sales, so none of that should be a problem for you, should it?

Buy some books. There are many good books on effective business writing.[33] Almost everyone I know has one on their bookshelf. Books on effective business writing often provide lots of practical examples and exercises. It's worth buying one. If you buy one, please read it – more than once.

In addition to a business-oriented writing guide, I like to have a more general-purpose style guide[34] at my elbow when I'm writing, because these provide more detailed guidance on grammar and currently acceptable usage. There are many good style guides on the shelves of your local bookstore – choose one that fits in with your business needs and suits your personal writing style.

Finally, use a dictionary, not just to check spelling, but also to make sure you are using the correct word to convey your meaning. Meanings change over the years, and while that change is in progress, it is sometimes better to avoid words that can be ambiguous.

For example "Your new TV will be delivered momentarily" can have multiple meanings. If the writer is fresh out of school, it probably means "Your TV will arrive in the next day or so". But someone slightly older will interpret the statement more literally as: "Your TV will arrive almost immediately – just wait a couple of seconds." Someone over fifty, or an English speaker from outside the US, might expect the TV to appear and disappear again right away, because for them *momentarily* means *for a moment*, not *in a moment*.

Keep to the point. In business, the biggest sin in written work is *rambling*. Nowadays, most people who work for a living don't have the time and patience to decode a document that hides the message from them. People do crossword puzzles and read medieval poetry and detective novels for relaxation in the evening, or on

---

[33] There are dozens of books on business writing around. Most of them are quite well-written. Please browse your local bookstore to find one that appeals to you, as the choice is enormous. You might start be looking at: *The Business Writer's Handbook*, Alred, Brusaw, Oliu (Bedford, 2002); *The Elements of Business Writing*, Blake and Bly (Macmillan, 1992).

[34] For Example: *Elements of Style* by Strunk and White (Macmillan); *Woe is I: The Grammarphobes Guide to Better English in Plain English* by Patricia T. Connor (Riverhead Trade); *The Chicago Manual of Style* (Chicago University Press); *The Economist Style Guide* (very useful if you write documents in English for non-US readers); *Eats, Shoots and Leaves: The Zero Tolerance Approach to Punctuation* by Profile Books, 2003; Gotham, 2004).

vacation. At work, they want something simpler so they can get home and spend some time with the family.

People really do ramble on and on… in proposal documents, in e-mail messages, and even in their personal résumés. And sometimes even in books on sales management, I've got to admit. The key to avoiding rambling is to be clear what you want to achieve. Write down one sentence on a scrap of paper before you start. For example: "This report will convince the board to employ two more sales people." Or, "This document will convince Reallybig Corp that they can save millions by buying our inventory management system." Or, "This e-mail message will let Sally know that she really did a great job at the trade show." If you like, think of this scrap-paper sentence as a *mission statement* for each piece of writing. Then, as you write, and as you review, *test each sentence against that mission statement*. Does it help achieve my purpose? Does it get in the way? Throw out anything that doesn't help you achieve your purpose, even if it's a brilliant piece of prose.

This takes time and effort. Blaise Pascal once admitted in a letter to a friend: "I have made this longer, because I have not had the time to make it shorter."[35] If you want to convey a message to a customer or a colleague, you will make that effort. Your choice is this: spend a few extra minutes making sure your message is clear, or force your readers to spend those minutes and take the chance that they won't bother.

Don't get hung up on grammatical niceties. Consider this sentence: "Almost everyone I know has one on their bookshelf." I used it earlier on in this section. Did you notice the deliberate error? The sentence is, of course, grammatically incorrect – some might say inept. Some grammar textbooks, and the grammar checker built into my word processor, will try to make me write: "Almost everyone I know has one on his or her bookshelf." Is this second form somehow better than the first? Is it easier to understand? When you read the first sentence, did it make you halt in mid-paragraph thinking: "What on earth did Stu mean by '*their* bookshelf'? I'm confused."

Understanding the rules of grammar is important, but slavish adherence to them is not necessary. Remember that these rules change over the years and decades. I predict that the use of *their* in place of *his or her* after an indefinite singular antecedent[36] will very soon be completely acceptable. Nowadays, splitting sentences at a conjunction for purposes of emphasis hardly raises any eyebrows. So I *am* permitted to write, if I so wish: "Understanding the rules of

---

[35] *Lettres Provinciales*, Blaise Pascal (First published 1657; Oxford University Press, 1989).
[36] As my copy of Webster's puts it.

grammar is important. But slavish adherence to them is not necessary."

Don't throw away the rulebook. Keep your word processor grammar checker switched on, but use it for highlighting possible problems, don't let it tell you how to write. If it suggests you should sacrifice clarity and conciseness to obey one of last century's rules, choose to break the rule.

Get a second opinion. Once upon a time, hardly any sales person or sales manager prepared documents that were seen by outsiders. In those days, professional typists processed all finished documents, including proposals, reports and letters. Typists invariably had a much better grasp of English grammar and spelling than the people who drafted the documents. Big salaries were, apparently, paid for qualities other than literacy, and that remains true today. Typists provided an essential *quality control* step in the production of documents. Such a step is missing in many organizations today.

If you are writing an important document or e-mail message, especially one to a customer, it can be useful to ask someone you trust to check it. This is not to suggest that the person who is doing the checking is in some way more capable than you are. A fresh eye is likely to spot errors you have missed, and when you, in turn, check his or her work, you will no doubt make suggestions for improvement too.

Sometimes you can provide your own second opinion. If the document can wait a day, then sleep on it. Read your prose the next day, and you will almost certainly find something that can be improved. (Don't take that to extremes though. A great work of literature might never see the light of day because the author sleeps on it for years, in search of perfection.)

Writing Sales Proposals. As a sales person, I have written or contributed to hundreds of sales proposals. (As a manager I have received and evaluated a good number too. It would be wonderful if everyone who writes proposals could be obliged to spend some time evaluating proposals as part of their apprenticeship, but unfortunately it usually doesn't work out that way.)

Typically, proposals for complex technology products contain far too much information that the customer has not asked for. Often, they are illogically structured, repetitive, and too long. Remarkably often, they don't make it easy for the evaluators to find the answers to the only two questions that matter: "Will this solution give me the business results I'm looking for?" and "Is this solution better value for money than any of the others that I have to consider?" Make it quick and easy for the evaluator to conclude that the answer to both questions is "yes" and you already have a head start on most competitors.

Here are my basic rules for making your proposal documents less rambling, and more focused, readable and persuasive:

- **Address the customer's specific needs.** Focus the entire proposal on what *interests* the customer. Limit the body of the proposal to providing the information the customer asked for in the RFP[37]. It is clearly a big mistake to believe that more is always better – but some people don't know how to use copy-and-paste with discretion. This results in bloated proposals that become difficult to read, and make evaluators comatose with boredom. Be ruthless: test every section and every sentence against the document mission statement to weed out unnecessary material. Less is more.

- **Prove your value.** People buy for many reasons, many of which have nothing to do with the contents of a proposal document. But whatever else drives them, they need to be convinced that they are getting value for money. You should provide clear and convincing demonstrations of business value throughout the proposal. Once people know the price, they often cease to read and think objectively. For that reason, I like to place my numbers near the end of the document. (I know, some people turn straight to it anyway. The best thing to do is to make sure that the number does not make them go into shock. You need to build a good relationship with the customer and manage their expectations long before the proposal hits their desk.)

- **Ensure a customer orientation throughout.** Every sentence should talk primarily about your customer, not about you, the supplier. For example avoid writing things like: "SupplierCo provides state of the art administration products that increase user productivity." Instead, write: "CustomerCo will benefit from increased user productivity by implementing our state-of-the art administration products."

- **Keep to the preferred response format.** If your customer has defined a format for your bid response, use it. You might think you have a better format, and perhaps you do. But if by using

---

[37] RFP is Request for Proposal. This is a document prepared by the customer. It requests you, the vendor, to provide a Proposal. Seems simple enough, so why do some sales people call their proposal an RFP? Maybe they mean Response to Request for Proposal, which would be an RRFP. They should just call it a Proposal and stop confusing everyone.

your own layout you make it more difficult for the evaluator to find information and to assess your proposal, you'll lose points.

- **Make the Executive Summary a summary, not a rewrite.** I once had to make a contribution to a proposal that grew and grew until it became a small encyclopedia. The executive summary alone ran to about twenty pages. Too much detail in an executive summary makes it difficult to make an impact. Use the summary to *assert* your case, use the body of the proposal to *explain* it.

- **Use appendices.** Appendices are useful for providing fine detail to back up the information in the body of the proposal. Restrict appendices to providing elaboration, detailed explanation, and extra detail that will be useful to the customer and enhance your credibility. Don't include an appendix unless it there is a relevant need in the body of the document to make a relevant reference to it.

E-mail messages. Most business communication is by e-mail these days, yet many people don't approach writing e-mail messages with any care. Some people say this is because writing an e-mail note is too easy, so people just don't bother. Well, making a pot of coffee is easy too, and we all know that some people make great coffee, and others can't – perhaps they 'just don't bother'. People can still tell the difference when they drink it, and maybe they don't say much but it still makes an impact on the subconscious, as well as on the taste buds.

With a little care, anyone can make good coffee. And anyone can create reasonable e-mail messages that leave a pleasant taste in the mouth. Here are my basic rules for writing e-mail messages that boost your credibility rather than demolish it:

- **Send one e-mail message for each topic.** E-mail is cheap. Given the way that most people file and manage their e-mail messages, it is courteous to break e-mail correspondence up into bite-size chunks. Try to have one distinct topic per e-mail, with an appropriate subject heading, and keep your e-mail messages brief. It is fine to ask two or three related questions about one customer account in one e-mail message. But it is not so acceptable to ask questions about two or three different customer accounts, all in one message.

- **Use an informative subject line.** A heading such as "Meeting" will be lost in a busy in-tray, while "Meeting July 15 – Account Planning" will be helpful to the people who receive it, and they will be able to find it when they need it.

- **Use sentences, with capital letters and punctuation.** "This guy wants to sell me a two million dollar computer system and he doesn't know where to find the shift key. What kind of technical support service can that company provide?"

- **End with a call to action.** Many e-mail messages fail to invoke a response because the writer doesn't ask for one. If you want the recipient to do something, then just write it down. "Now that you have this information, please complete your report and send it to everyone in the team for review by the end of the week."

- **Use a spellchecker, and review your text.** Spelling errors and typos can demolish your credibility. No matter how brilliant you are, your fingers can still hit the wrong keys. A spellchecker can help you spot these errors. But spellcheckers are not very good at understanding context, so sometimes they miss errors. "Let's meet for lunch and I'll introduce you to my good fried Bob..." would not be picked up as a spelling error, but it's probably not what you intended to type. Read everything through carefully before you send it.

- **Read it out loud before you press the 'send' button.** Reading out loud is the best way to identify clumsy or ambiguous statements. E-mail messages can sound angry and confrontational even if you don't feel that way. People tend to write e-mail messages as if they are speaking, but when the recipient reads them, they may get the tone of voice quite wrong.

  Read this sentence out loud: "If I don't receive your numbers by 5 pm, I'll take a guess at them myself." Try it in an angry tone of voice, a neutral tone, and in a friendly helpful tone. Depending on the tone the message can be threatening, simply informative, or helpfully cooperative. Decide what tone you want to convey, and add a word or two to give the reader a clue. If you intend to be helpful, say something like "I know you're busy, so if I don't receive your numbers by 5pm then I'm happy to estimate them myself." If you intend to imply a rebuke for failure to deliver then say something like: "Your input would be useful, but if you fail to send me your numbers by 5pm, then I'll have to estimate them myself to meet our deadline."

  Remember, the printed page (or screen) is unable to convey tone of voice, so make up for that with well-chosen words.

E-mail is a powerful business tool. Used well, it can enhance communication and accelerate business decisions. Carelessly written e-mail messages can demolish your credibility with customers, and cause confusion and concern. If your messages contain typos and are muddled, customers will think that you have no eye for detail, no quality standards and don't really care. They are very likely to assume that your company is just the same.

On the other hand, since so many e-mail messages are sloppy, if yours are well-crafted and lucid, then you will create a good impression and win an edge over your competitors.

Thanks for the Memories

How many books are there in the bookstores on improving your memory skills? I don't know, or perhaps I forgot. In any case I know there are plenty. There is a big market for 'improve your memory' books.

My theory is that over the ages, ancient human beings learned to give priority room space in their brains to items that were important for survival, such as where to find food, the location of big holes in the ground that you might fall into, types of creature that might eat you, and partners who were prepared to mate with you.

Fast forward a few millennia and today most people have no difficulty remembering how to get to their favorite restaurant and the safest places to cross city streets and survive. They also remember people who proved to be less than truthful in their business dealings so that they can avoid doing business with them in the future. People remember dates from when they were teenagers, and relatives who died years ago.

But the same people can't remember the name of the business contact they met at lunch the day before yesterday.

Some people and events are memorable; others aren't so easily etched. Unless you work at it, you're not going to remember much about that tedious person you met at a conference who insisted on telling you about the many benefits of having a hemi engine in your SUV. Trouble is, that was the president of a company that turned up on the top of your prospect list several months later. You should have remembered.

Remembering people is so important. A person's name is one of their most valuable possessions – so treat it with respect by remembering it and using it appropriately. Forgetting someone's name within a couple of minutes does happen. It's embarrassing (yes, I've done it too) and it could cost you business.

In the natural course of events, your mind will remember things that your subconscious decides are important. And your mind will forget those things that your subconscious decides are unimportant. The trouble is, what your subconscious mind wants is not always aligned to the everyday needs of your business life. This means that you need to find some way of investing items of information with additional importance and tagging them for later recovery.

Over the years people have come up with an array of tricks and techniques for mentally tagging pieces of information so that they are more memorable. Using mnemonics, rhymes, association pairs and so on. Read one of the many books on the subject[38], try out some of the approaches they suggest and find a few that work for you.

As with everything else, you can only acquire and improve the skill of remembering things by learning, understanding and practicing.

But please don't try to keep everything in your head. Also learn to use one or two of the many tools that are available to you. You and your team probably have to record information in your company's prospect management or CRM system anyway. So instead of viewing this as a chore, make a point of learning about the system's capabilities and use it to organize your contact information, track your calls and meetings. If you learn to make the most of the tool, then using it will become a built-in part of the way you do work, not a chore. PDAs and electronic organizers work for some people, others prefer notebooks, others rely on their trusty 3x5 filing cards. Whatever you use, make it a habit. Use it everyday until you don't have to think about it any more, because it's just the way you do things.

People are not all the same, to be sure. Some people have no short term memory like Dory in *Finding Nemo*[39]. Others have 'total recall'. But for people in the middle of the range, which is most of us, memory skills are somewhat imperfect - but quite wonderful just the same, when you think about it. It seems that the main difference between the person who remembers things and the forgetful person, is that the first consciously works at memory skills, and the other one doesn't bother, or maybe just forgets how important this is.

Whatever tricks and techniques you decide to adopt, there is one simple thing that everyone can do to help them remember who you've met. When you meet a person, listen for his or her name, repeat it and use it several times as soon as possible. That will help to embed it in your mind. People regard their names as part of themselves, and using it shows that you that you regard them as a person not just as another hand to shake.

---

[38] There are thousands of memory training books out there. I don't want to recommend one in particular, because their styles vary so much, and the one that you like will depend on your personal taste. Do you like your self-improvement books in an academic style, patronizing or gushing? Psychologists have researched memory intensively in the last hundred years, and most books on the topic that are based on this research have something useful to offer.

[39] *Finding Nemo* (Pixar, 2003). Dory was played by Ellen deGeneres.

Negotiating Skills

Customers always want the best price and the most value, and competition is always there to increase the pressure. Negotiation is a fact of life today, as indeed as it has always been.

Sales people need negotiating skills, and sales managers should always be ready and willing to help their team develop negotiating strategies and tactics.

How do you decide whether to agree to customer demands and when to give in? How do you recognize and handle the tactics that customers use to get a better deal?

We all negotiate every day. We negotiate when we're buying or selling a car, or a sofa. Negotiations take place between parents and teenagers, every time there's a late night party going on somewhere, which seems to be almost every night. We negotiate when we apply for a new job, or, if we're sitting on the other side of the table, recruiting someone. We negotiate about pay rises, house purchase, and what color to paint the dining room.

Where two or more individuals have to come to common ground to gain agreement, you negotiate.

One style of negotiating is all about understanding and changing the position of power, or changing the perception of the position of power. In 1981, the air traffic controllers in the US went on strike. The public generally thought that the air traffic controllers were in a strong position: with no flights able to take off or land, the economy would undoubtedly suffer. Without a doubt, it looked pretty good for the controllers, who were confident they could hold out to get their demands met. President Reagan and his negotiating team reversed the power perception by questioning a basic assumption: only the present cadre of air traffic controllers could do the job. Reagan reminded the strikers that their actions were illegal, and told them to come to an agreement with their employers and report for work, or else. Or else they would all be fired and replaced by newly trained controllers who were eager to have their jobs. They failed to settle so he fired them.

This is an example of confrontational negotiation in which both sides adopt a firm position, and the outcome can only be one side winning and the other side losing. Nothing in this confrontation indicated that the parties were willing to seek a win-win solution.

At the time public reaction to the outcome was mixed, and attitudes divided along fairly predictable political lines. My point in bringing up this story is that the balance of power is critical in negotiation, and the most important step in changing the balance of power is to question the assumptions that underpin assessments of power positions.

Whatever happens your negotiations with customers should never degenerate into a confrontational impasse and or reach the level of acrimony that was reached during the air traffic strike: that wouldn't be good for repeat business!

In negotiating with our clients we need to always think win-win for both our company and our client. Anything short of this will hurt us in the long run. The customer needs to feel that they negotiated well and walked away with good value that your competition could not offer. Your aim should be to win the battle, and lay the foundation for winning the war. Not to win one battle and kill the relationship.

The science of negotiation is pretty well developed, and you can be sure that decision-makers in companies you are dealing with have received some negotiation training. If you and your team are not similarly skilled, you will lose business, or you will win business only at disadvantageous terms. It is therefore vital to *learn negotiating tactics*. You need to understand the negotiating tactics (and tricks) that people use. Civilization has evolved these tactics over thousands of years, so don't expect to pick them up overnight by osmosis: take a course, or read a book. You need to understand tactics not only so you can use them yourself, but also so you are prepared to neutralize them when they are being used against you.

There are a number of good training courses available to help people learn the techniques and disciplines of negotiation. You should make sure that everyone on your team attends at least one. Don't forget about some of the veterans, who maybe went to a negotiation skills workshop many years ago. Repeat training can help to remind people of tactics that they've forgotten about. People who have been on the job for some time also have more experiences – successes and failures – that they can relate to the training material.

And as always, it's very useful to buy and read the right books.[40]

I've found that in my negotiations with customers, some situations arise again and again. Here are some general principles that may be useful to bear in mind as you negotiate.

Let the customer win. In many negotiations, there is a winner and a loser. In negotiating a sales deal the situation is quite different: your aim is to create two winners, and no losers (except your competitors, who are not party to your negotiations anyway). You

---

[40] One book that I like is *Getting to Yes* by Roger Fisher and William Ury (Penguin Books, 1991). It achieves a great synthesis of hard and soft negotiating styles that takes a tough-minded approach to achieving positions of mutual interest.

want the customer to accept your offer with some enthusiasm. Customers like to feel they have earned a concession by fighting for it. Giving them everything they ask for means that they value the concession less. Your customer also wants to be able to buy with confidence that there will be no 'buyer's remorse' downstream. Sales negotiation is all about constructing a deal in which both parties truly win. Equally, your positioning of the offer must suggest that by saying 'no', both parties lose.

Information really is power. The more you know about your customer's real needs, pressures, motivations and constraints, the better you can position your offering to make saying 'yes' as painless as possible.

'No' isn't always 'no'. For me, NO stands for Never Over. On more than one occasion I have been able to secure a deal after the customer has told me 'No thanks'. How does that work? It is at the point of saying 'no' when a customer feels most able to explain *exactly* why they don't want to accept your offer. Up to that point, some customers feel a reluctance to be explicit about all their concerns and revelations. When a customer says 'no', a sales person must use that opportunity to find out why. In every case, the discussion will be a useful learning experience that can provide pointers to how to handle future negotiations with that customer and others. And sometimes it provides a pretty simple way of re-building the offer so there are no longer any reasons to refuse. Now, please don't expect to turn every refusal into an enthusiastic acceptance. But it can be done, and you should never assume it's over too early. In one case I was able to reverse a decision *after a competitor had started work on the project*. In this case our competitor helped me to establish credibility by behaving exactly in the way I'd predicted, thus bringing the customer back to the safe hands of my company.

Understand your own value. When businesses sell to businesses, the buyer is looking for benefits. The astute seller will understand the buyer's business well enough to be able to express the benefits in concrete terms that ring true for the customer. It is essential that you and your team understand your own value relative to competitors. But you should also be able to express that value in multiple ways for various different customers with different priorities and personalities. Just being able to recite a formula expressing value is not enough. With a true *understanding* of value you will be able to appreciate the impact of your products and services on your customer's business, and adapt your value propositions accordingly.

Don't let a feeling of insecurity drive the price down. Many times, sales people want to offer bigger and bigger discounts and incentives to encourage the customer to make a decision and sign a deal. They are convinced they are behind the field and the only way to overtake the competitors is to cut the price. This type of insecurity is generally evidence that the relationship with the customer is not close enough for the sales person to make an accurate assessment of the likelihood of successful closure. Knowledgeable customers know that they just have to take their time signing, and some salespeople will roll out yet another price reduction. Don't let your team get caught in this trap – it can prove to be expensive.

Take cultural differences into account. If you are dealing with a customer from outside the US, take some time to familiarize yourself with their culture. People who work in China for example, are often surprised how easy it is to get the customer to say yes, but how difficult it is to close the deal. 'Yes' doesn't always mean 'I agree'; often it means 'I understand what you say'. When the USA and North Vietnam delegations turned up in Paris for the Vietnam peace talks, they were facing some serious negotiation. But from the start they were on different wavelengths. The US delegation, keen to get the business finished, rented some hotel rooms; the Vietnamese *bought* a hotel. Cultural differences change the flow of negotiation significantly. The French, German and Swedes may all be European, but their approach to business varies a lot.[41] And don't make the big mistake of thinking that the British think like Americans just because they speak a similar language.

Don't play silly games. Some sales people like to increase the pressure by inventing offers and special deals. "If you sign today I can give you another 5% off, but only if you sign today." Business buyers aren't taken in by this type of approach any more, and always know how to reverse the pressure. That sales person has just informed the customer that there's another five percent saving to be had. The smart customer will respond with something like: "I'm not prepared to sign today, so it's too bad we can't do business. Tell you what – if you change your mind come back to me with another quote including the extra five percent and I'll think about it again."

In sales, negotiating is not just a power-play game. You can only negotiate in the context of the type of relationship you have built. If your aim is to secure a steady stream of ongoing work, your negotiations have to take place in an atmosphere of trust and co-operation. It's still business, and it's still negotiation. But it's not war.

---

[41] For a start, take a look at *Riding the Waves of Culture: Understanding Diversity in Global Business*, Charles Hampden-Turner, Fons Trompenaars (McGraw-Hill, 1997). Then find individual books specializing in various different cultures, according to your needs.

A Last Word on Skills

As I said at the beginning of this chapter, skills are important to sales people, just as they are important to athletes: skilled people play the game much better.

Acquiring skills takes training, and it takes practice, and it takes persistence. It takes twenty-one days, so they say, to break a bad habit. It takes twenty-one days to acquire a new one.

Encourage your team to build skills continuously. Spending one month on consecutive training courses and then trying to consolidate five new major skills at one time is not efficient.

Phase your team's training programs over the year, and make sure you help them make opportunities to practice and absorb the lessons.

Make sure you address training and experience needs in your regular one-on-one conversations with every team member. Use every opportunity to transfer your knowledge and skills by coaching and by example.

Above all, as a sales team leader, you must set an example. Your own behavior provides evidence to others of your skills. If you know you are deficient in any skills areas, don't assume that it doesn't matter just because you're now a manager and no one expects you to know much about the practicalities. In sales, the best team leaders provide hands-on practical support to their team members, and this means that they have to know what to do, at least as well as the people in their team.

I know that in some departments, managers can get away with the attitude that their management skills are paramount, and they don't need to understand the messy details. That just doesn't work in sales. Sometimes you need to get into the mess. In sales, if you don't understand what your people face every day, and are unable to support and coach them as they develop the skills they need, then you are failing in your duty. If you couple that deficiency with similar ineptitude in a couple of other areas, then you might qualify as a klink.

Chapter 4
Building Relationships

A sound relationship between buyer and seller helps the buyer to 'leap the decision gap'. Another way of looking at this is that it helps the seller to close deals.

We all need to understand better how to build sound, lasting relationships. Being sociable, being interested, and being there is a good start.

Leaping the Decision Gap – Why Relationships Matter

Our lives revolve around relationships with other people. Relationships define who we are and what we value. What we think of other people influences how we act towards them. How others think of us, influences how they behave towards us.

In selling, relationships are important. People buy from other people. The relationship between the buying person and the selling person is fundamentally important – how could it be any other way?

Relationships don't necessarily dominate every selling transaction. When you just need to run out to a store to buy some of, for example, your favorite blue cheese, then this is not likely to be a relationship-critical transaction. However, even then, your choice of store may be influenced somewhat if you know that the cheese-loving assistant at one store in particular will be delighted to give you advice on alternatives if your favorite happens to be out of stock. And she'll entertain you with stories of cheese experiences around the world while you make your decision. You trust this cheese expert, and she makes the necessary trip to the store to buy cheese so much more interesting.

Now if the existence or non-existence of a "relationship" can make a difference in a transaction like buying a chunk of Roquefort, how important is it going to be to someone who has to make a decision on a multi-million dollar technology project? If it goes wrong, the decision maker can lose face, lose credibility in their company, or even lose their job.

When it comes to making a really complex decision, people tend to work at two levels: the scientific level and the emotional level.

> *When it comes to making a complex decision, people work at two levels: the scientific level and the emotional level.*

Most people insist that they make buying decisions based on hard evidence – a scientific approach. Will this product do the job that I need it to do? Will it perform according to specification? Will it reduce the operational costs as much as I need it to? In reality, people ask these questions, and endeavor to find a fact-based 'scientific' answer. But when someone is thinking about buying a highly complex technology solution, sometimes there is no real way of proving the solution will deliver everything. Except by actually doing it.

How much hard work and analysis, how many facts, are going to *prove* without question that a solution will do a specific job well; that the price will be fair; and that the solution supplier will fix any unforeseen problems that arise? It is not possible in practice for customers to assess all of the variables, consider every conceivable option, and allow for every contingency. Customers can only hope to achieve a sufficient level of confidence in their supplier. Some of that confidence comes from facts. The balance comes from the relationship.

Eventually the customer must be prepared, after balancing all the options and weighing probabilities, to make a leap into the dark, and buy something. This is an emotion-based decision.

Leaping the decision gap is always scary for a customer. So it is the job of the sales person to make that gap as small as possible, to reduce the sense of danger.

> *Leaping the decision gap is scary for a customer. So it is the job of the sales person to make that gap as small as possible.*

Lead times for complex project sales are generally very long – six to eighteen months, or even more. One of the reasons is this gap: the customer needs scientific evidence of the worth of the solution; but no one can ever *prove* the solution without actually doing the job for free to demonstrate how great it is. And even then the customer might not be convinced that all possibilities have been covered.

To fill this scientific gap, every buyer always has to take a leap based on an emotional judgment that is grounded in a relationship.

In the eyes of a customer, a sound relationship lowers perceived risk.

Think of it this way. The buyer and the seller are standing on opposite banks of a river. There are lots of lego-like building blocks lying around on the seller's side. They are labeled *fact bricks*. The seller starts to throw factual building blocks across the river to the buyer. Some of the blocks land in the water and sink, but enough of them reach the other bank for the buyer to start constructing a bridge across the flowing river.

This is hard work. The seller has to throw these facts a long way, and the buyer has to spend time, and brainpower assembling them.

The structure takes shape, but eventually the seller runs out of facts, and the gap is still too big for the buyer to jump. Then the seller sees some more blocks, partly concealed by undergrowth. They're kind of fuzzier, rounded at the corners, but bigger than the fact bricks.

They're labeled *relationship bricks*. The seller finds that it's a whole lot easier to stack these relationship bricks up on his side of the river, while the buyer takes note of what is happening, with interest.

Soon they are face to face, just a short step apart. The gap is small enough that they can shake hands. Deal closed.

The sales person goes home that evening and mulls over the events of the day. "If I'd started building my side of the bridge earlier using those weird fuzzy bricks, then we'd have got closer a lot sooner. Also I wouldn't have had to throw those sharp-edged fact bricks so far, and maybe not so many would have dropped in the water."

Fortunately the exhausted sales person fell asleep before he was totally overcome by allegorical excess.

Different companies seem to have different perspectives on how important fact-based scientific bricks are, compared to relation-based bricks.

Some technology companies tend to approach the sale on the assumption that if they give the customer enough facts, they'll win the deal. The reality is that a company could have the fastest, most reliable and least expensive technology solution, and still fail to win the deal because of the lack of a relationship.

On the other hand, some companies win vast amounts of business by working very hard on personal relationships, to the extent that the capability of the technology being offered becomes less and less important.[42]

The most successful companies understand that being able to provide factual evidence that the technology will work, combined with a strong buyer-seller relationship is the best and most consistent winning approach. Relationships build trust, giving the customer the comfortable sense that even if there are problems along the way – as there will be – the seller will address those problems, and will fix them in a responsible and fair way.

A few years ago I was selling large-scale computer systems. Our major competitor was a company that got the balance right: solid products and a proven ability to build strong long-lasting relationships.

One incident in particular drove home to me how important relationships are.

---

[42] In the high-tech sector in recent years, this approach has resulted in some IT projects failing spectacularly and disastrously. This amounts to a confidence trick. I am not advocating the sale of shoddy goods in this way, even though some of our biggest name companies have made a pile of money doing it. Remember integrity?

My company had (I still believe) better products that were lower-priced and less expensive to maintain. Many times I had lost a bid in head-to-head competition, and I was struggling to understand why.

Our prospect was a software application company, and I was trying to persuade them to resell our hardware and software, bundled with their application. This reseller had been with our competitor for at least ten years.

I worked with this prospect for a whole year. We developed a solid working relationship. We went together to seminars on our products and services. We developed some really attractive financial incentives to do business with our company.

We gave them one of our systems for six months to try out. We helped them successfully convert their software to our platform and operating system.

But eventually, when it came to decision time, the customer just could not make the leap. This is what he told me about his relationship with his existing supplier, my competitor: "I've known Joe for ten years. We've been through ups and downs in our relationship, but he has been there for me in both the tough times and good times. He's a real partner in this business. I feel as if I would be cheating on Joe if I took on another platform for my software".

Even though he and I had built a good relationship of trust and support, I could not surpass the relationship he had with Joe. Even though our products were demonstrably better, the relationship with Joe was the most important factor in his decision.

Here's another example of misdirected effort caused by forgetting how important relationships are in winning business. This is from a few years ago, when I was probably still a bit naïve. A customer who we had never done any business with approached us unexpectedly. They asked our sales rep to put together a quotation and provide full configuration details for a fairly complex solution.

Excited, we all set to work. This was a great opportunity to break into a new client. Over the course of the next couple of weeks we worked long hours to put the bid together. We tested our approach with the client as we went along and the client was helpful enough to suggest at least seven changes to the configuration over a period of two weeks.

When the customer received the final quote he said he would notify our sales person the next day of the decision. True to his word, next day we learned that the job had been awarded to their incumbent supplier – our main competitor.

We soon found out that our competitor's sales rep had been on site every day for weeks working through the customer needs in great detail, and identifying potential issues and setting project success criteria. They knew we had seriously wanted to break into this account for years – so *they* had told the customer to ask us to bid for the business. Our competitor was always in complete control. Every change the customer asked us for had been suggested by our competitor. Every change we submitted was assessed jointly by our 'prospect' and our competitor! This was our competitor's way of reinforcing the relationship, building more trust, and being seen to be open and honest.

In our enthusiasm to follow up this great opportunity, we simply focused on getting the configuration and the price right and establishing 'value'. We forgot that value, while essential, is never enough by itself. We never established a relationship with the customer, and never found out their real needs. We just worked hard for two weeks, fueled by hope that turned out to be unfounded.

Every one in sales does this from time to time – it's one of the downsides of possessing exuberant optimism. But when you're assessing the likelihood of success, always take a reality check, and if you don't have a flourishing productive relationship in place, cut your expectation of success by, say, 90% .

...if you don't have a flourishing productive relationship in place, cut your expectation of success by say, 90%.

A company I know conducted an analysis of all the deals they had won over a year, based on the customers' impressions of what made the difference. It turned out that 82% of deals were won because of the strength of relationship with the customer *plus* a solid value proposition. The remaining 18% were won because of the relationship alone. They found that a strong relationship had been the foundation for *every single deal*.

A good relationship makes it easier for the sales person to communicate effectively. A strong relationship gives the customer a warm feeling that, even if it's not possible to prove it scientifically, the solution provider really is going to: deliver a solution that will do the job well; charge a fair price; and fix any unforeseen problems that arise. And this warm feeling is what makes it possible for a customer to leap that decision gap more confidently and sign the deal.

115

The Customer Really Does Come First

No matter what industry you work in and no matter what products or services you sell, a key factor in achieving sales team success is to have sales people who have a genuine *desire to please*.

If a sales person believes that the customer really does come first, and follows this through with genuine customer-oriented support, then this is a great foundation for building a relationship that will lead to sales. If the sales person only sees the customer as a way to generate a commission check, then that sales person will be less successful.

The sales team leader's attitude will ripple down to the sales team. You, as a manager, must understand the importance of placing the customer's business needs in a position of prime importance.

That means that managers should not browbeat sales people to push products and services that are not really what the customer needs.

...managers should not browbeat sales people to push products and services that are not really what the customer needs.

When I bring a new sales person into my team, I take the time to tell them that, for me, "the customer comes first" is not just empty talk. I try to find out how customer-oriented a sales person is, really – everyone says the right things, but not everyone acts accordingly. Here's the sort of thing I discuss with my team members to reinforce this viewpoint...

Successful sales people don't think about themselves all the time – it really is all about the customer. It's not even about the commission, not primarily - it's about the customer, and taking best care of the customer's need. It's about going the extra mile and not worrying about whether or not there's more dollars involved. It's about doing what is right. It's that simple.

It's also about admitting it if you made a mistake: you 'fess up to it, no excuses, no ifs, ands or buts!

A customer can always tell the intent and motives of the sales person. They know that commissions are part of the motivation, and that's all right. But if a customer senses, even for an instant, that your desire for rewards takes precedence over what's right for them, they'll run a mile. And I would too. Wouldn't you if you were a customer?

The customer must always be the focus of your attention, and the conversation should always revolve around the customer. One time, a client said to me, only partly joking, "Now that I'm done talking about myself, why don't you spend some time talking about me".

If you don't make the effort to learn about the customer, then I guarantee they won't be interested in finding out about you. It might be a two-way street when we deal with customers but in this street, the customer always gets priority.

Over the long haul, the most successful sales person is the one who is always there during the tough times, when there are problems and down times, even when there is no personal financial benefit at the time. This is a sales person who puts the "person" before "sales", who honestly cares, and respects and values their client and the relationships they have inside the company. This is the type of sales person who keeps close to the customer, even when the customer is being indecisive and frustrating. This is the type of sales person who wants to make sure the customer makes the right decision – even when this might mean losing a sale.

At this point in our conversation, I usually get a response. Sometimes it's an unbelieving smile, sometimes it's a frown. "Did I hear that right Stu? Sometimes you want me to let the sale go rather than sell the customer something that isn't quite perfect?"

I explain that in our type of business, selling the wrong thing can ruin a relationship for years, maybe forever. If a system is going to be in place for five, maybe ten years, and it just doesn't work well, then for ten years, everyone is going to be reminded how we sold them a lemon.

Repeat business is important – it's easier to sell again to a satisfied customer than to a new customer. But it's easier to sell to a new customer than to a previous customer who had a bad experience with your company, so making a customer unhappy is a very, very bad idea.

Actually, keeping the customer in the front of your mind, and working always in the customer's interest is not so hard, for people with the right perspective, not just on customers, but on their relationships with people in general.

I ask my sales team to think hard about their own perspectives, and whether they have the urge to please that will really help them when it comes to building relationships. I say something like…

There are two types of people in this world, givers and takers. Givers are people who put others first and want to help and

117

support other people. Takers put themselves first, expect others to do things for them and are generally not around when hard work is needed.

I know this is a broad generalization, and real human beings are neither pure givers nor pure takers: everyone is sometimes selfish, sometimes selfless. However broad generalizations serve a purpose and we all know people we think of as 'takers' and others who are clearly 'givers'.

Now in general, do you suppose that customers prefer the people who sell to them to be givers or takers? This is not a trick question. The answer is obvious: customers like to buy from givers.

Givers want to please their customers. They will make special efforts to make sure things go right. They will spend time and energy learning about the customer's business to make sure they can offer the right products and services. Givers are always there for their customers.

This doesn't mean that givers don't understand that their products and services have a monetary value that has to be paid. And it certainly doesn't mean that they won't welcome sales commissions that they have earned. But psychologically, givers get great satisfaction from helping their customers and always understand that sales compensation is the by-product of taking care of the customer. They know that their success is based on what they do for the customer, period.

Takers are different. In fact many customers can identify very well with takers, but that doesn't mean they will buy from them. Takers talk more than they listen, and often talk about themselves, their successes, who they know and how busy they are. Their sense of urgency is based on their own priorities, not the customer's. Takers are not around when there are problems. They like to be around only during the easy times when the limelight makes them look good.

I once attended a seminar in which we performed a short experiment that I found quite eye-opening. There were about forty students on the course and we had all got to know each other a little over the previous days. We each had to go round the group in turn, and tell each person whether he or she behaved more as a giver or as a taker. This was done with no discussion and analysis: we just relied on the impressions we had of the others formed over the couple of days we had worked closely together.

When the exercise was complete, everyone tallied up their scores. The course leader then lined us up in order from taker #1 (the same as giver #40) to taker #40 (or giver #1).

Then came the interesting bit. The course leader asked "How many of you would like to be better givers?" The fifteen or so people who raised their hands were all at the givers end of the line. Not one taker raised a hand. It seems that takers don't want to give, and givers want to give more.

To be fair, we must recognize that those people who are extreme takers have attributes that makes them very useful in some professions where, for example, braggadocio is more important than insight, and where imperviousness to criticism counts for more than willingness to learn. But sales is not one of those professions.

When there is work to be done in your community, or your sports club, or your church, are you one of the first to be there to help? Are you the sort of person who sees a problem and wants to step in and provide support wherever you can? Are you one of those people with a reputation for willingly helping out neighbors? If so, then genuinely putting the customer first will not be a problem for you.

On the other hand, perhaps you're not so willing in the "helping others" department. You'll help out if asked, or cajoled, but it's really not your thing to step forward. There's nothing wrong with this, it's just that you have a different personality, and a different attitude to the people around you.

Consider this situation. A friend asks you to speak to a class of Eighth Graders about your career, or your hobby, or maybe about the reality of being a sales person... How would *you* react? Would you immediately invent an excuse to be somewhere else? Do you say yes, hoping to think of a way out later on? Do you do it, but wish you hadn't agreed because you really don't have time, and you're only doing it for a friend? Think about it.

Someone with sales in the bloodstream would check the date, and if they could be there, they would. No ifs or buts. Maybe you'd have mixed motives, including loving to hear yourself speak, getting a kick out of the audience response, and just doing a good turn for a pal. But above all to help out, to join in, to *be involved*. Does this sound familiar? Does it sound like you? Are you the type of sales person that truly values the relationships you have, and will go out of your way to help?

Your attitude towards relationships in general, will show through in your attitudes to customers. Do you put the customers' needs first? Do you seek and cherish involvement? Do you really want to help?

Many years ago, a manager told me: "When you are at your client's office, you want them to think you're 51% on their side and 49% on your company's side. Back at your office, you want your company to think you're 51% on their side and 49% on your client's." I think that the intention of what he was saying is generally right, and I won't argue about the percentages. But when you look at it from the perspective that doing what is best for the customer pays back to you big time, then it's sometimes possible for you to be 100% on the customer's side, *and* 100% on your company's side.

For some people this sounds odd, but it's true. Focus just on winning business, and the customers will be reluctant to give you any. Work on what's good for the customer, and they'll give you their business. That's a good deal for both sides.

> *Focus just on winning business and the customers will be reluctant to give you any. Work on what's good for the customer, and they'll give you their business.*

Working at Relationships

Earlier in this book we looked at two areas that are critical to success in sales and in sales management. They were Attitude and Skills. Having the right skills and the right attitude are essential to creating good relationships.

Having skills and knowledge establishes **credibility**. Sales people must understand not only their products and services, but also their customers' businesses. They must know how to present the case, negotiate a deal, and ensure that the deal is delivered. Proficiency in all the skills described in Chapter 3 help to establish a relationship by boosting credibility. Absence of these skills diminishes credibility, and in a sales context, gets in the way of a strong relationship.

Attitude can help or hinder the establishment of a relationship. A positive attitude, as I described earlier, creates a working atmosphere conducive to relationship building. A negative attitude does the opposite. There is considerable evidence that people think well of people who display a positive attitude: they are seen as more capable and trustworthy! So a positive attitude is not only helpful in itself, it reinforces people's assessments of your good points and helps them overlook your defects... being viewed positively is clearly very helpful in building relationships.

As a manager, I will work with my team members in both these areas, knowing that there will be multiple pay-offs, including laying a foundation for strong relationships.

But is this sufficient?

Not really. People have to work at building a relationship in a purposeful way. Assuming that a sales rep already understands the important of skills and attitude in building relationships, what else should he or she do? What makes the difference?

My experience is that there are three things that a sales person must do to build a strong relationship. They need to **be sociable**, **be interested** and **be there**. When I work with my sales team on these three perspectives, these are some of the points I try to make...

Be sociable. In some people's minds, building a relationship is primarily – maybe exclusively – about being sociable. For me, sociability is not everything, but it is highly important.

To build relationships you have to be socially *attractive*. I'm not talking about your physical characteristics, but your personality and the manner in which you interact with others. To put it bluntly, some people behave in a way that makes others want to be around them. Some people behave in a way that makes people want to be some place else.

Being sociable also involves proactively making things happen in a social sense. As a sales person you have to understand that it is your responsibility to manage every interaction with your client, to make sure that there is no awkwardness or embarrassment. (Maybe that's a pretty limited view of 'social responsibility' but this is a book for sales managers and sales professionals, not for politicians.) Here are some of my rules for sociable behavior when dealing with clients.

- **Maintain eye contact.** Customers[43] believe, rightly or wrongly, that people who will not look them in the eyes are untrustworthy. They may be right. Or the person may have an ocular problem. Don't make them make that judgment. Look people in the eye. Smile. Nod. Be reassuring. You find that difficult? Then what are you trying to hide?

- **Meet face-to-face whenever possible.** No one is more enthusiastic than me about the wonders of modern telecommunications; after all, I've sold my share of it. However I still believe that nothing beats face-to-face encounters for getting issues cleared up, improving understanding – and building relationships. Whenever you need to discuss something important, make the journey.

- **Plan your meetings, manage the time.** Whenever you arrange a meeting with a client, recognize that your client's time is valuable, and plan the meeting so that it's productive. Have an agenda, understand what you want to achieve, and when you've achieved it, depart. Don't assume that because you've made a two-hour journey to be there, your client will be happy for you to hang around. If it takes ten minutes, take ten minutes. Then go.

- **Listen.** Read the section on listening in Chapter 3. I don't want to be repetitious so I'll only say it one more time: let the customer tell you things. Get it? Let the customer tell you things.

- **Don't be a blowhard.** I have seen too many sales professionals brag about what customers they have sold to and what high level relationships they have. But they can never get an appointment with them. No wonder. Customers don't like people whose egos get in the way of intelligent conversation. An

---

[43] These comments refer to customers in the US and some Western European countries. Be aware that people from other countries interpret eye contact differently – you can be seen as hostile rather than friendly if you get this wrong.

over-inflated ego can be the death of a sales person. A sure symptom of excessive ego: a sales person who finishes sentences for the customer.

- **Have fun, but choose the occasion carefully.** Sometimes it's right to take someone out for dinner or for a game of golf so you can get to know each other. Later, you can get down to business. But with some people, it's better to get to know them at a few business meetings before inviting them to dinner or golf. It all depends on the client. You have to have the empathy and awareness to judge which is best. It's not what you prefer – it's what the client prefers. Sometimes, it won't be dinner or golf, it could be hang-gliding or opera. How badly do you want the deal?

Be interested. So, you're a sales person. What motivates you? What is of value to you? The crunch question when it comes to building relationships is this: are you interested in others or only interested in your own well-being?

Customers want your interest. They are only human. They respond well if you show a genuine concern for their problems and challenges, and a genuine desire to help them succeed.

Notice that uncomfortable word: 'genuine'. Customers can see straight through insincerity, so don't believe you can build a relationship on your acting ability alone. Maybe some people can, but if you're that good you should be in movies.

Customers need more than a superficial show of interest. You need to address their concerns, and make an honest attempt to help them, in so far as you and your company can do that. Sympathy is great, and always welcome, but action (or suggestions for action) that can help is even better. A true sales person will try to help even if there isn't a sale on the horizon. Maybe the payback will come later. But even if there is no direct payback, the true sales person will still feel that they've done the right thing by trying to help.

I read the results of a client survey not so long ago. The survey found that the majority of clients felt that sales professionals are mostly competent and honest when talking about their products and services. But mostly sales people did not convince the customers that they had genuine *interest and concern*. Many times the sales person would respond to whatever they could solve, instead of what was really important to the client. They would leap into presentation mode the moment they heard about something that maybe could lead to a sale. The customers saw this as shallow. And they were right.

Without real interest and concern, there is nothing on which to build a trusting relationship.

Clients will always decide whether or not to move forward on the sales cycle. The client will base this decision on an emotional judgment: does this sales person really *care*?

One sign of caring (but only one) is that you do your homework. Customers respect and value a sales person who is constantly trying to understand their business, their market and the direction it is heading in. You cannot make a decision for the customer, but you can help them with the knowledge you obtain by being involved in their business and in their industry.

Whatever industry you're in, there are many organizations that you can join that can give you insight into what is going on and what the future might look like. Be interested.

Chambers of Commerce are often an excellent source of information, as well as a source of contacts. Many Chambers have committees that support executive conferences, luncheons and seminars. Get involved, and get your sales team involved.

You and your team, and indeed your company, should also participate in industry-specific organizations. If your company is serious about doing business in a specific industry sector, you should persuade your corporate leaders to support participation at the corporate level. Some industry organizations provide a great opportunity to learn, to influence and to network.

I had a manager in a software company crying on my shoulder one day. He had been charged with leading an initiative to sell more software products in the telecom sector. But company executives had just decided not to spend company money supporting the activities of the Tele-Management Forum, a worldwide telecom sector association that focuses on the software platforms and processes needed to run telecom operations. He had been denied a very cost-effective avenue to meet with industry decision makers, and company software developers had been denied ready access to the people in the industry who were influencing software strategic direction.

Every industry sector has its array of specialist organizations, and I admit that some are of more value than others. But some involvement almost always pays off. They arrange conferences, seminars and working groups that provide intelligence, influence and contacts. At the very least, joining in shows interest and helps to establish credibility. Be interested. Join in.

Be **there**. Good relationships with customers means keeping in touch. There always will be good times and bad times in the life of a company, or even an entire industry.

124

From March 2000 through 2003 the stock market plunged and the telecom market especially cratered. Previously solid stocks like Nortel, Lucent, Cisco and Alcatel went from all time highs to all time lows.

I had a number of high-tech companies as my customers. As they struggled to cut costs and took emergency action to regain financial balance, I heard the same thing from many of them: "We won't be able to use your services any time in the foreseeable future."

In these circumstances it would be easy to spend your time looking elsewhere for business. But it would be a serious mistake to lose touch. Even though my customers weren't giving me business, I still kept in touch. We exchanged information and insights on the industry and where it was going. I was able to help them extend the life of some products until time was better. Sometimes I was just a friendly ear to listen to their problems.

Eventually, things got better, at least for those businesses that survived. Eventually, the companies in the telecom sector were ready to buy again. The vendors that stayed in touch won business. Those who had wandered off to new pastures had to start again with customers who now viewed them only as 'fair-weather friends'.

Relationships take time to build. Furthermore, relationships must persist through good times and bad. Just look at what it takes to build a marriage: every marriage has its trials and tribulations, ups and downs, agreements and disagreements. Why should it be any different with a client? Except, of course for the sleeping arrangements.

Working through differences, being around when times are tough, being there not just to sell things but to support the customer – these are things that all help to build a strong and lasting relationship between vendor and client. Being there for them.

Be sociable. Be interested. Be there. A few years ago, I had extreme back pain. At that time I was running twenty-five miles a week, I was pretty fit, and I'd never had any serious back trouble before. I went for an X-ray, which showed a 'bulging disk'. Anxious for relief from the terrible pain, I went to an orthopedic surgeon, who was supposed to be the best in town. I get an appointment for right after lunch. But he comes in one hour late. Is that alcohol I smell? This is not reassuring.

He completely fails to put me at ease, because he lacks any social graces. Our conversation lasts three minutes, but he does almost all the talking. I never get a chance to ask questions. He didn't even make an attempt to examine me. The fourth minute of our consultation, he tells me that it's really important that he should operate on me right away, and he is, after all, the best in town at back surgery.

Is there any other option? Nope, it's the only way to fix the pain quickly.

You can imagine my thoughts at this time! Now, twenty-five years later, I can reflect a little more calmly, and I find it useful to think of this experience in the context of 'building relationships': be sociable, be interested, be there.

Was he sociable? Arriving late, smelling of booze, monopolizing the conversation, avoiding small talk, making no reassuring noises, his abrupt manner – altogether he failed to lay any foundation for a relationship of trust.

Was he interested? Only in notching up another back operation. With no investigation of background and facts, no physical examination, no discussion of different options that might be suitable for me, his lack of interest was obvious.

In the circumstances there was no way I was going to agree to a rush operation.

Was he there for me? This was the first time I had met him. He had had no opportunity to display any continuing commitment to me his patient. He would have had to be very sociable and genuinely interested to even start to overcome this shortfall. He could have suggested we work together for a few sessions to find out what was really happening with my back. He could have deferred the decision and then called me a couple of times to find out how I was doing. He could have been more patient with his patient, and recognizing my concerns, he could have made an effort, over a period, to address those concerns and help me to trust him.

Instead, what I got was what appeared to be an off-the-cuff decision to cut me open. Take it or leave it. I left it.

I was totally cured within a month by a chiropractor. I liked the way he related to me, and to his other patients. He was the team chiropractor for the Boston Celtics, and he was always there for them – on the bench – during games. He quickly won my trust and confidence. I trusted him to fix me, and he did.

Customers pay close attention to the way sales people behave. They make no distinction between behavior in the office, in the boardroom, on the golf course, in a restaurant, or at a ball game. Behavior is behavior, and bad behavior is never good.

For example, people can learn a lot about each other playing golf for a few hours. That's why sales people like to take customers on the golf course. It's a relaxed atmosphere that can encourage customers to open up and provide useful information that may lead to a sales opportunity and a sale. But at the same time, a golf outing gives the customer the chance to assess the sales person in a different environment... Does she or he play the game in the right spirit? "Hmm... I wonder if that score's been massaged. Why is he asking for so many mulligans[44]? She didn't try a kick wedge on that ball did she? Ouch – what a temper!

Customers (and potential customers) will learn lessons about a sales person's character, attitude and trustworthiness on the golf course or in a restaurant, or in any situation, and will inevitably translate those lessons into the business world. The longer sales people work with customers, the more opportunities there are for them to demonstrate their true character. For good or ill.

It is, in all honesty, really difficult to sell anything complex, risky or expensive without a sound relationship to provide a basis of trust and honest communication. You and your team must invest in relationships, and the investment is mainly one of time, patience and consideration.

Good relationships cannot be built overnight. The essential ingredients are always the same. Setting the scene by being friendly, approachable, and a good listener. Being genuinely concerned to find out what is really going on, and what your customer really needs. Establishing trust and credibility by providing support, help and your presence over a period of time. Being sociable, being interested, and being there.

> *Good relationships cannot be built overnight.*

'Working at Relationships' may sound, to some people, like just too much hard work. But don't be daunted. In my experience most people who are in sales actually enjoy building relationships – it's one of the reasons that they were attracted to the sales profession in the first place. Most people in sales do get some sort of a mental kick from working with people, getting to know them, learning what they like and dislike, adjusting to their style, being helpful and *building relationships*.

If you and all your team members are like that, then you stand a great chance of succeeding – but you should never forget that it still takes time and some hard work. If none of this comes naturally to you, then being in sales won't ever be much fun: maybe you should move on before you evolve into a klink.

---

[44] A "mulligan" is when a player is allowed to take a poor shot over again. A 'do-over'.

The Relationshipless Contact – Cold Calling

Many sales people dread calling customers they don't know and are fearful of their response, which they imagine will be rejection, more often than not. As a sales manager, I'm always careful not to throw a sales novice into cold calling right away. If people get the idea that sales is mainly about cold calling, they can lose enthusiasm very quickly.

Introducing someone to the sales profession by making them do cold calls would be like Edison introducing electricity to the world by demonstrating the electric chair.[45] So as a sales manager I don't give a novice sales person a long list of cold calls on the first day, and tell him or her "Don't just stand there, sell something."

A cold call is a sales call with no pre-existing relationship in place. In some markets, sales people spend a high proportion of their time cold-calling. But that's not the case in complex high-tech sales: in this world, sound relationships are so important that it is hardly surprising that cold calls are difficult, and rarely successful.

So, cold calls are difficult. Cold calls mostly fail. These are true statements that sometimes lead sales managers to one of two extreme conclusions. They might decide that cold calls are not worth the effort and so all focus should be on building on existing relationships. Some sales managers take the opposite view, and insist on sales people making a very large number of cold calls to make up for their low success rate.

In the world I inhabit – complex solution sales in the high-tech sector – neither of these extremes will work.

You cannot abandon cold calling entirely, because every business needs new customers, and you can't rely just on bumping into decision-makers on the golf course.

And you cannot adopt the 'more is better' approach, because if you focus just on making first contacts, you cannot spend time establishing the relationships that will lead to sales.

---

[45] Due credit: I heard something like this at a presentation by Bob Kaiser. Trivial background info: Thomas Edison did in fact play a part in the invention of the electric chair, and it did have something to do with selling... Edison wanted to show the world in as dramatic a way as possible that AC power, used by his competitor Westinghouse, was more dangerous than DC power supplied by the Edison Company.

Here are my rules for developing cold calling strategies: be selective, be prepared, be patient.

Be selective. The application of some intelligence and planning to a cold calling program can pay dividends.

Statistically, the least effective type of cold calling involves working through the phone book, or a trade directory from A to Z, without any sifting or discrimination.

When I was just a beginner in sales, I was given a list of cold calls to make. Out of 1000 phone calls, I only reached fifty live voices. I eventually made one sale out of that list, and that was to someone who already knew us. Cold calling can produce a result, but as a sales manager you have to weigh up if it's the best way for your team to spend their time.

Some sort of connection or lead is much better than making a call from thin air. The chances of getting to a second conversation are much higher when the first conversation is based on something more substantial than "I called you because you're next in the alphabet".

Hot leads are always great to get, but they don't always arrive exactly when you need them. If you need to stimulate business by cold calling, try to create a list of 'suspects' that, while not exactly hot, are not freezing cold either. How do you create such a list? Here are some suggestions...

- **Stimulate customer interest**. Companies who engage in blanket, unselective cold-calling are using sales effort to replace marketing effort. As a sales manager, you have a responsibility to get whoever is responsible for marketing in your company to do more than create awareness, more even than building a positive image of your company and products.

  You need the experts in marketing to create real sales leads, and they should be measured on their success in doing that. They can do this through the right type of advertising, on the web as well as in traditional media, through trade shows, and company-sponsored events. You need to work with the marketing team to ensure that you follow up, evaluate and report on every lead you and your team receive. Above all – give them all the success stories you can, to encourage them to do more.

- **Be on the lookout**[46] for target companies with characteristics that are likely to place them in the market for your solutions. Trade publications and the industry grapevine often produce

---

[46] Police forces call this BOLO – Be On the LookOut. Simply keeping your eyes, ears and brain on alert is useful for sales people as well as for the police.

clues about a company's intentions, plans and concerns. If, for example, your product has helped your customers to reduce their software support costs, then be on the lookout for companies who are talking about their software support costs being too high, or initiating an action program to slice out waste in that area.

- **Build and use your network.** Your network of contacts needs to be constantly extended and kept warm. Your network includes customer contacts, friends, and people you meet at industry shows, chambers of commerce, seminars and conferences. When you meet people face-to-face you can start to get to know them much more effectively than when you just talk over a telephone.

Your network is powerful, and should be one of the most fruitful sources of leads. Leads can come from the most unlikely of conversations. If you have built the right sort of relationships, you can have easy conversations that will uncover useful information about opportunities in other departments, in partner companies, and even in competitors. People know and have relationships with each other across company boundaries. It's so useful to be able to lift the phone and start off the conversation with something like: "Hi there Lou. Pat Smith over at Amalgamated suggested I should give you a call..."

By being selective about who you choose to cold call, you can increase your success rate tremendously. This is not too much hard work. It's a whole lot easier than working through the phone book from top to bottom.

Be prepared. There is no point in a sales person making a call without any idea of what to say to the customer. At the same time, sales people should beware of going to every customer, with a too detailed script that must be followed no matter what the customer says.

As a sales manager, you need to ensure that your team members are properly prepared for their discussions with customers. Once you get in the door, you only get one chance to make a first impression, and we all know how important first impressions are.

The initial conversation with a new customer is the sales person's opportunity to do just three things:

- Learn enough about the customer to assess whether they are likely to need and be attracted to your company's products and services.

- Explain enough about the value of your company, your products and services to engage interest.

- Prepare the ground for further conversations with your contact or other decision makers, along the path leading to a sale.

Some people like to have a script, but customers aren't impressed by a mindless recitation of facts. Sales people really need to carry in their heads just a short checklist of points, to make sure they cover the ground. The way these points are expressed will depend on the personality of the customer contact, on the type of company and their needs. If a sales person really knows the products and understands their value, then customizing them on the fly for any situation, should be effortless. Mental checklists should contain more questions than answers, and more prompts for the customer than prompts for the sales person. This is because the first call is primarily to start to build the relationship between the sales person and the customer.

All customers are different. But actually they do tend to follow a limited numbers of patterns of response. That means that if a sales person makes enough 'first calls' he or she will build a repertoire of responses to ensure the conversation continues to flow in the right direction.

My son Greg used to sell for a lawn service company, and most of his calls were cold calls. Greg made one sale in his first week, three in the second and he continued to gradually win more and more business for several months. By the end of the year he won the 'rookie of the year' award before moving on. I asked him how he managed to convert cold calls into sales so successfully, and he said that it was all a matter of becoming familiar with customer reactions, having the appropriate response ready, and delivering it with confidence.

The same thing surely applies to more complex sales. "Having the answers" is great for credibility and there's no better way to have the answers at your fingertips than to prepare, practice, and do it. Cold calling is not easy, but it becomes easier the more you do it.

Be patient. A first contact should never be made for the purpose of making a sale at least not in the business of business solutions. A first contact is the first step in establishing a relationship that will enable you to make a sale.[47]

Your cold call program must include adequate time for follow-up calls, and for building that relationship. Listening and understanding what you hear takes time. Sales managers must allow for some period

---

[47] Of course, you will point out, there are exceptions. I agree. Selling corn dogs from a stand at the State Fair is one of the exceptions.

of uncertainty after contact is made, and before the rep can decide whether the prospect is a good one or not.

If a sales manager mandates too many cold calls, sales reps will not have time to investigate and develop each prospect adequately before moving on to the next one.

You also need to establish clear qualification criteria[48], so people in your team know when to keep going, and equally, to back off if there is not a real likelihood of making a sale.

Sales people may need to invest some time in a prospect before coming to a conclusion that the relationship isn't going anywhere useful. Once you really understand a prospect's business needs and priorities, you may come to the conclusion that the real business need for your offering just isn't there. Everyone should understand when a prospect should be made a lower priority, and placed on the back burner.

I still have social contact with people I met first in the context of a 'cold call' but I never had the opportunity to sell them anything, because they turned out to have no real need for, or interest in, what I was selling. I still keep in touch. Why? Because I've come to value the relationships in their own right; because the more people there are in my network the more opportunities I have to find out what's going on in the industry; and because one day, I might just be there when they really need me.

Cold calling will never be easy. Cold calls will never generate 100% success. But it *is* possible for a sales manager to make the cold calling chore easier and more productive. Remember that the reason for making a cold call is hardly ever to close a sale: it's to start a relationship. This means that the sales manager and everyone in the sales team must all: be selective, be prepared, and be patient.

The reason for making a cold call is hardly ever to close a sale, it's to start a relationship.

[48] There's a lot more about Qualification in *Don't Just Stand There, Sell Something - Volume 2*.

132

Trustworthiness: A Long-term Investment

If you and your team want to build long term relationships with your customers, then your customers must trust you and your team; your team must trust you; and you must be able to trust your team. Deception can occasionally pay off, but you can only fool most people one time. Being trustworthy pays off as an investment. Trustworthiness wins customer loyalty, it reduces stress in the workplace, and everyone sleeps better at night.

There are three ways people generally approach being 'trustworthy' in business.

- There's the *obvious* way - being honest with people, honoring commitments, doing what's best for the customers and stockholders. This is the approach that I'm most comfortable with, and that I demand from all my sales people. But others take a different line…

- There's the *expedient* way - telling the truth only when lying is too risky. If you can get away with it, you do what is immediately advantageous even if it's not right; you lie and cheat, but only in moderation. If you're smart, then you can get away this for a long time, maybe for a whole career.

- There's the *cynical* way - lie, cheat and steal all the time, but stand up in front of stockholders and customers and boast about your integrity. Eventually you'll get found out. But you'll have made a pile of money meantime, and chances are you won't have to give very much of it back, even if you have to wait a few months in jail before you get to enjoy spending what's left.

I believe there's no short cut here. The only way to gain trust, lasting trust, is to be trustworthy. Really. This is not something that you can pretend about and hope to get away with it. Being trustworthy is a *fundamental* decision people make about the way they run their lives. You can't choose to turn integrity on and off, just as it suits the immediate circumstances. Occasional integrity is not good enough.

> *…there's no short cut here. The only way to gain trust, lasting trust, is to be trustworthy.*

Look around you, not just at people in sales, but in all roles in business. It seems that every week there is some new big scandal about executive dishonesty hitting the headlines: phony accounting, opaque corporate structures, or diversion of company funds for personal purposes.

There are many more cases of business graft that reach the courts, but don't make the national headlines. There is also a constant flow of arbitration disputes between customers and suppliers in which one or the other is claiming that the other failed to honor commitments, lied about capabilities or did something else that led to a complete break down of trust. These are less visible than the court cases, because of the confidentiality built into the arbitration process, but they're there.

And there are maybe thousands of instances of petty deception that people just accept as the way business is done these days. I often come across little examples of people being deceitful to further their own objectives, even if it's not good for their customers, and downright damaging to the company they work for.

With all this positively un-trustworthy behavior around us, why bother doing anything but the minimum needed to keep out of trouble? Why do I make such a big deal about *being* trustworthy, not just *appearing to be* trustworthy?

If I thought that people could get to be successful in sales and sales management just by pretending to be trustworthy, then there wouldn't be a separate section in this book on the topic of Trustworthiness. If I thought that appearance was more important than reality, I'd include some advice in the Relationships section about how to fool most of your customers most of the time. But that would be wrong, because ultimately, reality counts, in many different ways.

For one thing, it's really hard work to sustain a false impression over the months it takes to build a relationship and over the years you should expect that relationship to last. Relationships based on falsehood will one day fall apart.

At another level: think about the sort of business society we are building if we base everything on falsehood and deceit. If no one can take anything on trust, then business life becomes more and more complicated and risky until ultimately even the simplest business transaction involves lots of hard work checking and cross-referencing everything.

We can see signs of this happening already in a number of small ways.

We are inundated with e-mail messages that attempt to con us into spending our money on worthless goods, or are laden with computer viruses, spyware and malware. As a result of this deluge, no one opens e-mail messages from people they don't know. This means that e-mail is no longer available for honest companies to use to introduce prospective customers to their goods and services.

We are so used to advertisements that mislead or exaggerate, that many people are becoming increasingly immune to ads in any form, or simply ignore them completely. Even people who work in advertising buy a Tivo so that can watch TV without having to sit through the ads. To get through to customers, ads have to be even more subtle – or even more misleading. To have any impact on the market, companies have to buy more and more advertising, and as people become saturated, they turn off even more.

I admit that one time I was taken in by dishonest advertising. Being a little on the heavy side, I was persuaded to buy some pills that guaranteed you would lose ten pounds in ten days. Then I read the small print. Sure, I just had to take one pill a day, but I had to take it at 5pm, and then not eat anything until the next morning. It seemed to me that if I could manage not to eat a thing for more than fourteen hours out of every twenty-four, sure I was going to lose weight. Unfortunately the pills didn't magically increase my will power or make it easy not to eat anything. An aspirin every day would have been just as effective, and a whole lot cheaper. I got my money back, but after an argument and waiting for two months. There may be some wonderful new diet products out there that could help me lose weight, safely and surely. But one bad experience means it's difficult to trust anyone who makes such claims, and so as far as I am concerned, and probably thousands of others, those 'good' products are likely to stay on the shelves.

Many years ago, I wasted an hour or so listening to a pitch for a water filter for our new house when I first moved to Texas. (If you've ever experienced the muddy taste of unfiltered Dallas water in high summer, you'll know why I was interested in a filter system.) The rep arrived half an hour late, wearing a sports coat from two decades ago and a toupee that was on slightly crooked. Being fashionable isn't really too important, but being presentable is; I've got nothing against toupees, providing they're on straight. First this rep asked me to tell him how much I spent on clothes each month, and on detergent, and on coffee. I gave him some rough figures, which he didn't like so he doubled or tripled each one of them. (How could I be so frugal?) He pulled out a calculator and figured that I would save around $3000 a year on clothes, coffee and detergent, because with great filtered water flowing into the house, our clothes would last longer, we could use less coffee in our filter machine, and we could use less detergent. Now all I had to do was write him a check for $130 each month for five years and I would actually save $120 a month.

Now, underneath all this nonsense there might have been some real facts – I am sure a really good filter system can make my coffee taste better. But he made so many dishonest claims that if there were any real facts in there, I missed them. He used his own figures for the calculation, not mine. He made assertions about the huge savings that were possible without providing any evidence. And he was evasive about what I would really have to pay for the system. Naturally I asked him to leave, but as he went I remembered to ask him for my free 'no obligation' phone that he had promised me for listening to his pitch. The phone broke the first time I used it.

This sort of sales approach must have a fairly low success rate, but I guess it's high enough that they keep doing it. Why? If the company has a good product at a fair price, then a deceptive sales pitch isn't going to help. In fact, it can turn customers (like me) off. And no one is going to recommend a product to their friends and business colleagues if they feel they've been suckered.

Being less than honest with customers isn't limited to companies operating at the margins of respectability. We have seen how some large energy companies fraudulently manipulated the market to raise prices to end customers. Financial scandals keep appearing in all industry sectors – in insurance, investment companies, telecom companies, software businesses. In the high tech sector we have seen examples of situations where customers placed their trust in sales people who said – trust us, we're the best, we'll look after you no matter what happens, we'll guarantee success." But when the customer is given a legally binding contract to sign, it contains words that say, in effect, no matter how unsatisfactory our work is, you can't blame us – oh, and if we decide to fix any problems, we'll charge you extra.[49] And they do.

During the high-tech boom, some analysts reckoned that failed IT projects cost the US economy at least $145 billion in 2001 alone.[50] Now maybe some of the blame can be laid at the door of customers for buying the wrong things, but looked at simplistically, that still represents a lot of high-tech suppliers failing to meet commitments to their customers. Some of that was the responsibility of sales people who knowingly over-committed. And some was the responsibility of sales people who over-committed without realizing that their company lacked the delivery capability it claimed to have.

---

[49] I've seen this in a contract: *We do not warrant that this work will be fit for any business purpose.*
[50] *Optimize Magazine*, July 2002. The same issue also includes results from the Standish survey of 2001, briefly: according to customers, only 9% of IT projects met time, budget and performance expectations; 29% of projects were complete failures.

What many of us observed at that time was an increasing lack of customer confidence – customers simply couldn't be certain that any major investment in information technology would actually pay off in business terms. Many projects were running way over budget. Many failed to deliver the improvements in performance and functionality that were promised. With large complex projects, it's pretty difficult to pack it up and send it back to the store, especially if a big chunk of the money has been paid up front. It's just a hunch, but perhaps one of the reasons for the dramatic swing from boom to bust was the sudden failure of trust – companies that needed new technology became more and more skeptical of the claims of companies who sold and delivered that new technology.

Most people suffer in such times of economic downturn. (A few prosper, but that's another story.) People and companies lose money, big institutions and small investors alike. People lose jobs, suffer stress, and sometimes ill-health. People become less entrepreneurial, more cautious and cynical.

See what I mean? Lying, cheating and stealing just isn't healthy.

Cheer up! Maybe this is just a phase we're going through. Today the world might appear to be excessively cynical, cautious and untrusting. But these things, I believe, have an ability to be self-adjusting. I am an upbeat type of person and so instead of viewing all these problems as a problem, I think they are really an opportunity.

As I travel around the country and around the world, I come across plenty of people who are really offended by the level of corporate dishonesty and deception that we've seen in recent years. People know it's a problem, and they don't like it. The reason they don't like it is that it is so much at odds with their fundamental values and personal code of behavior. Those values are shared by many of us, probably the majority. There are still lots of people who I trust, and who trust me, and so we can still continue to do effective, mutually profitable business together. Business still goes on, and most deals are still based on relationships, and those relationships are based on trust.

The untrustworthy people I've come across are actually in the minority, and pretty well known to be untrustworthy by everyone. Word gets around.

People continue to seek out sound, trustworthy people to do business with, because doing business with cheats and liars is risky, not to mention hard work. There has always been a big benefit in being trustworthy. Today, the premium is even bigger. Being honest pays off.

But surely the dishonest win sometimes? Sure, they do, but the gain is only short-term. Sales managers who push their sales people to lie, cheat or mislead their customers to achieve short-term gains, are short-sighted people – they are klinks. Sales people who go along with that sort of pressure are laying a foundation of distrust that can ruin their sales career. The word gets around, and if someone is caught in a lie, or lets a customer down after shaking on a deal, then people will get to know it. Sales reps who use deception to build undeserved trust are building on sand. It is hard to build a reputation for trustworthiness, but very easy to demolish one. I've seen it happen many times.

So the reality is, being ethical and playing the game with integrity helps me and my team make more sales. Telling the truth generates more sales than bending the truth? Yes. In sales, you become a long-term success by building a long-term reputation. Investment in integrity generates a real payback.

There is, I suppose, another reason why I stick to decent business values, and coach my team to do the same thing. It makes me feel good about what I do every day. I was brought up to understand the difference between right and wrong, and I still hold to those values. If I behaved any other way, I couldn't sleep at night, which wouldn't do much for my performance during the daytime.

Building Trust

Building trust involves more than saying: "Trust me." While politicians and CEOs can do this and get away with it (occasionally), sales people always have to demonstrate that they can be trusted by their actions, not just their words.

Customers want to know you sincerely want to do the best thing for them. Of course, they know that sales people work for salaries, commissions, bonuses, trips to Hawaii and so on. They know that this isn't a hobby or a charity mission. Nevertheless they need to know that your desire for commission payments will not take precedence over your desire to do the right thing.

As a sales manager, I make it my business to be very clear with my team: I expect trustworthy behavior at all times. There are four 'rules of trust' we can use to discuss this; each one of these presents an opportunity to behave well, or badly, in the eyes of the customer. These rules of trust are:

- Telling the truth, always.
- Honoring commitments.
- Handling problems.
- Giving trust to get trust.

Telling the truth, always, sounds to some people like an impossibility. To others it doesn't seem to be a problem. Why is this? The answer is that it is impossible to tell just one lie. Tell one, and you have to tell another to cover up the first one. Then you've got to spin the same story to other people to appear to be consistent. Then you have to remember who you told what story too. One lie breeds plenty more.

It follows that the golden rule of truthfulness is simple: avoid telling the first lie. This is easier than it sounds. I'm often amazed at how easy it is for some people to fall into a chain of unnecessary deception.

The customer asks, "Do you have a box that does x, y and z?" The sales rep knows that there is a box available that does x and y, but only some of z.

"Sure thing" the rep says, "in fact our model AB4321 was designed especially for people like you who need x, y and z all in one box." Internally a voice is screaming at him: "How am I going to cover up the fact it does only part of z? Maybe they don't really need it all and we can bluff our way to a sale. Perhaps I can get the development guys to write a quick mod. I'm going to get in trouble again. Why am I always getting in trouble?"

In fact, every seasoned sales person can find some words that explain the real situation without throwing away the opportunity for a sale. Customers are always more pragmatic than inexperienced sales people expect.

"You know, not many people need all of x, y and z in just one box. We have several boxes that are close, maybe the AB4321 would be OK. Exactly what parts of z are you going to need? Then I can work out the best way to put something together to meet your exact requirements."

All sales reps need to learn, really quickly, that if they want to permanently destroy a relationship with a customer, just tell them one lie.

> *All sales reps need to learn that if they want to permanently destroy a relationship with a customer, just tell them one lie.*

How hard is this? Step one: understand what you and your company can deliver, and what you can't. Step two: sell the stuff you can do, and work round the stuff you can't do.

Being up front and honest is always the easiest path, and the least stressful, and in my experience customers always welcome and appreciate candor from a sales rep. Sometimes complete honesty might lead to a "no" from the customer, but if the answer is going to be "no" eventually, isn't it better to find out as soon as possible?

And don't forget that "I don't know" is not a sign of weakness, providing you follow it with "… but I know how to find out."

Honoring commitments. The job of a sales rep (and the sales manager) does not end when a deal is signed. Part of the job has to be making sure that the customer gets what has been promised.

A regular complaint from customers is that their suppliers fail to meet their commitments. Deliveries arrive just one or two days late. A product doesn't quite meet specification. A project more or less delivers what is expected, but not exactly.

What is exasperating about many of these cases is that so often the customer would have been quite prepared to accept a delivery date one or two days later, or would have been quite happy with a slightly different project scope – *if only they had known up front.*

If a sales rep tells the truth during the sale, and is honest about what can or can't be done, how can there be a problem honoring commitments made to customers? If you can't do it, you shouldn't have promised it.

This applies to verbal commitments as well as to written commitments. If there's a difference between what is written down and what has been said, then go back one step and read the "Telling the truth" section above.

However, we all know that sometimes things go wrong. Even so, *you* still have a commitment. That means *you* have a problem to handle.

Handling problems. The deal is done, the customer is happy at first, but then something goes wrong. Perhaps there's a problem during delivery, perhaps it's a problem in the first few weeks of operation. Who should fix it?

Anyone in the company who can help should be mobilized to sort things out for a customer who has a problem. It often falls to the sales team to make the phone calls, cajole people, get them to work late, whatever it takes to rescue the situation. Sales people often complain when they have to do this. Stop complaining, it's your opportunity to shine in the eyes of the customer. Other departments in the company may have forgotten that ultimately it's the customers who pay everyone's salary, but you won't forget that. You're in sales!

It is unforgivable for a sales person to sit back and do nothing when a customer has a problem. I've seen every evasive tactic. One approach is to simply refuse to take the phone call, hoping the mess will go away by itself. Another futile approach is to fight back: provide endless excuses and lame justifications for what has happened, but do nothing to make things better. Blaming someone else is always easy: "Our shipping contractor lost the shipment. We were sent some faulty components from Taiwan. The dog ate it."

Forget the evasion and excuses. The best use for your energy and creativity is to work with other people in your company and partners to evaluate what has happened, what needs to be done, and fix it. Sometimes the sales person has to step up and phone an executive late at night to get the OK for out-of-the-ordinary action. Do it.

And meantime, make sure that you talk to the customer, tell them what you are doing, and listen to their response. If they yell at you, sympathize. You can get so much closer to customers if you hear them out and feel their frustration. If they are in a state of panic, reassure them. They need to know that you are on their side, and are doing everything possible to solve the problem for them.

When the problem is fixed, make sure someone in your company works out *why* the problem happened, and takes steps to prevent it ever happening again.

Sales people spend time carefully building a relationship with customers – that's how you make sales. So when something goes wrong, it's only natural that customers should reach out to the sales person. Tell your team: make the call, follow it through, and be glad you had the chance to demonstrate your concern, and your commitment.

Give trust to get trust. Building trust has to work both ways. Think about it. Is there anyone you trust totally, who does not trust you? Is there anyone who trusts you totally, but you don't trust him or her at all? Both situations are pretty unlikely.

> *Give trust to get trust. Building trust has to work both ways.*

Trust between two people tends to be built up step by step, with each one gradually accumulating more and more trust based on their experience of positive actions and trustworthy behavior.

If you encounter someone who, at the first meeting clearly doesn't trust you, how easy is it for you to trust that person? I have found that usually people who are not prepared to give any trust at all are themselves untrustworthy.

So if you want to assist the building of trust, one thing you might consider is to give some trust early, to build confidence.

This applies to your relationships with customers and, if you are a sales manager, to members of your team. (I do not suggest that you naïvely offer complete trust to everyone unthinkingly. This is the twenty-first century after all.)

One of the simplest things a sales rep can do to show trust is this: *trust the customer to understand.* Sometimes sales people hide the nasty truth from customers, fearful that the customer will walk away. In fact most customers are realistic and understanding if you give them a chance. You can't deliver your specialist cooling equipment in less than six weeks? Tell the customer, even if they have said they want it tomorrow. Chances are, the customer understands perfectly well what typical lead times are for this type of equipment and already has plans to wait. In any case, it's better for the customer to be mildly annoyed now, than to be furious in two weeks time when the cooling gear doesn't turn up.

Customers live in the real world, just as you do. They'll make a big deal of expecting perfection from suppliers, but it's their job to be demanding. They really know that perfection is a goal to aim for; they want you to get as close as possible; they certainly want you to strive for perfection. But if your company falls slightly short sometimes, that can be forgiven. What they will not forgive is a failure to be honest about shortcomings, attempts to cover up, and willful deception in any form.

Here is a simple example to illustrate the above points. So many people have had unsatisfactory experiences with car sales people that I just have to tell you about Dave Reasoner. Through his actions Dave rapidly gained my trust, which is quite something when it comes to buying used cars.

A couple of years ago, my son Greg needed a car and somehow we ended up visiting Dave at Baillargeon. Greg wanted a really reliable car, economical on gas, and his budget was between $5,000 and $8,000.

Dave promised to look out for likely suspects, even though we were shopping at the lower end of the price range for that dealership... But he kept his word and soon came back to tell us that a car had just come in that we might like to look at. It looked good, but Dave told me straight up front that the car hadn't been inspected yet, so he couldn't vouch for its reliability. It turned out that the inspection revealed that the car had been in an accident and so Dave suggested that this would not be a good buy for us. If he hadn't told us, we would never have been able to detect this by ourselves. Apparently they have some machine that measures the thickness of the paint to identify irregularities resulting from repair work.

A week later, another call from Dave. It was a four-year old Mitsubishi Galant, fully loaded, sunroof, only 26,000 miles. Greg and I liked it, but we were sure it would be too expensive, at least $10,000. But Dave hadn't forgotten about our budget, and offered it to us for $7,700. That was a great deal. I'm sure Dave didn't make much money on it, but he knew I'd likely come back again.

He was right. A couple of months later, I wanted to find a suitable car for my youngest son Bryan, who was turning sixteen. I went back to Dave and he started work on it. He gave me an update just about every day on the cars he was finding, checking out with me which ones we liked, and advising me which ones he would recommend – and which we should avoid. Before too long, he called me and said he'd found the perfect car for Bryan. A 1993 Infiniti G20 with 122,000 miles – but in mint condition with one owner.

How do you know whether to believe the sales person when he says it's perfect and a great bargain? It's all about trust. Dave had built my confidence by delivering the first time, and being honest with me throughout. So this time, although it looked more risky, I took Dave's word. This car turned out to be just what Dave had said: a great bargain at $4,300, and perfect for Bryan. Dave turned out to be quite different from car sales people I'd dealt with in the past: because of the trust his customers have in him, he gets repeat business while other more typical sales guys are struggling to find customers.

We're now thinking about my daughter's next car. Guess where Rachael and I will be going? In fact Dave has done such a good job in establishing trust and credibility, my kids will probably go to him when they need to buy something really special for me!

The special element of trust will always put one sales person ahead of another. When a customer has a need, which sales rep gets the call? The person who has built a strong relationship based on trust.

> *The special element of trust will always put one sales person ahead of another.*

As a sales manager you need to be trusted by your team members and you need to be trusted by your customers. You also need to exercise active leadership over your team members to ensure that their customers trust them too – and so you can trust them.

An important part of your leadership role is simply setting a good example.

I first went into sales in Birmingham, Alabama in 1983. There I met Bobby Thomas who was to become my mentor and a good friend. Bobby and I were very different. I was just starting in sales, and he was very experienced with an excellent record of achievement in selling high-tech equipment. He was from Alabama and I was from New York. He was courteous, calm and never got flustered; Bobby could be described as a real southern gentleman, and I – well, whatever I was, I wasn't one of those.

As I watched Bobby in customer situations, I noted that he always said what he meant and meant what he said. When Bobby made a promise, he always kept it. He always followed through and looked after the customer's interests after the deal was signed. If any problems came up, he would be honest about what was going on, work hard to get the problem fixed, and never make excuses. I never, not once, saw Bobby lose his temper, get frustrated, blame others for problems, or use foul language. Bobby was naturally a man of integrity, he didn't have to work at it, he didn't have to pretend. He was the same in front of customers as he was with his business colleagues and with his friends.

All Bobby's customers knew that Bobby was a man of his word, and recognized his complete commitment to doing the best thing for his customers. As a result, customers trusted Bobby completely, and were always happy to do business with him.

As a sales person, Bobby Thomas was highly successful. And I believe that he was successful in sales because he was successful as a human being – a man of balance and integrity. He was a tremendous early influence on me in my business life, and eventually on my personal life. He helped me recognize the importance of having beliefs and values and living them out all the time. Bobby was a sincere Christian who did not talk about his deep beliefs. He simply lived according to them.

Bobby showed me, and many other sales people, how behaving with integrity was a key factor in being successful. He demonstrated every day that behaving with integrity is not something that should be switched on and off. The way to build trust is simple: the integrity switch should always be in the on position.

The way to build trust is simple: the integrity switch should always be in the on position.

Question Your Motives

Why are you doing this? Your underlying motivation for being in sales is important. Obviously being in sales is one way of earning a living. It might even be a way to get rich. So earning money is one of the reasons people are attracted to sales. In my experience, if you are good at it, and you choose to work for the sort of company that values the contribution that sales people can make to the financial health of the business, then there's plenty of money to be made.

But there's money to be made in lots of other roles in this world. So leaving the money aside, a better question to ask is: Why did you choose sales as a way to earn a living, rather than something else. Why sales instead of being a production engineer, a server in a cocktail bar, an investment analyst, an oil well firefighter or a circus performer?

When I discuss this topic with new sales people, or people planning to enter the sales profession, I get lots of different answers. There is, of course, no single 'right' answer. But I expect to hear from sales people that they enjoy meeting other people, feel that they are good at building relationships and get a buzz out of working with people and helping them solve their business problems. When people tell me this, I like to look them in the eyes - I think I can judge whether someone is speaking sincerely, or just giving me the answers I expect to hear.

In any case I can soon find out by the way they behave with customers. Not only that, their customers will also be able to tell what the underlying motivation is.

What's all this got to do with "trust" and "relationships"? A lot. This is what I tell my sales team...

Customers know you are in sales to earn money, but if they believe that your actions are driven purely by money, they will back away. Customers start to lose trust in sales people if they feel they are pressured to sign *today* just so the sales person can book an order this month instead of next; when they find out the sales person has added a few unneeded products and services to the order to boost the order value; or when it becomes evident that the sales person is recommending a solution because it's the most expensive, not because it's the best.

Sales people who are genuinely driven by the right motivation of responsibility to the customer simply will not make these mistakes. People who are motivated primarily by greed will repeatedly make such errors and their relationships with customers will suffer as a result.

So look inside yourself and be honest with yourself about the type of person you are, and what really motivates you – that is, what really gives you satisfaction in your daily work. If you have to admit that the answer is money, pure and simple, you will never be able to build long-lasting trust with customers because you will automatically do the wrong thing from time to time, driven by your single ambition, to make more money.

There's something of a paradox here. Sales is a great way of making money, if you're good at it. But if you do it just to make money, and if making money is the main focus of your attention, then you probably won't be very good at it, and so you won't make as much money as you might hope for.

If money is your only objective, then you might never earn enough to be happy in a sales job.

> *If money is your only objective, then you might never earn enough to be happy in a sales job.*

The Bible tells us: "Whoever loves money never has money enough."[51] In other words, *if money is too important to you, no matter how rich you get, you won't be happy.* This is true, but it's not my point here. King Solomon was not in sales, but if he had been, he might also have pointed out that *if money is too important to you, your customers will be turned off, and you won't even get to be rich.*

---

[51] *Ecclesiastes 5:10.* This is thought to have been written by King Solomon, who probably knew something about money.

Relationships and Repeat Business

Every sales person and every sales manager is someone's customer too. Think about where you choose to buy clothes, where you choose to buy a car, where you choose to dine out. It's surprising how big a part relationships play in even simple purchasing decisions.

I must admit that around where I live and work, there are just a few restaurants that I visit regularly and where I take clients. Sure, I'm looking for friendly service, and consistently attractive and edible food, and no unpleasant surprises. And of course I visit new places to try them out. But it turns out that the restaurants I keep going back to are those places where people have made an effort to build a relationship with me, and of course I respond. These are places where they know my name, and remember my special favorites, and what I don't like so much. These are places where I feel that my guests and I are getting an especially warm welcome and even special treatment. At the same time I know that in some places, *everyone* feels they're getting special treatment – and that's what makes these places special. As a result people keep coming back.

Repeat business is built on relationships.

I buy most of my clothes from one clothes store (J.A. Bank Clothiers). I like the quality and though they're not the most inexpensive, they're good value for the money. Yet I don't go to their branch store closest to my home. I always go to the store where Steve Gollis takes care of me. I've been going there for over sixteen years and Steve has been there all that time. He believes in the company, their products and their business standards. But above all he understands what I like and value, and helps me choose clothes like a friend does. He won't press me to buy the most expensive if it won't work for me. He'll take items back – any time at all – if there is a problem. He is honest about what looks good on me and what doesn't. Since my wife usually approves of the end result, I guess he's doing a good job. I value his opinion and trust his judgment, and so I keep going back.

I have been a member of Bally's health club for fifteen years. I used to go to my closest Bally's but I now go to one that's farther away, even though it's less convenient. When one Bally's is pretty much as well equipped as another, why would I make that extra effort? Because Bob Coe, the manager, knows who I am, and takes an interest in my progress. He seems to always be there and I believe he makes everyone feel just as welcome. Because I expressed a casual interest, he once took me into the maintenance room to explain the renovation being made to the steam bath. The new steam room is great, but the reason I continue to go there is because of Bob. His passion for his club and his enthusiasm for building relationships with his customers make all the difference.

Both Steve and Bob are great examples of how relationships can influence how people can spend money. Not the clothes, not the exercise machines. Not even the plumbing in the steam room. It's the people, and the relationships that they build, that encourage me to spend money with them, and not with others, and that is what sales is all about.

There's something else that all of us in sales should remember. While relationships make sales, it isn't always sales people who have the winning relationships.

I've seen an on-site service technician build a relationship that earned his company millions. Ron's job was really just to support some IT gear on the customers premises, but Ron took his company's 'commitment to service' seriously. He felt he was there to help, in any role, and he grew to become an integral part of a customer's operation – a valued advisor. He would suggest changes to the IT environment, and the customer would listen. When the customer had a problem, Ron would get involved in the discussion and his contribution would be valued. Now Ron could easily have avoided this level of involvement – there was nothing special in this for him. Equally, his boss could have taken klinkish exception to Ron using his time in this way. Did he really have to be on site full-time? Maybe we could save some money by giving him another customer to support? Fortunately, Ron's manager was smart, Ron stayed, and his relationship with the customer led to more business, more equipment for Ron to look after, and more profits for our company.

Everyone in every company is in sales in one way or another. And anyone can help the sales effort by working on building great relationships with customers, in one way or another, in big ways or small ways. The way a company is managed from the top can make a big difference to the behavior of individual employees and a big difference to the bottom line.

Everyone in every company is in sales in one way or another.

Here's a simple example. Many years ago I relocated from Birmingham, Alabama to Dallas, Texas. One day I was flying with my three children who at that time were respectively around four years old, three and one-and-a-half. Quite a handful. We were at the bulkhead near the front, and the beverage cart started its trip from front to back. Now my kids are fairly normal kids and were starting to get a bit boisterous. They had never been on an airplane before and I wasn't having much success in reducing their excitement level. Now every father knows that, when in doubt, you feed kids. So I asked the flight attendant for some extra bags of peanuts to help keep them occupied, and hopefully quiet. I could see passengers around me nodding in agreement – for heaven's sakes, give them some peanuts. The flight attendant was very short with me: "Sir, we'll let you know when we are done serving if we have any bags of peanuts left over, but you'll have to wait." It seemed like many hours later in that "flight from hell" that she stopped by and gave me two more of those little tiny bags of peanuts. We'd already started the descent to Dallas.

About a year later, I was visiting my parents up in Virginia, just outside of Washington, D.C. Again, it was just me and my three children, now a year older, but no quieter. But this time, a different airline, and we were way at the back of the plane. Eventually, the beverage cart started to make its move, again from front to back. I couldn't wait for the cart and stopped a passing flight attendant... "Can I get some extra peanuts for the kids?"

You would have thought I was an elephant in a zoo! The flight attendant smiled at me and gave us about twenty bags of peanuts and this was before everyone else was served. When they eventually reached us with the cart they gave us our drinks – and about ten more bags of peanuts, plus pins with eagles wings, decks of cards for each of them and cartoon character hats for them to wear! When we landed I thanked the entire crew and told them I would be flying with them again.

And I did fly with them again. I always felt welcome when I climbed on to their planes. I felt that I had a *relationship* with that airline, and clearly they were concerned to build a *relationship* with me. About ten years later I was regularly being offered free upgrades to first class. I noticed that I'd flown over 1.7 million miles with that airline, the one with the generous peanut policy and the smiling attendants.

Out of interest I checked how many miles I'd flown with the first airline – the one with the parsimonious peanut lady: a puny 8000.

That early peanut experience started me in a certain direction and made me inclined to choose one airline over another. But their continued warm behavior and consideration for me as a customer reinforced my loyalty and kept me coming back. To the airline, the cost of being relationship-oriented was, literally, peanuts. The payback in increased business was beyond peanuts.

One day, back in the early eighties, a friend showed me the latest annual report of Coca Cola. On the front cover of the annual report was a very long row of people sitting and working away on computer terminals and personal computers. In front of the scene, was a guy obviously helping out one of the computer users. I seem to remember he had his arm around her shoulder, so clearly he was being helpful.

My friend asked: "Do you know who he is?"

I couldn't guess. A model? A movie star? The CEO of Coca Cola? I had no idea.

It turned out that the star of the front cover was the IBM sales rep.

I was impressed. Clearly, this individual had created a warm and deep relationship with the company to be chosen to be on the front cover of the annual report.

Actually I was also more than a little dismayed: I had just been recruited as a sales rep for one of IBM's competitors, and Coca Cola was one of our targeted accounts. I was starting from nowhere, and my biggest competitor was already part of the family, and it turned out, had been family for several years.

This proved to be an extraordinarily difficult account for competitors to break into. IBM did a great job. Sure, they delivered value for the customer. But they created a strong and highly supportive relationship too.

I had a client in Alabama a few years ago. I got to know the CEO really well and he often asked my opinion when he had important decisions to make - not just when he wanted to buy something from me! Our relationship extended way beyond me just selling to his company. One time he told me that his sales force was struggling, and asked me if I had any ideas for improving success. Maybe I could spend a little time with a couple of reps and find out how they could close more deals?

That's right, instead of spending my time selling to his company, I should spend some time helping to sell his products! Now, I know that many people in sales would make a show of helping but really they would be reluctant to spend too much time on something that didn't pay commission, especially when they have other accounts to manage. But I always like to help so my first reaction was to get out there and see what I could do. Then I thought about it a little more. I figured that if this company wasn't growing, then they wouldn't need to buy more of my services and products. And I also knew that my relationship with the company was so good that if they needed anything they would buy it from me. The logical approach was to help in any way I could. My emotional response and my logic were both telling me the same thing: help my customer.

I made over thirty calls over six months with their sales reps. We worked together on building relationships and all the other stuff I write about in this book. Over the next twelve months, their sales tripled. As a consequence, my revenue grew too – much more than if I'd spent the same time waiting for an order instead of actively helping my customer.

My relationship with the customer made it possible for me to have the opportunity to help. My help made them more successful. Their success gave me more business – and it made our working partnership even stronger. Win-win.

The relationship between a sales person (or team) and a customer can evolve through different levels. Some sales people talk in terms of "Preferred Supplier", "Trusted Advisor", "Strategic Partner" and so on.

These labels used to be quite useful when they were used objectively. But in recent years I've found that companies use these terms in ways that can be quite misleading.

For example some companies *only* do business with companies who are on their "preferred supplier" list; since every supplier is "preferred" there is, for them, no such thing as a simple "supplier", except perhaps for the lunch counter that sends round sandwiches for meetings.

One company I encountered decided to describe all its customers – and prospective customers – as "Partners" even if they had never done any business with them. This not only devalues the term, it can be positively counter-productive. Not every customer wants to be described as a "Partner" when all they want to do is buy some boxes.

In some cases, companies will insist that they are "Trusted Advisors" to their customers. True, they will provide advice on their own products and services – but every supplier does that. As I understand the term, the idea was to be engaged with the customer at a level of strategic planning that was quite independent of the portfolio of services offered. Not many companies achieve that quite as well as they imagine they do. Many of those who do get involved in corporate strategy are consulting companies who are actually paid for their strategic input: it's just a service. They may be trusted to supply it, but then so are electrical contractors.

I'd like to return to a more objective way of assessing the level and quality of relationship a company has with its customers: one that removes some of the subjectivity from the assessment by using terms that are somewhat verifiable.

Here are my own definitions of four levels of customer-supplier relationship:

- Who are they?
- One among many.
- The first choice.
- The only choice.

Who are they? This is where most companies start off, before there is any meaningful relationship with the customer. This does not necessarily mean that the customer has never heard of you, just that you do not automatically spring to mind when the customer needs something you can offer. If your company is in this position, the chances are there are one or more companies who already do business with your customer/prospect and who have a superior relationship.

When you are in this category, you will know because:

- You always phone them, they never phone you except when they want to complain.
- You always have to remind them to include you on the bidder list.
- You lose, more often than not; and if you win, it's really hard work.

If you have a 'Who are they?' relationship with a customer or a prospect, you have a lot of hard work ahead of you to elevate your status. However it can be done. All your customers' favorite companies today were in this category once.

A slightly superior status is **one among many**. This means that normally the customer will be happy to assess your offering alongside the offerings of other suppliers, although they won't necessarily think of it. In this category, relationships are generally cordial rather than warm.

- You will be given no special notice of opportunities.
- Most large jobs will be subject to competitive tender, unless there is a supplier in place with a superior relationship, in which case you won't even be asked to bid.
- If there is an RFP, you're unlikely to be asked to make any suggestions for its contents.

While 'One among many' is preferable to 'Who are they' it still does not signify a special relationship. Don't be confused if the customer describes you as a 'preferred vendor'. That just means they prefer you to a company they've never heard of.

The first level at which you should be entitled to congratulate yourself and your team for building a special relationship is the **first choice** level.

When you are a first choice company, some or all of these things will happen, based on the level of trust that comes with the relationship you have built:

- You are the first choice company for the products and services you offer, and you receive contracts on a non-competitive basis and other companies rarely do.

- When a deal has to go out to competitive tender, you are sometimes asked for your opinions about the contents of the RFP.

- You are asked to quote special prices for long-term deals – stretching several years ahead.

- Your company and their company talk at executive level, and you know something about their future plans.

Being a 'first choice' supplier is a great position to be in. This is the minimum you should aim for. Successful companies can achieve this level with multiple clients. Those companies generally understand the importance of building relationships, and make it possible for their employees to spend time and energy doing just that.

The black belt level of relationship building is when you achieve **only choice** status with your customer. You'll know you've arrived at this level when:

- You automatically receive all non-competitive orders for the products and services you offer. No competitors are considered unless the project is big enough that company rules demand a formal competitive tender.

- When a deal has to go out to competitive tender, you are always asked for your opinions about the contents of the RFP. Usually you write most of it.

- The customer is always happy to negotiate big deals, binding both parties for years.

- The executives of the two companies know each other's future plans, and regularly work together to map out strategic possibilities.

Being an 'only choice' company is a wonderful place for a company to be. Some vendors exist for years without this happening. This status provides dependable revenue streams and removes a lot of the uncertainty from forecasting. It often takes years of relationship building to reach this position. Companies need to take relationships very seriously, at all levels of contact, to achieve 'only choice' status.

Being an 'only choice' company has it's disadvantages: the only way is down, and all your competitors are working really hard to make that happen. You will also encounter jealousy and discomfort in some places in your customer's organization: you need to be sensitive to these things and work to keep everyone on your side. Your company's integrity needs to be bulletproof, because many people will look for any slight excuse to bring you down. This leaves no room for complacency. Privilege has its responsibilities. Still, it's a much better place to be than 'Who are they?

Everyone in sales looks for repeat business. We all know that it takes a fraction of the effort to close a deal with a repeat customer than with a customer who we are working with for the first time.

The main force that creates repeat business is the quality of the relationship between the people in your company and the people in the company you sell to.

All other things being equal, a company that has a good relationship with a customer will always win business against a customer that has a poor relationship, or no relationship.

Everyone in your company should be mobilized and motivated to build strong customer relationships – aiming to be an 'only choice' supplier wherever you can.

> *The force that creates repeat business is the quality of the relationship between the people in your company and the people in the company you sell to.*

The Manager's Role in Building Customer Relationships

The sales team manager is uniquely able to motivate relationship building – or to get in the way.

The **first** step for a manager is to avoid the klink trap of believing that sales are made purely on price and logic. Price and logic play a part, as do other scientific approaches: proof of concept studies, return on investment analyses, price-performance calculations and so on.

But sometimes a sales person cannot even get an opportunity to present the compelling logic of a proposal without building a strong enough relationship to get a hearing. So very often, without a good customer relationship strategy, a company with sound products and services can fail to win business and fail to win business against competitors who might even have inferior products.

So a sales manager (and indeed all company executives) must understand that facts, while important, aren't everything. Facts rarely are sufficient to close a sale without some help from a relationship.

The **second** contribution that a sales manager can make is to give sales people – and other employees – space, time, authority and motivation to get close to the customer. In many businesses today, decision lead times are long. Complex and risky decisions take longer. As we have seen, building a relationship is critical to giving the customer the confidence to take the leap required to make a decision.

Managers do not help when, impatient for results, they move sales reps from one account to another. Or let some people go when they haven't managed to close a deal in the time frame allowed by the company.

High staff turnover is the enemy of relationship building. Obviously you don't want to hang on to people who can't do the job. But not closing a large complex deal in a few short months doesn't necessarily indicate incompetence. Sometimes it does, sometimes it doesn't, and a sales manager must be smart enough to tell the difference, not jump to a conclusion, as klinks do, that lack of immediate results is evidence of lack of ability.

Unfortunately, too many managers have a short-term perspective. Metrics sometimes drive behavior in a thoughtless way, and this can result in managers taking counter-productive decisions. In some environments it takes the sales person some months to establish a level of customer confidence sufficient to start real selling. And then the decision lead-time can be some months more.

The only way to accelerate sales is to build strong relationships. So if people are replaced because they can't achieve success quickly, then success will never come.

Why would any customer buy from a company that sends a new sales person along every few months? The customer is going to think: "They don't value me, they don't value their sales people, they don't value our relationship. Maybe they're not the right people to do business with."

The **third** thing that seems to make a big difference in building relationships is: get your people on site. This applies not just to sales people but to your delivery and support people too. Site visits should be encouraged, just to keep in touch, make sure that existing products and contracts are running well. If possible make them get support contracts that demand regular site visits and progress meetings! The delivery people may worry about the cost, but it provides a regular channel for gathering information, making contacts – and building relationships.

I once had the opportunity to get some office space at the office of my number one client. As we discussed how I would support them on site part time, I told their company president: "Think about it this way. I'm working for you and you're not paying me anything. How bad can that be?" This worked out great. The customer loved the support. We loved helping them, and we loved the ongoing growth in business that this produced. This relationship was very strong, and very productive, and lasted five years until I moved on.

Finally, a sales manager must provide *active backup* for their team members at all times. This means not just sitting around and waiting to step in when something goes wrong, but actively seeking ways to help and get involved.

It is essential that every customer should know you, the sales team leader, nearly as well as they know the sales rep assigned to them. Why? It provides the customer with an additional level of reassurance that your company is interested in them. You may be able to bring a more experienced perspective to critical customer conversations, which can help to smooth the path to a sale. If the customer does have any concerns about the capabilities of the sales rep, they are much more likely to confide in you if they already know you. And at a basic practical level, if the rep is not around for some reason (such as vacation, influenza, skiing accident, divorce proceedings) then they will have you around as a backup, a familiar face, and someone who knows them and their business.

To make all this work, you must get involved. This means making regular visits to the customer with your sales rep – not every time, but often enough to be remembered. You should do your homework – research the company, go to their seminars, visit their stand at trade shows. You should tag along now and again on golf trips and other social events.

You *must* try to develop relationships with people higher up in the company hierarchy than your sales rep's contacts. Sometimes the only way into an account is from the top. Use those executive-level contacts to influence decision making as well as to understand their company's challenges so you can be proactive in helping to address them. You should also become an advocate to support the customers' needs at the corporate level within your own company.

When your sales rep closes a big deal, be there for the event, not as a VIP visitor, but as a trusted member of the team. Give credit where it is due – to the sales rep. By showing that you value your team members, you are showing that you value what they are doing for your customer, and customers appreciate that. And when your customer is successful, congratulate them, and celebrate success with them.

Chapter 5
Thinking and Planning

Thinking ahead is good for everybody. Being action-oriented is a good thing, but acting without thinking can have horrible consequences.

Too many sales managers say "Don't just stand there, sell something" believing that the only way to sell anything is to get in front of the customer, now. Wrong.

The only way to sell something is to get in front of the customer with something useful and intelligent to say.

Thinking, Planning – and Acting

Anyone who has been trained in project management learns early that time spent planning pays off big time when you start to actually do the work. Often I've been told that a day spent planning saves two days in execution. Whether that is a verifiable statistic, I don't know. But I've seen many well-planned projects and I've seen many poorly planned projects in my career. There is absolutely no doubt that there is a strong correlation: well-planned projects are much more likely to deliver the expected results on time and within budget; poorly planned projects hardly ever do.

'Projects' are everywhere in business, if you look at it in the right way. Running a marketing campaign is a 'project'. Building a relationship with a customer is a 'project'. Selling a deal is a 'project'. Delivering promised results is a 'project'.

Other 'projects' are: recruiting a new sales team, running a training event, designing and implementing a new sales prospect management system.

Don't think that just because I describe something as a project, that you need to load up project management software on your computer, and set up a lot of formal management procedures. Those things will always help, especially for a large or complicated initiative. I'm simply suggesting that some of the techniques and methods that make large, formal projects successful also help in driving more everyday initiatives to success.

Foremost among these tools is the simple notion of 'thinking ahead' – also known as *planning.*

Talking with many people in all sorts of different businesses, I have never found anyone who is prepared to argue that effective planning is a waste of time. Not one. So how come so many people seem to forget all these tried and tested principles, and want to dive straight into doing things without thinking it through? Nowadays this is particularly noticeable in many sales organizations, with clueless managers pressing for action for its own sake, instead of encouraging their teams into purposeful effective action.

Typically, you can expect to hear klinks say things like:

- "Don't hold things up worrying about call objectives. Just go and get the appointments and figure out what to say when you get there."

- "We don't seem to be making much progress. I'm going to reorganize the team."

- "Don't worry about what *they* think they need. Just get out there and sell our gear to them."

- "OK team, I've already committed to revenue targets for you all. Let me know how you're going to achieve them in the next couple of days."

- "Account strategy? What account strategy?"

Klinks make rapid decisions without weighing options and without attempting to assess possible consequences. And when things go wrong, klinks never accept that they were part of the problem.

Part of the klink problem is that they misunderstand what "action orientation" is all about.

An action-oriented company gets things done. But getting things done demands a certain amount of research, analysis and planning before some more obvious things can be done properly. Research, analysis and planning are actions too!

An action-oriented business certainly tries to avoid endless debate and reworking of plans, which amounts to displacement activity and results in delays and disappointments. It is one thing to say, as an action-oriented manager will say: "Let's plan well, but quickly." It's quite another thing to say, as a klink will say: "We don't have time to plan, let's just do it."

An action-oriented approach gives due weight to thinking as a useful activity. A klink fails to respect the process of thinking things through, and therefore only attaches value to more obvious actions – producing reports, submitting proposals, making appointments – even when those actions have no payoff in terms of business won.

Purposeful and well-directed research, analysis and planning always pay dividends, but these activities will irritate klinks. A klink is like a small child playing chess. It's my turn - gotta move *now*! Successful chess players think ahead several moves, assess patterns and explore options *inside their heads* before making a move. Who would criticize a chess player for not being action oriented, or for wasting too much time thinking and planning?

> *Purposeful and well-directed research, analysis and planning always pay dividends...*

Many years ago, early in my sales career, I knew I had to establish credibility with my boss by clocking up some visits to a new account. I made the mistake of fixing an appointment before I'd done my basic research on the company. I was so pleased to get the appointment that I didn't take time to find out anything about their business - their financial performance, their mode of operation, operational challenges and so on.

The good news was that I achieved my objective of getting in to see an executive in that account, and my boss was pleased that I could put a check in the appropriate box. The bad news was that I had to overcome the embarrassment of that first visit and work really hard to restore credibility with the customer. In the end, I made it. But it took much more effort than it really should have done.

I quickly learned that as a sales person, I needed to question what I was told to do before going off and doing it. I learned to do what was effective in selling to my customers and not just what my boss expected. I never again made a visit without doing my homework. I learned that intelligent research could point me towards clients who were likely to do business with me, and help me avoid no-hopers. I learned that intelligent research and an account strategy could save months in a complex sale.

And now as a sales trainer, and sales team leader, I emphasize over and over again: thinking ahead is a valuable action. Do it.

While thinking and planning are essential, don't let yourself (or your team) spend so long on data gathering and analysis that you fail to act. The planning process must result in effective action. When you gather 'decision support data' you have to actually use it to support a purposeful decision.

Getting more information is always potentially useful, but there comes a time when even with imperfect information it's better to act than to freeze. Like when you walk over a cliff in the twilight, you grab the nearest shrub growing out of the rock face. You don't take too long weighing up all the options. Of course if you'd planned the hike properly, learned how to use a map and a compass, and asked for route-planning advice from locals, you'd be much less likely to walk over a cliff.

A solid leader/manager (a SMART manager) spends enough time gathering information and planning to set a direction that is reasonably likely to lead to success. If something goes wrong along the way, the good leader makes quick decisions, informed by extensive background knowledge.

This is the type of thoughtful and balanced behavior that sales managers should aim for, and should encourage in their teams.

Changing the Way Things are Done Around Here

Many managers wants to change things. Good leader/managers want to improve things. Good managers also understand that not all change is improvement.

Changing the wrong things or changing things unnecessarily can cause confusion and disruption.

Let's be clear: all organizations have to change and evolve. Everyone knows that change is a fact of business life. But not all changes have equal merit.

> *Good managers understand that not all change is improvement.*

Reorganizing a field sales team may, in some circumstances, rationalize responsibilities, improve accountability and eliminate decision bottlenecks. Great stuff – it's like giving your car a tune up to get better performance and better gas consumption. A similarly intentioned reorganization that's not properly thought through may introduce conflicts, and slow everything down while increasing overhead costs. You've added a fifth wheel to your car assuming that five wheels will make it go faster than four.

Real leader/managers can tell the difference between a change that will create a real improvement and a change that is, well, just a change.

When evaluating opportunities for change, there are, broadly two important things that require the application of intelligent thought and analysis:

- If there is a problem to be solved, what are the root causes of that problem?

- When considering a possible fix for a problem, what are the side effects of the change going to be?

Real leader/managers solve the cause of a problem; klinks tackle the symptoms. The ability to tell the difference between a cause and a symptom would not seem to require a lot of brainpower. Believe me, in many business settings, while the symptoms are obvious, the real causes can be well hidden.

A company selling complex business management software found that its sales were dropping gradually month by month. First reaction: it's the economy of course, each sales is harder work these days; let's reduce the price a little, increase incentives for the sales force, and recruit a couple more people to the sales force, so we can get back on target and keep the stockholders happy.

The downward trend continued. Deeper investigation showed that maybe the product didn't quite match the market leaders in some special areas of functionality: clearly some investment in product upgrade was called for.

A couple of releases later, and the downward trend was still continuing. Eventually, some one had the bright idea of talking to existing and prospective customers about what they liked about the product – and what was not so likeable. It turned out that post-sales implementation and product support was really poor, and everyone in the industry seemed to know that except for the people who were building and selling the product.

This was a fixable problem, but by acting without investigating the true cause of the sales downturn, someone in that company spent a lot of money unnecessarily and delayed effective action by more than a year.

Sometimes putting a patch on in one place causes an explosion somewhere else. Leader/managers are good at impact assessment, and weigh all the pros and cons of an action before going ahead. Leader/managers know ahead of time what problems are likely to arise and have plans to handle them. They avoid the impulse to rush ahead without the benefit of due thought process every time they have a bright idea.

I once knew a sales manager who was in charge of a big national team selling a wide range of complex products. This manager wanted to stir his team to action – he thought they needed to become more aggressive and hungry for business. The manager realized (correctly) that many of the products they were selling did pretty much the same thing. Sales people were expected to work with their customers to choose the most appropriate product from the range, and this was sometimes a time-consuming process.

The sales manager decided that he could get a great increase in sales performance by reducing the products available to each sales person, so they wouldn't have to learn so much complex technology. Furthermore, instead of assigning each customer to one sales person, he let every sales rep in a region sell to every customer. This seemed to be logical, to ensure that customers still had access to the full range of products. What was exciting about this gee-whiz idea was that now his sales people would be competing with each other for business, and competition is a good thing, right?

Customers certainly liked it. While they no longer had the

opportunity to review options reasonably objectively with one sales expert, instead they had been handed tremendous power to play one sales person against another to get bigger and bigger discounts.

This ploy indubitably achieved the objective of stimulating aggressiveness in the sales force. They worked longer hours, made more visits and traveled further. However this all achieved no overall increase in units sold. Revenues and margins were reduced significantly and each sale took much more effort than before. And half the sales force found new jobs. A success?

In any company there are many opportunities for unthinking change and all of these may have unexpected side effects that need to be taken into account. Changing performance measurements, compensation rules, reporting lines are all popular things to do to save spending time finding out what is really needed.

Changing computer systems is another favorite, but these days even a klink may shrink from that activity, because it involves so much time effort and money to implement a corporate level system. Even so, that has not prevented lots of companies spending hundreds of thousands of dollars on customer relationship management systems (CRM) that languish only partly used, because no one took into account the need for training, process re-engineering and analysis effort required to make the investment in the software application worthwhile.

The biggest opportunity for klink-driven disruption in sales management is in the organization of the sales department. It just seems like an irresistible opportunity to meddle. Apparently no special skills or knowledge are required to decide who should report to whom, or how field sales force territories should be charted.

In many companies, the answer to every problem is to reorganize. If we're not achieving the numbers, let's reorganize. If we introduce a new product, let's reorganize. If we recruit a new sales manager, let's reorganize. If we hit our numbers, let's find a way to reorganize to do even better! Look, the leaves on the trees are turning yellow: time for reorganization.

Companies agonize constantly whether to arrange their sales teams in product silos, by industry sector, by geographical region or by assigning reps to companies according to the golf handicaps of their CEOs. (Maybe there's not a lot wrong with that last option.)

Often companies create a complex mix of these factors in the quest for

I've seen companies change their client alignment strategy twice a year and three years later, they're right back where they started.

perfection. I've seen companies change their client alignment strategy twice a year and three years later, they're right back where they started. Their customers haven't changed, and very little of value has been achieved.

If you are determined to reorganize the sales organization in your company, I offer you these four principles to keep in mind:

- The perfect sales organization structure does not exist, for any company.

- What works for one company may not work for another.

- For successful sales, continuity of relationships between sales reps and customers is much more important than the way the sales department is organized.

- Where there is a real problem to be solved, reorganization is hardly ever the best way to solve it.

I worked in a company in the 1980s where the leadership team exercised a management philosophy we all called "birdcage management". Birdcage management applied at all levels of the organization, sales teams, sales department, executive team, company board.

Imagine everyone in your sales department sitting on perches in a big wire cage. The Head of Unnecessary Reorganization comes along and shakes the cage. All the parakeets fly around squawking for a while and land in different positions. After all the excitement, the Head of Unnecessary Reorganization gets a bonus. The cage of parakeets still contains the same parakeets. Once they've smoothed their ruffled feathers and learned to get comfortable on their new perches, business goes on pretty much as before.

The Sales Process

CLosing a deal in not just an event, it's the result of a process. Let's look at that process at a high level, and consider the sales manager's role in ensuring that the company-prescribed processes help and support the sales team in their mission to win business, not get in the way. I like to break down the process into these four big steps:

- **Unknown to Prospect:** There are thousands of business opportunities out there, most of them unknown to the sales person. The first step in making a sale is identifying just a few of those unknown opportunities to work on. Some of those 'suspects' are more likely opportunities than others, and become 'prospects'.

- **Prospect to Qualified Prospect:** Not every prospect is worth the investment of the time and effort needed to close a deal, and so every sales process includes a qualification step. To qualify a prospect we need to start to build a relationship, uncover their real needs and assess their real readiness and ability to buy. Qualification is an essential discipline, and is often overlooked, resulting in wasted effort. At the same time the customer is evaluating your company as a potential supplier!

- **Qualified Prospect to Customer:** If the prospect has been properly qualified, and the sales person has built a sound relationship, then there should be a reasonable rate of success in closing deals. Sales people need to learn how to make contacts within the client company, identify decision makers, handle competitive threats, and convincingly demonstrate the value the solution, leading to a customer order.

- **Customer to Repeat Customer:** The sales person's work doesn't stop when an order is signed! It's every sales person's ambition to follow the first deal with successive orders from the same customer. Repeat business is tremendously important to the company. Most sales people find that the time and effort involved in securing a repeat deal, based on a successful record of delivery and an increasingly close relationship, is a fraction of the effort needed to win business with a completely new customer. However, repeat business doesn't come automatically, and sales people must learn the skill of ongoing customer management to keep customers happy and loyal.

This step-by-step process takes the relationship between your company and the customer from 'Who are they?' to 'One among many' when you get the first order. Then it's a matter of consolidating and building that relationship through repeat business to 'First Choice' and ultimately to 'Only Choice'.[52] Then you have to keep it there!

Sales team leader/managers have two important management responsibilities related to managing the sales process:

- Designing and fine-tuning the process.

- Making sure people use the process effectively.

Most companies implement something close to the process described above. In fact I can't think of any company I have worked with that didn't provide some sort of structured management process to help people move through the steps from unknown to repeat customer. However the way different companies do this varies widely. There is no single standard for selling in corporate America, and every company tunes one of the standard processes to meet their own requirements and priorities.

All companies set some rules and guidelines for sales teams to follow. Some companies permit a sales team manager some freedom to tune the process and set rules for the team. Others are very non-permissive, usually because their sales operations have been damaged by klink-style managers in the past.

To the extent that the company allows sales team leaders to set rules, you should take that responsibility seriously. Think through all the implications of your decisions, make sure you understand the impact by discussing possibilities with everyone affected, in your team and elsewhere in the company. Weigh the options, then act intelligently.

As a competent sales manager, you should work within the constraints set by the company. But you also have a responsibility to question rules and restrictions that don't make sense.

As a sales team leader, you should not take any selling prescription at face value. You should base the way you lead your team's sales efforts on the wisdom and experience of others, but apply your own intelligence and perceptions to create your own approach, which takes into account the type of products or solutions you are selling, and the type of customers you are trying to sell to – and, to some extent, the type of people you have in your team.

---

[52] See the section on Relationship building in Chapter 4.

And sometimes you just have to bend the rules a little, especially where your company sales department is led by a klink. For example, I observed one sales team struggling to comply with a rule that said they should be closing deals after three visits to the customer. Unfortunately the complex and expensive services they were selling typically took around six months to close, and customers expected lots of interaction during that period. If people in the sales team had done exactly what the sales divisional manager mandated, they would have done no business at all. Fortunately the team was led by a sales manager who provided some shelter from senior management ineptitude, as described elsewhere in this book.[53]

In another company, the sales team manager expected each sales person to identify a unique customer decision-maker early in the engagement and focus all energy on that person. No visits to anyone else. You can sell some products to one person, but the decision to buy a complex solution is almost always influenced by several different executives. This is hardly surprising because complex solutions can often impact a company in multiple ways, across multiple departments. That sales team manager was a klink, and consequently his team, no matter how talented, could not be successful if they followed the rules.

Some companies create rules and guidelines that are helpful to the sales team. That's what sales management should aim for – to create an environment that generates success.

But some sales managers create rules that don't help inexperienced sales people, at the same time getting in the way of the experienced folk. If you are responsible for setting rules, avoid this mistake. And if you have rules imposed on you that don't make sense, argue.

Sales people need to know a lot, and need well-developed skills, to be successful. One of the basic skill sets needed is knowing how to work the sales process, starting with identifying likely prospects and culminating with closing deals with customers.

One of the first things that should happen when a sales person joins a new company is immersion training in the company's sales process. In general this is a good thing, so sales people shouldn't try to skip this on the grounds that they have been selling for years already. Every company has its own process variations and system customizations and it is in your own interest to ensure that your team members learn these things as early as possible in their career with the company.

---

[53] See the section: The Umbrella and The Oilcan in Chapter 6.

Your team needs to learn how to use the customer relationship management system for prospect tracking and customer information. You need to learn the company standards for proposals and contracts and how to document your orders.

When your sales people have learned the mechanics of working the company's sales process, you've taken a big step, but you're not done yet. Sales people need to learn what is expected of them as individuals, and what the rules of the game are in the company.

What does the company expect a sales person to deliver in the areas of prospecting, selling and post-sales support? And what parameters has the company management set, in their collective wisdom, to ensure that sales people deliver results. What are the rules for regular reporting? Do they demand that sales people clock up a certain number of visits every day? What counts as a visit? Are there mandatory qualification criteria? How fast do they expect a sales person to close a deal?

It is an essential part of the sales manager to ensure that every team member learns these things, because being ignorant of what is expected is never a good thing. If you and your team members choose to not comply with a company rule or guideline, you should do so consciously for good reason, not because you forgot to read the rulebook.

> *If you and your team members choose to not comply with a company rule you should do so consciously for a good reason, not because you forgot to read the rulebook.*

I accept that process isn't everything.
It is not possible for someone to win business *just* by working through a process, with no regard for building relationships, knowing the business and being trustworthy.

Still, process is important[54]. Process provides a context and a logical framework for applying skills and building relationships. Process is not a replacement for building relationships. Rather, relationship-building should be built into the process.

---

[54] So important that I need more space to do it justice: see *Don't Just Stand There, Sell Something - Volume 2*.

Avoiding The "Instant Success" trap

Today the sales profession keeps recruiting firms busy all the time, as people move ever more rapidly from company to company, or leave the profession, or die young. Moving sales people around from company to company is a great annuity for the recruiters.

It's now quite acceptable, apparently, for a sales person to have a resume that lists four jobs in four years. A few years ago that would have meant the person had some sort of problem.

Veterans remember when it was the norm to spend eight to ten years with one company in a sales position. Today, based on what I observe in the market, hardly anyone stays in one sales job for more than two years. I know of one extreme case in which a company went through 24 sales representatives on one four-person sales team in just five years. Some only lasted a few months.

More typically, in another company between 1997 and 2003 a sales representative lasted just nine months on average. In that company, selling high tech projects, it took more than nine months for a typical sales rep to understand the solution offerings, how the company ran, who could provide support and how to work around company politics and management idiosyncrasies. For a typical project the sales lead-time was way more than nine months, yet sales reps who did not deliver quick results had to leave.

How in the world did that company expect to establish a solid customer base, build relationships and establish credibility? What sort of relationship can you create with a customer if you change their representative every nine months? How did they think they could penetrate and grow new accounts? Changing out a sales force every year simply guarantees lack of new sales, especially sales from new accounts. The company is doomed to rely on renewal sales from existing customers and on bluebirds[55].

Every company needs some metrics to support management decisions: if you don't measure things, you're missing out on a valuable source of information. But measurements must be used with some degree of caution and judgment, and even intelligence.

Turnover in sales is the highest I've seen it in the last twenty years. I've observed many talented sales people being "moved on" before

---

[55] For those new to the sales profession, you need to know that a 'bluebird' is a chunk of business that flies in 'out of the blue'. It was not in your forecast. Bluebirds are serendipitous and sometimes undeserved. It's a freebie. Bluebirds are sometimes great news, but they sometimes fly in with a heap of problems: more about this later.

they have had a chance to achieve results, even though the underlying signs were good. And this is simply because their managers are klinks who don't really know how to evaluate the performance of a sales person. These managers don't participate, they don't coach or mentor, they fail to appreciate what is really going on, all because they lack the needed knowledge and expertise.

On the other hand, an experienced and talented sales leader-manager knows full well that the numbers are not likely to come right away. That doesn't mean that no decisions are made for nine months. On the contrary, the expert leader-manager can tell far earlier than any klink can whether a new recruit is going to make the grade, or if additional support and coaching is needed, or whether the sales person should be let go.

A sales leader-manager with sound judgment and a good understanding of the sales process can identify deadbeats early and remove them from the team. People with potential are recognized, encouraged and allowed to develop long enough to actually achieve some results.

Imagine this. You decide you want to grow some apple trees. You plant a few saplings in the garden, feed them a little water and encourage them to grow with motivational speeches. After a few months you realize that you haven't seen any apples yet. Outrage. Clearly, by any objective measure of performance these so-called apple trees just don't have what it takes in the apple-producing department. You phone around some more apple nurseries – send me some new apple saplings, I need some new talent around here. The old timers in the nursery have seen it all before – they're happy to sell you some new trees and you start all over again. And again.

Down the road there's another apple farm. They seem to be able to ship plenty apples to market, even though they don't seem to plant new trees all the time. Here's the typical klink response: I'm going to change out my saplings *even more often* so I can compete. That'll show them.

Knowing when to wait and when to act needs an understanding of the real underlying dynamics of a situation. This needs intelligent observation and analysis, and a weighing of possible options.

SMART managers know the difference between patience and complacency.

SMART leader/managers know the difference between patience and complacency. A good manager knows that sometimes the right action is to wait a little longer for things to mature. This is not the same as doing nothing because you don't know what to do or (worse) because you don't know there is a problem.

Strategies for Selling

Many people read lots of books about sales and selling strategies. Good idea. But as a result of this people get confused about what is a strategy, what is a tactic and by the way why is there all this talk about war in books about selling?

It is the job of good sales managers to help their team understand strategies and tactics, and also to apply strategic and tactical thinking effectively, and in the right places.

The terms *strategy* and *tactics* have been around for centuries, and yes, they are rooted in the ancient art of making war, which has been developed over many generations. The fear of death focuses the mind, and soldiers have tried very hard to work out the best ways of serving the needs of monarchs and politicians without causing the demise of too many people on their own side. Similarly, sales people need to work out the best ways of selling goods and services on behalf of their corporate masters.

In military terms strategy is about the big picture: defining the objectives, and planning the general approach to the war, to campaigns within a war, and to battles within a campaign. Strategies have two connected parts: the strategic objective (**what** must be achieved) and the strategic plan (what we must do to achieve it – the **how**.)

Tactical decisions relate to individual smaller-scale, shorter-term decisions: the way that individual actions and skirmishes are conducted.

Strategic weapons are big and powerful and limited use of them can affect the outcome of the battle or even the whole war. Tactical weapons are used to decide the outcome of individual actions.

We also need to remember that wars take place in a context – the context of political objectives. These are the objectives of one set of people to place themselves in a position of power relative to others – or to defend themselves against such positioning.

The military analogy is not perfect, but it can be useful especially if it throws light in areas that would otherwise be overlooked. To make the military analogy useful we need to stretch it just a little, along the following lines...

Corporate objectives correspond to political objectives. To move towards achieving corporate objectives, companies identify and define a *target market*. This is somewhat like declaring war in order to achieve political objectives.

Selecting a prospect is comparable to defining a campaign within a war. Developing the relationship with a prospect requires an *account strategy*; just as conducting a military campaign requires a campaign strategy.

Qualifying an opportunity corresponds to choosing a battle to fight. Winning a deal needs a *deal strategy*, just like winning a battle needs a battle strategy.

In the heat of a battle, or in the heat of trying to sell a deal, people constantly ask themselves: "What should I do next?" Tactical decisions are smaller-scale decisions within a battle or within the deal process. You need *selling tactics* to win an individual deal.

Tactical decisions seem to have less lasting impact, but cumulatively tactical successes lead to winning the battle. Winning battles leads to winning the war and the achievement of the political objectives that started the war in the first place. Similarly, the corporate objective of market dominance is achieved deal by individual deal, based on a succession of tactical decisions and actions. Win enough individual deals and you help your company achieve its business objectives.

Discussions of strategy often focus strongly on beating the competition. This is understandable, but misses something. Simply beating the competition is something you necessarily do when you win deals, but should not be your exclusive focus.

I remember one time viewing from the sidelines as two big companies competed for a project to upgrade a company's billing and customer administration systems. Projects like that always make the client feel uncomfortable: typically they end up costing more, taking longer and causing more disruption than anyone plans for. Migrating from the old systems environment to the new one is usually difficult and tedious.

The two chief contenders did such a great job in sowing seeds of fear, doubt and uncertainty in the mind of the customer, that the customer's executives decided that the risk, pain and cost of living with their old antiquated management system was less than the pain risk and cost of signing up for a new installation.

In this case, both competitors lost, and neither of them won. However they each achieved their main short-term objective, which was to ensure that the customer didn't do business with a competitor. But can that sort of containment really be counted as success?

Certainly, to win a customer order, you have to defeat the competition – that's logical. But to win a customer order you must persuade a customer that you can do the job, not simply that the competitor is too inept, overstretched, expensive, unreliable or corrupt to do it.

Why all this emphasis on beating the competition? Maybe because so much of the discussion about strategy and tactics is based on military and sporting analogies. In wars and competitive games there are usually two sides. One side wins, the other loses, at least that's the general idea. War and sports are sometimes more complicated than that. Selling things is *always* more complicated than that.

In sales, there are multiple 'sides' – you, plus a number of competitors. And then there's the customer.

The customer is not really on one side or another. The customer makes the decisions about who wins and who loses. No matter which side makes more mistakes, spends more money, does the most 'convincing' pitch, the customer gets to decide. The customer gets to decide whether a discussion of an issue over a latte in a corner coffee shop is worth more or worth less than a dinner in the fanciest restaurant in town. The customer gets to decide whether the 50-slide presentation with animation and sound effects is better or worse than the six flipcharts presented in twenty minutes by the other guys.

The customer doesn't weigh the proposal documents from company A and company B and say: "Good job, Company A, at three pounds, you clearly beat those slackers at company B who only managed to generate a few ounces of paperwork". No, the customer gets to read the documents, and make a decision based on whatever eccentric and irrational factors they want to include.

It's different on a battlefield, isn't it? Those fighting armies think they know the rules, and ultimately one army will 'win' and the other will accept defeat. But in sales there's someone looking down at the field of war – the customer – and making decisions maybe to a different set of rules.

On reflection, maybe that happens in war too.

So a winning selling strategy must aim to convince the customer that your company is the right company to do business with, not merely frighten the customer away from your competitors.

... a winning strategy must aim to convince the customer that your company is the right company to do business with, not merely frighten the customer away from your competitors.

The distinction between strategy and tactics is very useful, and military people usually maintain that traditional distinction. But outside the military, people more and more use the word 'strategy' to refer to things that are tactical rather than strategic. If the trend continues people will soon talk about their strategy for eating breakfast. This is unfortunate because if we adhere to these traditional meanings of the two words 'strategy' and 'tactics', this helps us to place some focus on certain aspects of the selling game that are often overlooked or undervalued.

When we think about planning for winning customer deals at those three levels – **corporate objectives, account strategy, deal strategy** – it helps us understand that success requires sound decisions, intelligent thought, purposeful planning and effective actions at *all three* levels. All of these things together are sometimes described as 'sales strategy' but looking at them individually really helps to highlight what is important.

Nothing can guarantee the success of a military operation but intelligent planning at all levels reduces risk and increases the probability of success. But all these levels of strategic thinking actually achieve nothing more than *setting a framework for action*. The plans only amount to something if someone takes action, and the real action is carried out in the field.

At the **corporate** level, a company needs to know why it's in business. On the surface all companies exist to sell products and services for profits, which can be used to pay employees and reward shareholders. But underneath the surface of each business there are additional motivations and imperatives, and some of these aren't even understood by the executives at the top of the company. Motivations of power, prestige, doing good in the world and more are all mixed in.

Companies are usually started by people who are good at something, and enthusiastic to do it, and want to make money out of it. Being good at something is not a trivial endeavor, as anyone knows who has tried to learn to juggle, ski, or play the xylophone. This base of skill and zeal establishes the core expertise of a company – making machinery, repairing motor vehicles, pulling teeth, or building bridges, or any of thousands of other business possibilities.

Note that being good at sales is rarely a good reason for setting up a company: you also need something worthwhile to sell!

The core expertise of the company needs to be matched to a set of customers who want to pay the company for the benefits of that expertise. And this is where the sales team comes in, because customers are rarely sitting around waiting to hand over money to the first company that offers them a gizmo. There are, thank goodness, the complicating factors of discernment, value-judgment, confusion and competitors to be taken into account. Sales people are there to help the company get goods and services to customers. All around the world, sales people form a communication bridge between the makers and the buyers and lubricate the path of commerce.

To make sure these sales people do the right thing for the company, the leaders of the company need to make some very clear decisions about the direction of the company and state them clearly.

- This is what we are good at. We are here to do those things we are good at for money to make profits. (There are many other things we might be good at or can imagine we are good at but we choose not to do those things so we can focus on doing what we know we can do.)[56]

- This is who we aim to sell our goods and services to. (There are many other people who might buy these things or whom we can imagine might buy these things, but we choose not to try to sell to them so we can focus on selling to those people we know are interested.)

- This is what we aim to achieve as a company in the long term, and in the near future, expressed in concrete, objective terms.

- When we make, sell and deliver our goods and services, these are the standards of business behavior we expect from all our people. (Values vary widely, but these are the values we have chosen and not some other set of values.)[57]

Putting together well thought-out statements provides the core of a corporate strategy: corporate vision, mission, values, policies and the associated business imperatives for products and customers. Corporate strategy consultants can earn good money getting executives to sit still long enough to write down statements like the above. That's the easy bit. It is very difficult to get a company to live up to those statements, to focus on its core expertise, on its target market and on its business values. But a company must focus, because unless everyone in the company is clear about these things, and acts accordingly, everything becomes muddled and ineffective. Getting it right is called effective leadership.

Emerging from all the heavy thinking that happens every day at the corporate level, the sales teams must be provided with *market objectives* (defined in the corporate market strategy) to provide a sense of direction, and to provide the guidelines for selecting those

---

[56] Incidentally, companies also need to recognize what they are *not* good at. Many companies dilute their strengths by straying from their core competencies. This could be something to do with greed or ego or another deadly sin.

[57] You can tell when a company is clear about these things. You ask anyone in the company why they're in business and how they go about it, and they can tell you, immediately. I've come across this clarity and purposefulness in companies like Avon (cosmetics), Johnson & Johnson, IBM and Dell.

customers who you should aim to sell to, and what you should sell to them.

Companies *must* set well-defined strategic objectives for the company and for the people in it, including the sales people. Without the clarity of purpose provided by those objectives, the obviously urgent matters will always take precedence over the less obvious but more important issues.

With no sense of corporate direction coming from the top, most people – including many in sales – will fight fires and waste time in unproductive bureaucracy. However, if given a clear direction and authority, people will *make* time for the important tasks that need to be tackled to deliver the company's objectives. Ask someone "What's your job?" and in many companies the answer will be a list of things they *do* every day. In a well-led company people will tell you what they are expected to *achieve*.

> *...if given a clear direction... people will make time for the important tasks that need to be tackled...*

Let's assume that, at corporate level, the leaders have laid down some clear statements about what is to be sold to what sort of customers, and they have also set some standards for behavior. Great.

With clarity in these areas, sales managers have the basic information needed to think about how to win business. Once those corporate politicians have laid out what they want to achieve, the responsibility passes down to the officers in the sales department – sales department managers and sales team leaders.

The first step is working out exactly who to sell to! Which **accounts** will you choose to give most of your attention to? Is it going to be more profitable to deal with a few large businesses or a lot of small ones? Should we think about the location of prospects, so we can control our traveling costs? Should we take into account whether prospects can actually afford to pay for our products and services?

Almost always, top of the list are those accounts you are already doing business with. These are already good prospects for further business. (Except in rare cases where you have been thrown out already.)

The more difficult question to answer is where your growth is going to come from. Which **new accounts** will you choose to give most of your attention to?

From the corporate level mission statement and marketing approach, you should already have a broad idea, expressed in the form of target markets, industry sector, company size, geographical location, and so on. Few companies can afford to be able to actively sell to every potential customer in the space, so it is necessary to sift and prioritize. Having a target market provides you with a mixed bag of potential customers who may or may not be ideal candidates for your sales efforts. At this stage, these companies are *suspects*, not *prospects*.

To move these suspects into the prospect category, you need to:

- establish *account selection criteria* (a management responsibility;
- gather *account intelligence* (a task for the sales reps)
- apply the selection rules to choose the best candidate accounts (a joint effort between sales team leader and sales reps).

Who sets the account selection criteria? The companies who do this best rely on a combination of analysis conducted by marketing people, and the experience of sales managers who know the business. Marketing analysis is a useful tool that provides an understanding of the characteristics of companies who have bought products and services in the past. If we can identify certain 'types' who like to buy our stuff, maybe other companies with the same characteristics will be good candidates too. Marketing departments should also have access to data on market trends and future possibilities in product evolution and changing customer needs.

Marketing departments should always start this process, but marketing should not finalize these criteria without input from sales. Sales people can add some additional color to the rules: sales people know not just who has bought, but how hard it was to close the deal and what factors were most significant in closing it. Sales people also know how easy or hard it is to maintain certain types of customer and win repeat business.

Working with your marketing experts you should be able to use market statistics and your experience to come up with a picture of 'ideal target' companies within your target industry sector. Ideal target companies are those companies that are most likely to have a need for your products and services and appreciate its value to them. An 'ideal target' description might look something like this:

"Our target is manufacturers of pharmaceuticals. Our ideal customers are those manufacturers with a wide range of traditional, generic products who are anxious to reduce unit costs to a minimum. Companies with sales over $500 million are more likely to buy our products than smaller companies. We want to focus on the Americas, because selling in other parts of the world is still not cost-effective for us. Companies that are growing by at least 5% per annum are likely to have the greatest need for our product, and those that are profitable or have large reserves of cash are most likely to be able to buy it! Avoid companies that have mostly PillcomCorp equipment installed because they are giving free upgrades for the next year and we can't match that."

This type of statement includes all the essential characteristics: type of company; business size; geographical location; financial situation; competitive barrier to entry.

The idea is to avoid wasted effort by narrowing down the number of companies you need to talk to, by eliminating low-priority candidates from the search early on. This improves your team's success rate and increases productivity.

If you still find that you have too many candidates to chase down, even after you have narrowed it down to ideal customers, then you need to narrow your definition even further, or perhaps develop a method of scoring and weighting each of these categories. By assigning scores, you have a tool that allows you to shelve or reject suspects with the lowest scores. Sometimes you have to say no so that when you say yes you can deliver.

Time spent working out these criteria, will save time, energy and heart-searching when it comes to making selection decisions. Devising these criteria, and the weighted scoring formula, is all part of planning. You can call it strategic planning if you like.

Before you can apply the selection rules to the list of suspects, you need to understand enough about the suspects to make an informed and intelligent decision. This brings us to the next step in gathering *account intelligence*.

What do we need to know about each suspect? Things like:

- What do they sell? Who do they sell it to? What is their direction of evolution? Do they have new products planned?

- Who are their competitors? Are the leading or following?

- Are they relatively successful, limping along, or doomed?

- Are they growing or shrinking in employee numbers? What are their staffing and productivity goals?

- What is their geographical coverage? How is that going to change?

- What are their business challenges and opportunities? Is their industry going to experience and disruptive changes in technology or business models?

- Who are their preferred suppliers today? (In other words, who are *our* competitors in this account? What does the suspect like about these suppliers? Are there any signs of dissatisfaction?

- Who makes purchasing decisions? Who influences purchasing decisions? Do we already have relationships with any of these decision-makers or influencers?

- What sort of people are they? What do *they* see as their most vital needs? What are their preferences and dislikes?

- How much money do they have available to spend? How much money have they budgeted for the solutions *we* offer?

Where do you and your team go to get all this information? You can start with the wealth of public domain information that is around these days:

- The company's web site;
- Brochures, flyers and press releases;
- Company annual reports and legal/government filings;
- Magazine and newspaper archives;
- On-line information services such as Factiva, LexusNexus, or Dialog[58];
- Your own marketing intelligence team;
- The target company's PR department.

Then you can move on to mine the seam of less formal information, which may have to be crosschecked and used with caution, but can sometimes be invaluable:

- Your network of industry contacts;
- Anyone you know in the target company (but don't push them to divulge company confidential information);
- Gossip on the Internet (assess with skepticism).

The objective at this stage is to gather just enough information so you and your team can confidently use the standard selection rules to 'score' their suspects and decide whether they should be promoted to prospect status, parked, or ignored. You may have to revise your decision later as you get to know even more about the company, but at least you've made rational start to selecting new accounts for close-in attention.

---

[58] www.factiva.com; www.lexusnexus.com; www.dialog.com.

Having chosen the accounts, you next have to work out the best way to get into the new account, build relationships and identify opportunities. For existing accounts you need to work out the best way of maintaining and growing business with the customer.

This needs a *sales account strategy*, which consists of *account objectives* plus an *account plan* to achieve the objective.

An account strategy *positions* the sales force to win customer deals..

All strategies need to start with an objective, which is *what* we are trying to achieve. The strategic plan is *how* that objective will be met.

Sales managers need to construct an objective for each existing account and each potential new account in the form of account targets. The target should be based on a practical assessment of what is possible and realistic. A revenue target is usual, but it sometimes does no harm to link that revenue target to specific products or services that market research indicates are more likely to be attractive to that specific account. That, at least, is one way of making sure that market analysis information is visible to the account sales rep!

Sometimes the objective is not simply to 'win business'. If the account is attractive because it is a stepping stone to other accounts, then that could increase the long term value of winning even a small deal, providing it is for the right type of services or products and it will be visible in the industry. This can be the case when a specific company is seen in an industry sector as a 'thought leader' (or 'trend-setter', as they used to be called).

It is important to decide the strategic value of each account up front and take into account in setting the objectives and devising the plan. This is helpful when it comes to offering special terms or discounts for 'strategic reasons'. In one company, where this process was not carefully managed, reps regularly sought 'strategic discounts' right at the end of a sales effort. Under the pressure of an imminent win/lose, it is never easy to think clearly about such things, which is why it is better to settle the 'strategic' perspective up front and define any special strategic aims explicitly as part of the account objectives.

Once the objectives are defined, you need a plan. The plan lists what you and your team are going to do to penetrate the account, if it's a new one; or to maintain and build the level of business, if it's an existing account.

Account planning – what a bore! Many sales managers find developing an account plan a chore and a waste of time: "Don't just stand there, sell something."

Please don't be one of those. Don't be a klink.

Account planning need not be painful, providing it is done with just one clear aim in mind: what do we need to do to build the sort of relationship with the customer that will give us a chance to win deals.

The account plan should include all of these elements:

- Individual monthly/quarterly sales targets based on the account objectives.

- A limit on expenditure for the business development effort on the account: it isn't worth spending a million dollars to earn a few hundred.

- Preliminary identification of products and services that might be attractive to this customer, and the types of value proposition that might be successful.

- If this is an existing account, or a new account in which intelligence gathering is already advanced, the plan should identify key decision makers, and specific customer needs and priorities.

- Steps we will take to gather even more detailed intelligence about the prospect.

- Steps we will take – at corporate level and sales team level - to make contact and to build relationships.

- Discount policy for this account, latitude to negotiate special deals.

The account plan provides account reps with a clear sense of direction and a practical to-do list for every account. The plan cannot define the detail of what has to be done, day-to-day, and you shouldn't try to make it do this. But the plan represents some conscious thinking that will precede the action needed to develop that account. And if that thinking can be something of a team effort, all the better. Two heads are often better than one.

Why all this thinking? Why not just get out and *sell*?

The answer is simple. The approach you take will depend on being informed about the customer and the customer's relationship with existing suppliers. For example, if the customer already has an 'Only choice' relationship with a supplier, you cannot expect to just get added to a vendor list by just asking. However that might be possible with a company that has no special relationship with any one supplier, and has several suppliers, each of which is just 'One among many'. Your approach (that is your strategy) will be different in these two cases: the level at which you need to interact and persuade, the number of customer decision-makers involved in the deal, the balance between price and performance and so on.

This up-front research and planning has a side-benefit: by the time first contact is made, your sales people can talk to the customer with confidence and credibility. They will talk to the right people. They will ask the right questions, and they will be able to listen carefully to the answers, because they will understand what the customer is talking about. And their feet will stay on the floor, not wander into their mouths.

Where has all this thinking brought us? We have a corporate strategy that defines where the business is going and how it's going to get there. The corporate strategy gives us target markets that provide the basis for identifying customers. Working with your marketing friends, you can work up some account selection criteria that will help you and your team decide which new customers to aim for, in addition to building up the business with existing customers. We have defined account objectives and account plans for every one of these potential customers, and for existing customers. Your sales representatives are already out there gathering more information and building relationships.

And now you have an actual selling opportunity! The launching platform for selling the deal is already there: it's a relationship generated by the account strategy.

Now we can get out and sell? Let's just do one more piece of thinking before we do that.

You need a *deal strategy* to define how you're going to approach an individual selling opportunity. The deal strategy defines the approach you are going to use to achieve the objective of winning the deal. Believe me, it pays to think a little more about exactly who you need to sell to, and what sort of value proposition will convince them. We also need to plan what to do if something goes wrong, and plan what to do when we win!

Over the years people have devised some standardized approaches to developing deal strategies. One of the most widely used is the Holden approach[59] which describes four distinct strategies: direct; indirect; divide and conquer; and containment.

I like to link these different strategies to the four levels of relationship we discussed in the chapter on Relationships.[60]

- Who are they?
- One among many.
- The first choice.

[59] *Power Base Selling*, Jim Holden (Wiley 1990)
[60] Chapter 4

- The only choice.

Your best strategy for winning a deal will depend very much on which of these relationship levels you are sitting at. You will not move from one relationship level to another without winning a deal. It goes like this: build relationship; win deal; use deal to consolidate and build more relationships; win more business; and so on.

As you win deals and build the relationship, your deal strategy will change.

The worst position to be in is the 'Who are they?' status. This would not be so bad if all your competitors were in the same position, but this is hardly ever the case. Usually one competitor is in a 'first choice' or 'only choice' situation.

Sometimes companies in this situation remind me of Donkey in the movie Shrek[61]. Jumping up and down at the back of the crowd shouting "Pick me, pick me!" over and over. This only worked for Donkey because there were no other volunteers. This will only work for you if there are no competitors.

For a company who is essentially unknown to a customer, there are two imperatives: become known, and establish trust. You need to make sure that all the decision makers are well-informed about your offerings, and know your record of success. Having good reference sites helps to establish confidence. Make sure your customer contacts pay attention by taking them there – don't rely on them to make the call. Organizing trips to good reference sites is much more valuable than organizing days out at a golf match or ball game when your relationship with the customer is in this early stage.

Make sure your value proposition clearly addresses all the benefits and features that your competitors will emphasize. You need to demonstrate superiority across the board. The incumbent has all the advantages: easy access to the customer, a track record, and – it's easier for the customer to stay put than to move into the unknown territory of a new relationship. The devil you know is better than the devil you don't know.

Your positioning relative to competitors may have to be one of 'containment' (in Holden terms). This means you must aim to win small victories from the incumbent, limiting the amount of new business they capture. Essentially containment is as much about restricting the growth of the incumbent in an account, as about winning substantial new business.

---

[61] *Shrek* (Dreamworks, 2001). Donkey was played by Eddie Murphy.

186

A more positive approach is to try to 'divide and conquer'. Essentially this means putting forward the argument that it is unwise to put all their eggs in one basket by relying on a single supplier. Having more than one vendor will keep the incumbent honest and competitive in their pricing. At least, you can point out, giving us a small project to prove what we can do will give you another option for the future if you should need it... Many successful client-supplier relationships have started off with a divide and conquer strategy.

Attempting to replace an incumbent completely is best done incrementally, not all at once. Customers need a good reason to change suppliers, but they don't need an especially good reason to stay with an incumbent. Allowing them to try you out on a small task reduces their risk and lays the foundation for you to take on more work later.

You need to give them good reasons to change by creating uncertainty about the value of the incumbent's offering. I believe that concentrating purely on criticizing the opposition does not impress most customers. It is much more effective to stress the positive aspects of your own offering, and then mention the ways in which your competitor's offerings fall short. Allow the customer to work some things out for themselves; this is the most convincing way to sow seeds of doubt.

When you are in this position you will be under a lot of pressure to provide give-aways and heavy discounts. You might have to give something away to win a first project, but be careful how you do it.[62] You're setting a precedent for the next job, and the one after, and it's usually very difficult to increase rates once the customer knows what you can afford. Make sure you label these discounts and freebies clearly as 'introductory offers'.

First projects with a new customer set the scene for future growth, so you should make sure that the first opportunity you go for is one that you can deliver on, without doubt. A first project that is too large, or in an area in which your company does not have deep expertise is a big risk. I'm not saying that you should never go for a big opportunity with a new customer, just be aware that it's going to be a tougher sell, and that you cannot afford to drip the ball in delivery. Fail in your first project and you will probably never get another chance, and rightly so. (Fall short in a similar project a couple of years into a relationship when you've already delivered many examples of good work, and the customer probably won't hold it against you nearly so badly.) The sales representative should always take an active interest in delivery, but this applies even more so in

---

[62] See the section on Negotiation in Chapter 3.

early projects with a new customer. Be there for the customer. Make it work.

If you are one step further up the relationship ladder – 'one among many' – you are only slightly better off. In this situation you will at least have done some business with them already. This means you don't need to restrict your reference sites to those with other customers. You can point to the resounding success of one or two of the customer's own projects.

(What if those projects weren't a 'resounding success'? If the customer was anything less than completely happy with your first projects, then you should be ashamed of yourself. See my comments above.)

At the 'one among many' level, you should have already built up a good working relationship with decision makers, and you can afford to go for bigger and more ambitious opportunities, providing you are pretty sure you can deliver and are prepared to move mountains if things go wrong. In this phase you are aiming to build more confidence and credibility.

Still, as far as the incumbent competitors are concerned the strategy remains essentially one of containment plus divide and conquer.

But you should also look out for opportunities to change the ground rules in your favor. You need to be close enough to the customer to identify opportunities to change the orientation of the project or the way in which a decision will be made. Use your growing relationship with the customer to work out ways to be different that moves the incumbent out of their usual area of expertise. Be creative.

If the customer asks for a solution based on a particular software package, then do some research and see if there is another approach that can meet the customer's requirements better and more economically, using a core application that the incumbent doesn't sell.

If the customer specifies a particular software architecture for a solution, critically assess the architecture and suggest ways to improve it.

If the customer insists a particular hardware platform to maintain compatibility with the legacy environment, develop a low-risk plan that can allow them to gradually migrate to a more modern, more cost-effective platform.

In all such cases, chances are the specific solution requested has been suggested by the incumbent. Pointing out exactly how the design is sub-optimal sends a useful message. Often it is the incumbent, rather than the customer, who is most comfortable working inside a limited range of technology products. You can upset this feeling of comfort by revealing possibilities to the customer that are better value – and that you know you can deliver better than the incumbent can.

Many companies stay at the 'one among many' level for years. Customers like to have a few fallback companies they can keep on hand, while maintaining loyal to their primary supplier, the incumbent.

Being able to displace an incumbent so you can move into the 'First choice' category needs a combination of persistence, skill, and maybe some luck. This is the most difficult step to take in building a relationship with a customer. Often the breakthrough comes because the incumbent makes a mistake – and someone is there, in position, and ready to move in. Who is likely to get the job when a rescue is needed? The company that is jumping up and down shouting "Pick me?" Or the company that has spent time getting to know the decision makers, learning about the business and being there for the customer?

Sometimes a company will award a contract to the incumbent, it turns out that the products and services delivered just do not meet the expectations that were presented to the customer. If you have made a good effort to convince the customer of the value of your offering earlier, then this could be your opportunity to step in and rescue the situation. Be there and be ready.

Being 'first choice' is great. Even though other companies are waiting in the wings and may pick up some of the business, you will always have an advantage. Your strategy should be to take advantage of your privileged position. With projects under way you have every reason to stay close to the customer. You should be able to hear earlier than others of new opportunities, and you may also be able to influence the statement of requirements. If an RFP is issued, you should endeavor to be in the position of 'trusted advisor' so that you can help to write the RFP document.

Being first choice still leaves opportunities for others. So use your first choice position to adopt a purposeful and direct approach to winning business. Make sure you reply faster than anyone else to requests for information and requests for proposals. You know how this customer works and thinks so take advantage of it. Spend time working with the customer to agree standard formats for statements of work and quotations so they get exactly the information they need, in the format they require it. You should try to get smaller jobs bundled up into a blanket contract or task order contract[63] - this makes it easy for the customer to give you all the small jobs instead of using these as opportunities to try out new suppliers.

Think back to when you were back in the 'one of many' position. Think about the things you wanted the incumbent not to do. And do those things now you are in the 'first choice' position.

While being 'first choice' is a great position to be in, 'only choice' is even better. Not many suppliers make it to this position, because most customers' policies try to ensure some level of competition among their suppliers. But you can get very close, and it's always something to aim for.

If you are lucky enough to work up to an 'only choice' position, what sort of deal strategy applies? Surely 'only choice' means that life becomes easy at last? Certainly, when you are an 'only choice' supplier, there's no excuse for losing a deal! But it's always possible to lose your privileged status.

The big enemy of 'only choice' suppliers is complacency. Somehow, the sales team and the delivery team must approach every new deal opportunity with freshness and creativity. At the same time, mistakes must not happen: it's so easy for people to do things that move you from top position to bottom in the customer's esteem. Yet it would be wrong to avoid risks by sticking within a narrow 'comfort zone'. Always look for opportunities to expand your service offering into new areas. Do this gradually, not in big steps, so that you can ensure quality is maintained and costs are kept low.

As an 'only choice' supplier to a major company, deals should come along regularly, big and small. Sometimes that means people focus just on these projects and lose sight of the underlying relationships. Don't let this happen to your team. Much of your effort needs to be devoted to 'hygiene' - keeping everything sweet in the account. Remember the account plan? Make sure you include specific actions for maintaining contacts, gathering intention and being

Should you offer discounts if you're an 'only choice' supplier? Some people like to milk these accounts for all they're worth. However that provides an easier way in for a newcomer who is prepared to offer a reasonable introductory discount. My approach is to stay highly competitive on price, but to link discounts to task order contracts or volume guarantees. That binds the customer even closer and reduces the opportunities for competitors.

---

[63] A blanket (or framework) contract usually includes no minimum purchase commitment by the customer. A task order (or call-off) contract is one form of 'indefinite delivery' contract which sets a minimum purchase level in return for special rates.

With the deal strategy in place, you and your team can actually sell! ("For heaven's sakes", I hear you saying, "it's about time.")

We have discussed the formulation of strategies at three levels: corporate, account, and deal. But don't get the idea that this is a simple linear process. In practice all levels of strategy are constantly being revisited and refined. And you don't have to wait until all the planning is finished before doing anything: in practice, thinking and acting are not completely separate. You don't completely avoid contact with the customer as you build your strategies. That would be disastrous.

But with a deal strategy in place, based on a sound account strategy, you can really start to move towards closing deals.

Putting together the proper strategy to win business is critical. When you are clear on your strategy, you're actions all make sense and help you to implement effectively. But in the heat of driving towards closing a deal, the sales manager needs to make sure that everyone keeps to the course determined by the strategy. The sales manager also needs to judge when it is best to alter that course when the underlying situation changes.

During the ascent from the first identification of a potential customer through to the successful conclusion of a deal there are many points where the application of thought will pay off, in terms of avoiding wasted effort and increasing the probability of success.

Understanding Value

Every day, a sales team manager has to think about value, from the customers' perspective. One of the essential duties a sales team leader has to perform is to constantly work with each sales rep to help establish value in the eyes of the customers. Sales reps often get too involved in the detail of the customer's needs and product feature. When this happens, it's often helpful if the sales manager can provide a broader perspective that more accurately pinpoints true value to the customer.

What does 'value' mean to a customer? There is a different answer for every customer. No two customers think quite the same - even two people who work for the same company - and the personality and preferences of the individual creep into the value analysis, no matter how objective someone tries to be. Ultimately each customer decides what constitutes value - no one else. Not you, nor your sales reps, nor the people in marketing who write value statements for the brochures.

When customers assess the value of a solution, there are two main factors they take into account. Business value, and personal value. Of course, the explicit discussion will be all about business value, but there is always a personal agenda.

Explicit business value is about either reducing cost or increasing revenues or both. Business value is never about product features and capabilities: it is about how some features and capabilities can improve the business so it makes money or saves money.

Business value is never about product features and capabilities: it is about how some features and capabilities can improve the business so it makes money or saves money.

When a sales person attempts to express value by listing an impressive array of features and functions, then clearly the sale is not likely to go anywhere fast. (This approach is known to sales veterans as 'spray and pray'.)

Instead, every feature needs to be linked to a business benefit, and then the customer's eyes will start to light up.

For example, suppose one of your sales reps is trying to sell a new inventory management solution to a manufacturer. She knows the product well, so she could list all the ways in which the database can display inventory, all the cross-checks and reconciliations that will be possible, the automatic links to the purchasing system that can be made. For the average C-level decision maker, this is too much hard work.

On the other hand she could, with your encouragement, lift her perspective and say the same thing, but this time leading with business benefits. "This is how you can reduce your spare parts stock holding by at least 10% saving you around $24 million per year. This is how you can make sure that your lowest cost supplier automatically replenishes your stocks exactly when needed, not too soon, not too late, allowing you to save 5% in buffer stocks and completely eliminating production line shut-downs."

It is the sales person's responsibility to help the customer join the dots, by explicitly linking features and functions to business benefits.

Because the impact of a solution will be different for every customer, the value proposition will be different for every customer. Suppose your company sells a new factory security system that costs just a few thousand dollars. If you talk to a customer that has no security problems – their automated cornflake management system confirms that 'wastage' losses are never more than a few dollars per week. – then the value of your system to that customer is very low, perhaps negligible. Offer the same system to a warehousing company that is experiencing product losses of hundreds of thousands of dollars of electronics per month, and the business value of the product is a whole lot different.

There are a number of ways in which business value can be expressed. Almost always the benefit is in terms of reducing costs or increasing revenues or both. Note that you don't always have to come up with hard numbers, as rough estimates are often good enough to provide a business justification for many projects. However the more explicit you are able to be, the more convincing will be your value proposition. This is why case studies of real implementations are so useful, and very powerful.

Here are just a few examples of the business benefits you can look for as you are preparing your value proposition.

This solution will:

- Reduce operational costs;
- Increase productivity;
- Reduce materials wastage;
- Improve cash flow;
- Reduce inventory;
- Shorten lead times for delivery to customers;

- Lower product defect rates;
- Reduce whole life total cost of ownership of equipment;
- Bring new product opportunities, and bring them faster;
- Open new markets for products
- Enable new products and services to be launched more quickly;
- ...and so on.

If you and your sales rep after a little research, analysis and thought, cannot pinpoint a couple of realistic and credible business benefits to discuss with the customer, then you have no value proposition. If you can't present business value, you can only present cost and pretend that the value is at least as big as the cost. You shouldn't waste that customer's time.

While business benefits are usually identifiable in terms of dollars, there are always non-financial components to any decision, and these are often individual and personal in nature. Understanding the personal agenda is often the key to a successful sale. While the reason given for a purchasing decision will almost always be a straightforward business benefit, the real (hidden) factor that clinches the sale might well be something more personal.

What sort of personal factors can affect a purchasing decision? Here are a few examples...

- I want my boss to stop pressuring me to fix this problem;
- It's about time the CEO realized that I exist;
- I'm looking for a promotion;
- I want to move within the company, and the faster I complete this project, the sooner I can go to a new job;
- My annual performance bonus depends on getting this done;
- I can see that this solution is going to make my life a whole lot less stressful;
- This will really show the COO who calls the shots around here;
- If I can initiate this project, I get to recruit six more people and that means I'll get a pay rise.

While these personal drivers are very important, there are two challenges: discovering the information; and using the intelligence effectively.

There's only one way to find out what is on your customer's personal agenda: build a trusting relationship, and listen. As we have seen, building a relationship underpins all successful sales and repeat business. Having access to your customer's thought processes is one of the benefits.

That same relationship will enable you to convey – with subtlety please – how your solution will help. Gentle reminders will often be enough to do the trick. "This is going to be a great solution for your company. I bet your CEO will love it. He'll probably say he thought of it first, it's so good." Use your imagination.

But be cautious. Selling purely on a personal agenda is not likely to convince anyone. The real and explicit value proposition is based purely on business benefit, and that must be convincing in its own right. Personal benefits then become the icing on the cake for the customer decision-maker.

Eventually, for any large deal, you are going to have to put something in writing that describes the value proposition[64] to the customer. As you're working with your sales rep to build a convincing statement of value, here are some things to keep in mind:

- **Say what your solution *is*.** Be explicit in describing what your customer will actually receive for their money. Too often sales people who know their own products and services well, just assume that the customer has a similar grasp of the detail. That is seldom the case, so always explain clearly what you are offering.

- **Say what your solution *does*.** This provides the logical and practical basis for the business benefits you will describe in the following sections. Note that this does not require an exhaustive list of features and functions – that comes later. But describe how the solution fits in to the business and what areas it will impact, and in what way.

- **Describe *all* the business benefits your solution will deliver.** In any big corporation, more than one person will influence the decision. A business benefit that knocks the socks of the CFO may just make the CTO yawn and vice versa. By the time you get to writing this down you should know exactly who makes the decision, who influences the decision and you should have a statement of business benefit that appeals to each and every one.

- **Explain how your solution is better than any other solution.** Your solution must promise some business benefits that cannot be obtained elsewhere at the same price. (Ideally it's great to

---

[64] I believe the term 'Value Proposition' may have been coined, or at least made popular currency, by Geoffrey Moore in his book *Crossing the Chasm* (HarperBusiness, 1991). For further insights into the principles behind value propositions and their application, this book is useful reading.

include some business benefits that can't be obtained anywhere else at any price, but that doesn't happen too often.)

Then, by all means go on to explain features, functions, bells, whistles and other details. But only when you have communicated, and firmly planted, the message of business value.

I find that in the area of developing value propositions, two minds working together produce more creative and comprehensive ideas than one mind working in isolation. It's fun to do this with your sales reps. And it's even more fun when you close deals as a result.

Chapter 6
Managing and Motivating your Team

Running the shop, and running it well means a lot more than sitting at a desk doing your e-mail.

A good sales manager needs to adopt an intelligent approach to recruitment and assignment; to motivating people; to incentives and sanctions, and to avoiding the pitfalls that de-motivate people.

Your Portfolio of People

First you plan and then you do. This Chapter is about doing: the everyday thrill (some might say "chore" or "grind") of making things happen. Doing things is not just about activity for its own sake. Doing things in business is about achieving results. And if you've done your planning right, you know exactly what results you're aiming to achieve, and you also have a pretty good idea of how you and your team are going to get there.

What the planning process cannot do, is to predict in fine detail everything that's going to happen. Things change: the economy fluctuates; your industry has ups and downs; people get sick; people falter; people succeed way beyond expectations; customers go out of business and new customers emerge from the woodwork.

You don't go back and rework your business plan every day. A good manager handles day-to-day occurrences as they arise – always keeping in mind the objectives and values that are important to the business, but not expecting to find a predefined formula answer to everything.

Good managers can do this. Good managers also know when things have changed so much that they need to return to the drawing board and update their plans and objectives.

Klinks, on the other hand, do not get this balance right. They either work without a plan and try to make everything up as they go along; or they move to the other extreme and become frozen in their executive chair whenever something happens that isn't included in the plan or covered in a documented procedure.

Your management style is critical for successful day to day running of your sales operation. There is no single correct management style: the best approach depends on the type of business you are in, the personalities of the people in your team and a host of other factors.

However there are some things that managers do that are almost always right, and other things that are always wrong. SMART managers usually do the right things, klinks mostly get things wrong.

All businesses want their sales professionals to be enthusiastic, energetic and effective. To attract those people and keep them motivated a business also needs – guess what? – enthusiastic, energetic and effective sales team managers.

The raw material that a sales manager has to work with is *the team*: your portfolio of people.

What is the most important thing a sales manager can do to build a successful team? Recruit the right people. Then you have to give those people responsibilities to match their style and approach.

Some sales managers do not apply enough thought and effort to these important areas.

I have seen a sales team leader recruit a friend of a friend into the team, without really testing whether the candidate stood any chance of being successful. In some companies, sales managers must sometimes accept new recruits that they have not chosen at all – they've been recruited by someone else in the company and they have to 'adopt' them. In some other cases, sales managers approach the serious task of recruitment with as little consideration as their choice of a sandwich for lunch. This is not a good idea. Choose the wrong sandwich and indigestion lasts for a few hours. Choose the wrong sales rep and you might not realize your mistake for months, and it could take months more to repair the damage.

Once you have a team of sales reps together, you know that they're not all the same, and you know that their personalities need to be matched to the personalities of their accounts. How do you do this? The most favorite way seems to be trial and error. You cannot eliminate trial and error completely, but you can continue to trial with a lower error rate by first of all understanding the personality of each account, and then by applying some careful thought to the way you assign sales reps to accounts.

In this section we'll look at recruitment first, and then at assignment, which seems like a logical order to me.

What should you look for in a potential recruit to your sales team? You will be trying to assess candidates (and this won't surprise you) in the following areas:

- their ability to exercise the basic **skills** of selling
- their **management** potential
- their **attitude** to the job
- their ability to build **relationships**, and
- their ability to **think and plan.**

In other words you are looking for most of the same basic attributes in a sales person as you would expect to find in a sales manager. The difference is mainly in the weight you give to each parameter. For example, a sales rep working alone on an account will survive better with limited management skills than a sales team leader could.

The candidate's résumé and cover letter may start to give you some insights into his or her abilities, but chances are it will be full of assertions, without evidence. You need to be able to read between the lines in a résumé to differentiate between real achievement and 'time served'. (Taking a new person into your team based on the contents of a résumé alone, or perhaps supported by a quick phone conversation, is such evident folly that no one would ever do it, would they? Well, I've seen it done, and noted the consequences.)

Taking written letters of recommendation at face value is just as dangerous as believing a résumé. Of course, all those fine words may be true, but it's your job as a sales manager to check. Without being too cynical you need to remember that people have been sued for being too honest in a reference letter, and so there's not much incentive for revealing bad things about people. In fact there is a tendency for managers to gloss over bad things and emphasize the good points, such as they may be. Just consider – if someone has a useless employee looking for a change of scenery, isn't there a tendency to give a helping hand?

Don't skip the important step of talking directly to the person who wrote that glowing review. Look for genuine enthusiasm for the candidate, not just the usual standard-letter platitudes which may hide everything from ordinary competence to dangerous ineptitude. One of my favorite questions to goes along these lines: "Suppose I recruit Ms. Smith... what would you advise me to do to help her be really successful in her new job?" This sort of open question helps to stimulates dialog about Ms. Smith's strengths weaknesses and preferences. Does she need lots of support? Does she work well in a team? Does she need structure? Direct questioning often fails to get down to these essentials, but the right open questions will usually open the floodgates of opinion and advice.

You should also phone other people in your network who might know the candidate and whose judgment you trust. Don't rely on idle speculation and rumor; but don't ignore it either. The purpose of this stage is to build up a list of searching questions and areas of discussion for the interview. What is unsaid in the résumé and unmentioned in the references is just as important as what is actually there.

And so we come to the interview. As I've already mentioned in Chapter 1, recruitment of staff at any level is not a small challenge, and managers need to pay more attention to how to do it well.

I have a suspicion that lots of otherwise good sales managers are not expert recruitment interviewers for two reasons. First they are naturally positive, up-beat people, who enjoy building constructive relationships with everybody. That's great for selling, but not necessarily good for buying, and when you're recruiting, you're buying. The second reason is that few sales managers bother to get formal training in recruitment interview techniques, and most companies don't insist that they do.

If you have a responsibility for recruiting sales people, make sure you get some substantial training. A quick rundown of hints and tips from a colleague over coffee is not sufficient. (Nor is merely reading this chapter: take a course or seminar on interviewing.)

Recruitment interviewing does share many aspects with the sort of conversations you conduct when you're in a selling role. You need to ask the right sort of open questions to reveal information. You need to actively listen and lead the conversation where you want it to go, while letting the candidate do most of the talking. Don't just ask about previous experience; test their knowledge, attitudes by asking them what they would do in various hypothetical selling situations. Everything in the section on Listening and Questioning in Chapter 3 continues to be relevant in recruitment interviews. But there are some differences, and special things to remember. For example…

Hunt in pairs. Never make a recruitment decision alone. Always work with a colleague, ideally one from a different department who has also been trained in recruitment interviewing. Sensibly, many companies now insist on that, as well as making sure the discussion is properly documented. You can conduct interviews separately or together, but two opinions are always better than one. Interviewing separately allows each interviewer to form an independent opinion. On the other hand, with two people conducting the interview together, you have more opportunity to observe behavior and attitudes, and more time to think of ways to steer the conversation to find out what you need to know.

Be a little bit mean. During the interview, despite what the text books say, don't try too hard to reassure the candidate and make sure he or she is at ease. Recruiting sales people is a special case: you want to find out if the candidate has the confidence and social skills necessary to make *you* feel comfortable, just as if you were a customer, which in a sense you are.

Reserve your judgment. In a recruitment interview, you need to be more **skeptical** and test the candidate's responses in a number of ways. Skepticism doesn't come easily to some of us who like to think the best of everyone, but a skeptical and searching approach can be acquired through good training that includes role-play interviews. (It's better to learn skepticism this way than as a result of making a succession of stupid recruitment decisions.) Skepticism leads to rigorous and comprehensive questioning that tests and validates the candidate's claims, including those made in the candidate's résumé.

Cover the ground. Your interview should also be **comprehensive.** With a customer, you are happy that the conversation should go to the customer's areas of interest so you can gather intelligence to enable you sell your products and services. With a job candidate you need to ensure that the conversation covers *all* the areas that *you* are interested in. That means that you will generally have to steer the conversation much more assertively than you would normally have to with a customer.

Look for substance, not just style. Let's face it; some people are really good at putting on a show. I expect all good sales people to be able to present well and conduct themselves with élan. However we've all met someone who is an 'empty suit': looks good, smells good, sounds good, but there's really nothing there. Look under the surface. Seeing through style to identify the real substance takes some special skills. When face-to-face with a candidate, a good interviewer needs to understand how to steer the conversation to find out the reality under the surface. Don't just ask questions. Probe. You have the right to probe, because you are the buyer. Use each answer to dig deeper. "Why would you do it that way?" "What other options are there?" "What could go wrong with that approach?"[65]

Don't buy a clone. A big mistake is to recruit someone *just like yourself.* So you're pretty good at your job, but how many photocopies do you need? Any good sales team needs a mix of personalities, skills and talents.

Don't be a klink. SMART managers look for and recruit people who are at least as talented as they are themselves, whenever possible. Klinks prefer to recruit subordinates who are not going to shine. When you come across someone totally incompetent in their job, you usually ask yourself: "How did this dolt land this position?" Sometimes you need to look at the immediate superior for the answer. Some people fear that they will be overshadowed if they bring people into their team who are particularly bright and capable. So they recruit dim people. When a klink recruits a dimwit into his or her team, this helps to perpetuate the chain of klinkdom. In due course these employees absorb bad management practices from their klinkish boss, get promoted, and live to carry klinkdom forward to another generation. A SMART manager aims to recruit bright and enthusiastic people so that every time, the average level of talent in the team goes *up.*

> *SMART managers look for and recruit people who are at least as talented as they are themselves.*

---

[65] To learn to do this properly, get some formal training. It will really pay off.

Allow plenty of time. You are about to make an important decision, on which the productivity, performance and happiness of your team will hang. Invest the level of time and effort that this task deserves. This is not just an investment by you, for your team. You are making an investment on behalf of your company, and so your recruits should have the potential to serve the company well for years.

Throughout this book, I have expressed some mild opinions about the prevalence of klinks in sales management and the high turnover of sales people. I know that there are many reasons underlying these problems, so I hope that I'm not being too simplistic when I suggest that if more sales managers set higher standards for recruitment of sales people, and applied them rigorously and consistently, maybe we'd have fewer klinks, and lower turnover.

Once you have a new person on your team, what next? You need to decide what role the individual will play in your team.

If the recruit is already experienced, you can plan to move him or her quite quickly into taking more responsibility – once you know that person's personality and preferences. If the recruit is a rookie, you need to make sure that the coaching and support needed will be there; you will personally have to spend time on this, as well as assigning him or her a trusted 'buddie' who has experience. By the way, you *need* rookies in your portfolio of people: they provide the raw material to grow the team, they bring new ideas, and they provide people for your veterans to mentor, which is good for them. (Teaching is the best way to learn.)

What accounts will the new rep work on? Is that person going to be in a lead role or in support? Is the rep going to be more productive winning new clients, or looking after existing clients? The answer to these questions will depend on the person's experience, obviously. But you will also need to take into account his or her personality and preferences.

Let's start by pointing out that at this stage you should not have to face the challenge of placing someone who is not very good at relationships, or someone who is a natural pessimist, or someone who is fearful of trying anything new. If you find that you have a person like that to assign to a role, then you have a real problem. Whoever recruited this person for your team got something wrong. If you made the choice yourself, you have only yourself to blame, and you should change your decision as soon as you realize you've made a mistake.

Every person on your team needs to be someone who starts off with the right attitude: optimistic, persistent, enthusiastic, resilient and affable. Every person on your team should have some level of selling skills, or be capable of learning quickly. Every person should be comfortable making contacts, and building and sustaining relationships.

In other words, this discussion is not about fitting square pegs into round holes. It's about finding the most closely fitting roundish holes for your various and variable, but still roundish, sales reps.

So when we think about the range of personality types in a typical sales team, we don't have to understand the full panoply of people in the world, including natural depressives, unpredictable geniuses, anti-social curmudgeons, and psychopaths. Psychologists and others have come up with a baffling number of different ways of classifying "personality types". Many of these psychological theories tell us the same thing in different ways, and each provides illumination in its own way. While it is interesting and entertaining to read the psychology textbooks, and it may help you in dealing with certain customers and top executives, don't think it's essential to read a shelf-full of psychology books in order to build a sound, well-performing sales team.

There are just three characteristics of my sales people that I always consider when I'm thinking about assigning account responsibilities. They are attitude, perspective, and relationship-building. In some cases it's difficult to get these assignments right on day one, so you should always observe how people are doing, and be prepared to reassign someone later, if that's what it takes for them to be successful.

> *There are just three characteristics of my sales people that I like to consider ... attitude, perspective and relationship-building.*

Attitude. The attitudes of sales people can vary – from 'Buoyant' to 'Unsinkable'. (Anything less than buoyant implies a tendency to sink. Many decent and talented people have a somewhat negative attitude, and are prone to cynicism and despair. They would flounder in a sales role, and they should not be in one. Fortunately most of these people know themselves well enough to not even consider a sales career.)

Buoyant people have a great sense of proportion, and failure doesn't dismay them for too long. Buoyant people bounce back quickly and get on with things. Buoyant people are almost always upbeat about life and their job.

Unsinkable people are more than just buoyant. They take failure in their stride, never missing a beat. As a result they have tremendous persistence and constant energy. If you need someone to work for months to break into a particularly difficult account, or to cold-call a long list of completely new prospects, you may need someone who is unsinkable rather than simply buoyant.

A reservation: some unsinkable people can also be insensitive, and the reason they are never down is that they don't listen or don't care, or both. This is dangerously close to megalomania, possibly useful for some jobs, but not for sales.

Perspective. Some people naturally love detail. They want to understand how everything works, and they have the patience to investigate and study. Others are 'Big Picture' or 'Overview' people: they see the woods, but aren't too concerned about the trees and the bushes, knowing there's someone out there tending to those things.

Both perspectives are useful in sales. Some people can move apparently without too much difficulty from detail to helicopter perspective and back again, as needed. But I have found that most sales reps are more comfortable in one mode or the other.

People who like to get into the detail usually get on well with technical and business specialists in the client company. They have the patience to learn about the business and its needs and can relate well to people who also understand the business at its functional level.

People who prefer to view the business from the big picture perspective relate best to customers who do the same thing. In general, this means the people in the company who are more interested in strategic direction than in the practicalities of how the strategic objectives will be achieved.

Broadly, in the customer's organization, detail people tend to be specialists in technical, operational and analytical roles, in first-line management and middle management. Senior management and board-level executives are more inclined to take a broad view of the company and its future. But this is just a generalization. Many CEOs are interested in, and are capable of understanding, the complexities of the technology used in their business. And many first-line managers are just as interested in the strategic and business relevance of technology decisions as in the technical details.

The point is, first understand your customer's perspective, and then choose a sales person who can provide that customer with the mix of overview and detailed perspective that will enable them to build a relationship and pitch a convincing value proposition.

> *First understand your customer's perspective ... and then choose a sales person...*

Relationship-building. All sales people must be good at making contacts, establishing relationships, and sustaining relationships. But they do this in slightly different ways. Some people seem to have the right mix of presence, affability and nerve to quickly establish relationships with new people. Others will get there eventually, but by a more gradual, steady process.

People who can establish immediate empathy are very useful for gathering new contacts in a networking situation, and for 'breaking and entering' into new accounts. Sometimes such sales people prefer the stimulus of always meeting new people, and so have less interest in maintaining a relationship over a longer period of time.

Those who have a slower and steadier approach to building relationships also seem to be more able to sustain close relationships over months and even years. Some customers are naturally cautious, and prefer to get to know people over a longer period of time, so if you are aware of this you shouldn't assign someone who will try to push the relationship too quickly – choose a slow and steady type instead. Slow and steady people are also very valuable as account managers for customers with whom your company has a long-term continuing stable relationship. They don't get bored and they delight in building that relationship over time, and becoming indispensable to the customer.

We can describe combinations of these personality types using a shorthand approach:

- Attitude: **B** for Buoyant, **U** for Unsinkable.
- Perspective: **D** for Detail, **O** for Overview.
- Relationship-building: **F** for Fast, **S** for Steady.

So if a sales rep has a normal positive attitude, an eye for technical detail, and takes time to build a solid relationship then I would describe him as a type BDS.

Remember these descriptions are not absolutes: **O** just means having a *preference* for the big picture – it doesn't mean the person has no interest in detail at all.

Also, establishing someone on the scale is not an entirely a scientific process. I usually talk with people and ask them their own views. Most people are pretty good at fixing themselves on these scales, and find it useful in establishing their areas of strength. I couple the person's own opinion with my own observations of behavior to draw a conclusion.

I think I am a BOS – Buoyant, Overview, Steady. I have probably changed over the years, which doesn't mean that I'm better or worse as a sales person, just different, with a *different balance* of strengths.

Let's look at a few examples of account opportunities, and the type of sales personality that's going to do best in those accounts.

In my first example, the target company has a CEO who is well known for his short attention span. He doesn't have much patience with anyone, and he is not interested in understanding the detail of how things are done, he just wants to decide where the company needs to go, and what needs to be done to get there. He will, without doubt, make the final purchasing decision in any complex expensive solution. What sort of sales personality would be best to assign to build a relationship with this CEO?

Clearly, we need someone who can grab this guy's attention and hold it. We don't want to risk losing his interest by discussing too much detail. Also it might take several attempts to get in here, and the CEO's irascible nature might discourage some people. My choice would be to go for someone who can get relationships going really quickly, a big picture person, and someone who is as near unsinkable as possible – a type UOF.

My next example involves a CTO who only makes decisions after amassing a huge amount of technical and financial information. She's also difficult to get to know, because she doesn't start to trust people until they've been around for a while. She has also shown in the past that she dislikes aggressive sales people, or indeed anyone who tries to push her faster than she wants to go.

My choice here would be the exact opposite of my choice for the first example. Here, we need someone who is willing to be slow and steady in building the relationship, who can patiently explain the detail, and thereby win the confidence of the CTO. Clearly this is going to be hard work, so the sales person needs to be buoyant, but an unsinkable might be too aggressive. This points to the ideal candidate being a type BDS.

At this stage you might think this is altogether too obvious. If that's what you think – great! Once you recognize the importance of these categories, it's not too hard to work out where to place each person on the spectrum. The idea is that if you can "type" each customer and each member of your sales team, then it's easier to choose a sales person who will complement and work well with a specific customer.

Third example: we need someone to spearhead a new campaign selling a new product to mostly unknown customers. We need someone who can lead the charge, undaunted by a low success rate, prepared to make contacts and establish the relationship and either make the first deal, or hand over to someone else who will nurture the account over a longer period. The product needs to be introduced by someone who can explain its unique technical advantages and the cost-savings that can be achieved in a complex operational process. I'd choose someone who is a type UDF, if I have one available on my team.

Final example. We have a long established account where we have achieved the great position of being 'only choice' supplier for just about everything that's in our portfolio. Our relationship is with a small exclusive team of close friends who run the company and make all the decisions: The CEO, CFO, CTO and COO. They like to bounce their strategic ideas off our account manager, who has become something of a trusted adviser. I need to plan to replace our account manager, who has decided to retire, move to an island, and write a best-selling novel. We have a few months to arrange a changeover, which will probably be needed, because it will certainly be a challenge to establish trust with this team. Fortunately our existing account manager will lubricate the process.

I need to find someone who can operate effectively at the same strategic level as the executive management team. This situation calls for someone who is thoughtful and measured, so I would go for a buoyant person who builds strong relationships steadily. My decision: a BOS.

The first step in creating a successful sales team: is to recruit the right people. Then, assign them jobs that play to their strengths.

You still have to manage your team, motivate them, plan the work, handle problems, work with them on building relationships and closing deals. But all of that becomes a whole lot easier if you already have worked out how to get the right people and put them in the right places.

The first step in creating a successful sales team is to recruit the right people. Then, assign them jobs that play to their strengths.

Motivating Your Team

Sales managers read lots of books about motivation, and attend training courses on how to generate enthusiasm and commitment in their team members. Mostly when people put the book down, or leave the training course, they think: "Well, that was pretty obvious" and go back to work with much the same approach as before. I've noticed that managers who were already good at motivating their team tend to do it a little better after some training. Managers who weren't good at motivating their team generally behave much the same as before.

This is because the ability to motivate others is just as much to do with your attitude as with any skills you might have learned. If you have the right attitude, learning some motivational skills will help you. If you have the wrong attitude it won't. The right attitude is about everything we discussed in Chapter 2. All those positive points that make someone cut out to be a sales person, also make them a good sales manager. Think of it this way: when you *sell* something, you're trying to motivate someone to buy.

And so, just like selling something, you can only motivate your team if you have built a sound, trusting relationship; if you have credibility with your team members; and if they buy the proposition that their enthusiasm and commitment will pay off. They need to feel that working with you is *great value* – just about the best way they can spend their time.

There are two aspects to motivation. Things you ought to do to make people more motivated. And things you shouldn't do because it will de-motivate people.

This book contains many examples of actions that can de-motivate a team. So in this section I want to concentrate on things that you can do to positively enthuse and energize people to be more successful as individuals, and to make the team more successful.

When people think of motivation, too often they just think about financial rewards, especially for people in sales. True, money can be a powerful motivator, and I'll deal with that in a separate section.

Another popular attitude is that motivation is all about special team-building sessions, company conferences and motivational speeches. These things work. But they only work really well when you've already laid a foundation by daily attention to motivational detail. Special events alone won't do the trick, indeed if the manager is a klink they could even make matters worse by making people more negative and cynical.

Here is a long list of things a manager can do every day to increase trust, gain commitment and enthusiasm. How many of these do you manage to pack into a day's work?

- **Be a coach.** Look for opportunities to help your team develop and exercise their selling skills. Sit down with each person in your team at least once a week to find out how he or she is doing, and what is getting in the way of success.

- **Be a mentor.** Extend your interest in your team – discuss development paths, career options and provide suggestions for ways in which each team member can be more successful in the sales profession. Recognize talent, and encourage more of it.

- **Listen.** The traffic of communication should be two-way. For most managers, that means they need to make an effort to talk less and listen more. Ask your team for feedback, and for their opinions, and for their perspective on challenges and opportunities, and listen to what they say. Then go away and think about it.

- **Understand the definition of success, and where success comes from.** A sales manager is successful if the team is successful. The team is successful if individuals in the team sell your products and services. Focus on helping them make that happen at every opportunity. You must want everyone to succeed.

- **How can I help?** Keep asking.

- **Trust your team – and challenge them**. Give them trust and responsibility and assume they will rise to the challenge. Set stretching targets. Believe that people can always do more than you might expect, given encouragement.

- **Value bright ideas**. Encourage creative thinking, and recognize that you might need to get twenty ideas to find one golden idea. If you don't encourage ideas #1 to #19, you might never hear #20.

- **Give.** Givers get more back than takers.

- **Reward your team.** Their sales commissions come first, before yours. Don't forget to say 'Thank you.' Publicize your team's success throughout the company.

- **Favor everyone.** Everyone in the team should think that he or she is your favorite sales rep.

- **Be honest.** Give your team members direct, constructive and understandable feedback. Tell them immediately when they've done something wrong, why it was wrong and how to do better next time. (As a result, your life will be less stressful, and so will theirs.)

- **Be on your team's side**. Take personal responsibility for your team's actions. Support them through all difficulties. Be there to help. Identify with them – if the team fails, you fail, if the team succeeds you'll succeed. Defend your team against the criticisms of others.

- **Create momentum**. Be proactive, make things happen. Help people set personal goals and help them achieve them. Encourage people constantly.

- **Set a good example**. If you do things right, your team will be encouraged to do things right too. If you don't do it right, you're team will quickly learn not to do it right. Setting a good example really can help to influence behavior. You, the sales manager, *you* set the tone, and you set the pace.

Financial Carrots

Carrots encourage people to do more of what you want them to do.
Companies often handle their sales people with a strange mixture of simplicity and complexity. On one hand they believe that sales people operate in a very straightforward way to monetary rewards and penalties. Following the money, they think, is a conditioned reflex for sales people. On the other hand some companies develop sales compensation schemes of such mind-numbing complexity that, often, sales people find it difficult to know exactly what is expected of them.

Indeed, sales people are motivated by financial rewards, as are most of us in today's world. But sales people are people too and can be motivated or de-motivated by the same sort of things that influence others. I have known many reps who have left lucrative sales positions because they have suffered under the rule of a klink for a boss. I have known others who have moved on because they cannot agree with a company's way of doing business or their underlying values. Clearly, there is more to motivating a sales team than money, but when we think of carrots for the sales force, the carrots usually are in the form of dollar signs, so we'll concentrate on that topic in this chapter. (Elsewhere in the book I discuss other ways in which managers can purposefully or by accident motivate – and de-motivate – sales people.)

Every company has a different way of paying their sales force based on what is being sold, the value of the deal and the length of the sales cycle. There is no single perfect formula for an incentive plan that drives the right behavior. But there are some general rules that companies need to follow. An effective compensation plan succeeds in motivating the sales team to close deals that deliver profitable revenues for the company. The company wins, the sales team wins. Any departure from the win-win formula will fail.

An unfair or unworkable compensation scheme reveals a lot about a company's attitude to their sales force. Some sales compensation schemes are often convoluted and packed with caveats, multiple thresholds and limits. These are designed to "protect" the company, but from what? To protect the company from getting too many sales? A company that values sales would not

> *An unfair or unworkable compensation scheme reveals a lot about a company's attitude to their sales force.*

choke at the thought of rewarding them for real results. A company that looks for ways to avoid rewarding people, even if they deliver results, is not just being cheap, it's being short-sighted. In an effort to ensure that the company always wins, they make the sales people lose. And so the company will lose the sales people.

This book is too slim for me to be able to provide a detailed primer on setting sales compensation. My purpose is to emphasize that getting a compensation plan right is (a) very important and (b) not very easy; and to provide some pointers on what to look out for.[66]

In my time as a sales rep and as a sales manager I have been on both sides of the compensation discussion. And I've been in the middle, trying to make sense of schemes that are handed down by corporate executive for me to apply to my team. There are some basic principles I look for in an effective compensation scheme for sales people.

For me, as both a business person and as a sales person, the basic business imperative for sales commission plans is that they should directly support company business objectives, not undermine them. In formulating the commission plan executives need to ask themselves more than "What can we do to maximize sales with minimum cost?" which seems to dominate most thinking on this subject. The plan should take into account a broader perspective on what the company is trying to achieve. What does the company need this year? More revenue? More profits? More market share?

The plan should steer the sales force in the direction the company wants to go. Should we push new product lines or milk the cash cows of established products and solutions? How much effort should go into breaking into new accounts, as against building add-on business in existing accounts?

All these board-level decisions should cascade down into management objectives and should be directly linked to the incentive plan.[67]

In a sound plan, I also look for some recognition that the wizards who created the scheme have taken into account the real nature of the business we are working in. Many executives move from one company to another, bringing with them a set of assumptions based

---

[66] For a sound guide to developing effective sales compensation schemes, consider these books: *Sales Compensation Handbook*, ed Stockton B. Colt (Amacom, 1998); *Compensating the Sales force: A Practical Guide to Designing Winning Sales Compensation Plans*, David J. Cichelli (McGraw-Hill, 2003).

[67] Perhaps we shouldn't be too surprised that corporate level objectives are rarely linked intelligently to sales incentives. It seems that in many companies, the executives can't even link company objectives to their own compensation in any rational way.

on what worked in their previous job. But no two industries are exactly the same, and within an industry, no two companies are exactly the same. Relying on misplaced assumptions is probably what has happened when an executive announces a new compensation plan with the words amounting to "This worked great when I was with Quack-rite Bathtoys Inc., it'll be a blast to try it on our guys selling high-availability servers."

Some companies sell projects and products to a relatively small number of customers in which the lead-time is long, the individual deal value is high. In these cases an unrealistic scheme can result in compensation that is more like winning the lottery than rewarding success. In one company I had a $60,000,000 annual budget (sales target) and a reasonable commission rate: but I had no existing accounts, the average deal was $15 million, and the sales cycle was typically two years long. I had to be very patient waiting for my first commission check. Unfortunately not everyone wants to be patient, or can afford to be, and when a sales person leaves after just a few months, the new person has to start again, building relationships. This costs companies money, which they could have chosen to spend maintaining loyalty during that long ramp-up period.

The other side of this coin is when a new person arrives on the team starts to work an existing well-established account, hits the jackpot based on the efforts of the previous sales person, and retires to set up a bed and breakfast in the Adirondacks.

In general, long lead-time projects of high value need sales people who are compensated with reasonable basic salary.

On the other hand, if the company is in a (relatively) low-priced high-volume market, the relationship between basic salary and commission can be quite different. Fast turnover provides fast feedback, so the sales person can survive, and management can make quicker and more accurate judgments about performance.

The nature of the business will also determine the most appropriate (that is effective and fair) answer to questions like:

- Should the company pay for sales bookings (i.e. when a deal is closed) or only as revenue comes in, or some combination?

- Should gross margins be part of the commission formula?

- Should the company pay sales commissions monthly, quarterly or annually?

- Should the company put a cap on commissions at some level?

- Should the company put a threshold in place, so that commissions are only paid if the sales person achieves, say 80% of quota?

Executives also need to work out how the compensation of sales managers be linked to their sales teams plan so that everyone is focused on the same goals. And in so far as executive's rewards are linked to sales success, the same applies to them too. The need for consistent treatment at all levels is not just a matter of fairness, though that is important. If rewards drive behavior (which is the whole point of incentive schemes) to have conflicting objectives at different levels of the company is sure to cause problems that will impact everyone's performance.

Good executives and sales managers balance the needs of the company with the needs of the sales people. The company needs to maintain its level of net profit and manage cash flow effectively. Sales people would love to be paid generously, but usually they will be satisfied with simply being paid fairly.

> *Good sales managers balance the needs of the company with the needs of the sales people.*

Generally if a company can be sure that the value of deals is pretty well fixed, and the likelihood of cancellation is low at the time of signature, then payment on bookings is relatively low risk, for both the company and the sales person. However for many companies today the actual value of the deal may be quite different by the end of the project. It could be higher as additional requirements are uncovered; or it could be lower as the real needs are uncovered during the course of the project. If the value of the deal is likely to change after the initial deal is closed, then it makes sense for the company to base at least part of the commission on actual revenue to reduce the need for *clawback* (paying back the commission payments to the company). It can make sense for the sales person too, if the result is payment for extra value delivered during the course of the contract.

The periodicity of commission payments also needs to be linked to company needs. Most sales people expect revenue-based commissions to be paid monthly, after the revenue is recognized in the accounts, and most companies are happy to do that. Smaller companies may ask a sales person to wait until the payment is actually received before passing on commission, which makes sense if cash flow is an issue. Most company accountants are reluctant to pay out money for bookings-based commissions until a revenue stream is visible, and sales people usually have to grin and live with this situation – accountants are influential at board level, and in this case, their reluctance makes financial sense.

On the other hand, some accountants also seem to like caps and thresholds, which generally sales people don't like very much at all.

A cap limits the amount of commission that can be paid in any period. When imposing a cap, companies are in effect saying "We want you to be successful, but not too successful." Is that what the company really wants? In a capped commission environment, sales people become adept at rationing their successes, especially if they are paid on bookings: anything that won't pay commission this period will be deferred until next period. If the cap is on revenue-based commission, this becomes a big disincentive to securing more business when the pipeline is already healthy. The decision to cap seems to be always subjective, and not based on a scientific assessment of the potential return to the company.

Thresholds are just as irritating as caps, and most sales people generally regard them as unfair and counter-productive. In a threshold-limited situation, especially if lead-times are long, the company is effectively denying the sales person compensation for success, unless it's big success. Does this mean that smaller wins are of no value to the company? If so, why do they attract any commission at all? As with caps, thresholds cause salespeople to feel less than happy with their relationship with the company, and drive them to spend time manipulating the system so that they spread their successes in such a way as to always achieve the threshold.

I'm not saying that caps and thresholds are never right, just that managers often overlook the impact of these techniques on sales team motivation, and the waste of time incurred when people work on manipulating the system instead of selling more deals. Caps and thresholds have become more and more common over the years. At the same time, sales turnover has become higher in most companies. Is there a link?

Suppose a sales person works hard in a difficult market to sell hundreds of thousands of dollars worth of profitable business, but only achieves 74% of quota when the threshold is 75%. That sales person will receive exactly zero in sales commissions. Such formulas are very common. What impact does that have on a sales person? I know one sales rep who sold $800K into a new account in his first few months in a company, and received no reward because he hadn't quite achieved the threshold. Yet over time that new account grew into the biggest account for the company, with annual sales of millions of dollars. The talented sales person concerned wasn't demotivated, he just moved on.

Sales people like straightforward proportional payments: flat rate, uncapped, no thresholds, sensible conditions. They like plans that directly link rewards to performance. If performance increases, the reward should increase. If the performance declines, the reward should decline: always, and without exception. Company executives don't seem to like to offer these things to their sales people. Yet company executives like the same things as their sales people do: they expect income to rise as they deliver more products, and they expect profitability to increase with growing revenue, not reduce. Why do they act surprised when sales people look for the same thing?

Getting rid of (or reducing) caps, thresholds, clawbacks and other complex conditions also makes plans more predictable, understandable, and therefore makes people (managers and sales people) more confident that the plan is fair and workable and will deliver the desired results. Complex compensation plans are highly prone to errors. If the sales numbers are posted one day too late or too early, that can make a big difference to the commission. When plans change, as they do too often, their complexity always means that it takes a few weeks for the algorithms to settle down. If there are complicated rules for which products count and which don't, that can be another source of errors.

Complicated plans are expensive to administer and often cause delays in payment, leading to more irritation, and less trust. Complicated plans produce errors. Errors waste everyone's time and energy, and cause frustration and discontent.

Companies need to make sure that the plan is written down and communicated in such a way that is fairly easy to understand. Sales people and managers should be able to interpret the rules without referring to a legal textbook or, worse, an actual lawyer. Obfuscation does more than obfuscate: it breeds suspicion.

Another company tactic that causes sales people dismay is the inclination of executives to change the plan whenever it looks as if it might become too generous. Plans should always be open to evolution to meet changing business needs and objectives, and nowadays that can be quite often. But plans should not be changed simply to try to avoid paying sales people for their successes. More than one time, I have seen a sales person bring in a huge deal early in the year only to have the company double their quota. This used to be unusual, but it is now becoming common. Executives should think a little more about the impact of these decisions.

Sales people should not have to worry about their compensation plan and fret about when or if they are going to get paid. They should be able to understand the rules and be confident that they will be applied in an even-handed way to everyone. They should be able to focus on selling and taking care of customers, winning profitable business for the company. They will not do this if they are spending time manipulating their work patterns to satisfy conditions in the compensation plan, if they are always having to check that the right payments are being made, or if they simply do not trust the company.

So - my basic principles for sound sales compensation schemes involve: relevance, simplicity and fairness. Schemes should be relevant to the industry, the company, its target customers, its business objectives, and to the needs of the sales force. They should be straightforward to understand and inexpensive to administer. And they should be recognized as offering a fair deal to the company and to the sales force. Only by following these principles will a compensation plan unambiguously drive sales behavior in ways that are entirely beneficial to the company. Isn't that what we all want?

Sticks

Carrots encourage people to do more of what you want them to do. Sticks discourage people from doing things you don't want them to do.

Some rules of the game are essential, so let's look at some of the things you, as a sales manager, *don't* want your team to do, and then consider some of the tools you need to help direct their behavior.

Most sales team managers are optimistic and positive by nature, and spend most of their time stimulating more of the right sort of behavior. This is how it should be. I've found that almost always, the easiest and most effective route is to use carrots to persuade people to move in the other direction.

However now and again, managers should be prepared to let people know that along with the carrots, there are sticks.

Here are just a few examples of the sort of things you don't want people in your team ever to do:

- Insult a customer.
- Be intoxicated within spotting distance of a customer, competitor, journalist, or gossip.
- Sell a competitor's products on the side.
- Spend time and energy manipulating bookings to get round caps, thresholds and other conditions placed on commission payments.
- Harass a colleague, a customer, or indeed anyone on company's time.
- Pick arguments all the time about commission payments.
- Spread rumors, talk negatively about the team and the company, spend too much hanging around the water cooler gossiping.

How do you deter and penalize such behavior? Some of the penalties might include, depending on the nature and severity of the offense:

- A mild private reprimand or slap on the wrist (metaphorically only - I discourage physical violence, as does the law).
- Withdrawal or reduction of sales commission.
- Public reprimand and derision.
- Reassignment, demotion or reduction in base salary.

- Dismissal.

Remember, the use of sticks is all about deterrence. If the tools of deterrence have to regularly be used for punishment, there is something seriously wrong. People should know the rules, and know for sure that they will be applied, otherwise these sticks have no deterrent value. If they don't deter people, the rules have failed.

But let's assume that someone has not been deterred, and has willfully committed a transgression against your company. Let's make the discussion simple (which it never really is in real life) by assuming that the facts of the matter are not in doubt. What do you do?

Without going into a whole lot of hypothetical detail, I'd like just to list some of the important things to remember when dealing with the occasional case of someone stepping *seriously* out of line.

- **Know your company's rules.** When you realize that you have to handle serious trouble, you ought to make sure you understand and stick to your company's rules. Often people don't realize that major corporations have teams of personnel specialists and attorneys working in the background writing all sorts of guidance for every imaginable situation. Those rules take into account any legal requirements that may apply in your industry and location. Most companies have standard procedures that usually include a 'second chance' for first offenders. – a probation period.

- **Apply your company's rules.** Apply the rules, or you might find yourself in trouble too. If in doubt contact your company's human resources experts. The rules take into account the seriousness of the action, and whether it was an isolated incident, or a recurring pattern. The purpose of the rules is to ensure fair and consistent treatment across the company, because inconsistency can lead to appeals and even legal action. Going through 'due process' might seem tedious to you, but it's even more bother doing it all over again because you got it wrong the first time, and don't even think about the amount of time you'll burn up if you have to show up in court.

- **Act promptly.** It's always a mistake to ignore unacceptable behavior. It's always a mistake to just wait and see if things improve. When something serious goes wrong, you must force the issue to the very top of your to-do list, because delay will make the problem bigger, not smaller.

- **Avoid theatrical over-reaction.** No matter how serious the situation, you won't improve things by shouting. Adopt a balanced, unemotional attitude to evaluating the situation, make a careful judgment, and do what you have to do. Calmly.

- **Seek advice.** A problem shared is still your problem, but you will find that your thoughts will become clearer if you are able to discuss it with a trusted colleague or your immediate superior. If you're going to fire someone, in some companies there is a process that involves others in the decision anyway. Don't look on this as an imposition – use it to make sure your thoughts are straight and to build confidence that you're doing the right thing.

- **Remember the rest of the team.** Although the impact of your decision will impact the guilty party most of all, remember that everyone in your team will be affected somehow. The penalty will serve as a reminder that certain standards of behavior are expected, and this is not just a game. In most teams, people expect to see people treated fairly, and that doesn't always mean with leniency. I know one manager who agonized for days whether to fire someone. When he did, all the other team members came to him and thanked him for getting rid of a passenger who just didn't share the standards of the rest of the team.

I remember one time a sales executive who was told to leave a customer's site. The customer told the sales VP that this person should be kept well away – he would never be welcomed back. Was this because of actual objectionable behavior, or simply a serious conflict of personalities. It's sometimes difficult to say, but since a prime responsibility of any sales person is to build a great relationship with the customer, I tend to think that if things go so badly wrong, the sales person must be out of line somewhere. Anyway on this occasion the VP reassigned the offender to another account. The 'stick' was that he kept the same quota, but the new account was much smaller and would generate much less revenue. In other words, he lost hard cash. At the same time he was also told clearly that if a similar incident happened again, he would be fired.

In situations like this, people will always have differences of opinion over whether the penalty was too harsh or too lenient. Should we have used a bigger stick or a smaller one? This will always come down to the personal judgment of the line manager responsible, and we should usually respect the judgment of the person on the spot. The actual decision is probably less important than the way it is handled. If the decision is reached in knowledge of all the knowable facts, if the situation is handled honestly, cleanly, quickly and with clarity, then the sales manager has done a decent job.

In this case there was no doubt that a recurrence would end in termination. The threat of being fired – 'the big stick' – worked in this case, which is how it's supposed to be. The stick is primarily a deterrent.

Sometimes it doesn't work as a deterrent, and then it has to be used, so that others know that it's a real solid stick; not one made of polystyrene. From time to time, sales people do have to be fired for lack of performance. But a good leader/manager will know for sure that the problem is due to incompetence or dishonesty. And incompetent or dishonest people have to go, there should be no doubt about that. But there is no point in sacking a competent person – the replacement is just as likely to fail if the underlying reasons for lack of success are not fixed.

If firing someone is up for consideration, there are three principles that need to be remembered:

- People should only be fired for incompetence or dishonesty or behavior that clearly does not fit in with the values of the company.

- The definition of what constitutes sackable behavior should be understood by everyone from the day they start in the job, and should not be changed every now and then by any manager on a whim.

- If someone has to be sacked, a manager should make the decision, face up to it and do it quickly and cleanly.

'Letting someone go', as people so delicately put it these days, is pretty hard when the reason is a drop in business activity, or a company reorganization, or because someone hasn't met budget. I find that difficult to do, as do most managers.

But if someone has behaved badly towards a customer or a colleague, if someone has been dishonest or corrupt, then firing someone isn't so hard. And it's certainly easier to live with the consequences of firing someone for good reason, than it is to live with the consequences of failing to fire someone when you should have.

The Umbrella, the Oilcan and the Pressure Gauge

For many people, sales management is mainly about incentives and punishment: carrots and sticks.

Of course, carrots and sticks are important implements for the well-equipped sales manager. Carrots encourage people to do more of what you want them to do. Sticks discourage people from doing things you don't want them to do. But a good manager has more to offer than these crude tools. Using only sticks and carrots is like driving a car using only the gas pedal and the brake. What about the steering wheel, direction indicators and windscreen wipers? Maybe you need to put in gas now and again too.

In my toolkit, I always like to have a selection of carrots and sticks. But there's other things in my box: for example, an umbrella, an oilcan, and a pressure gauge.

I use an umbrella to shelter my team from some of the unnecessary encumbrances that all companies tend to generate. For example...

Too much paperwork? Protect your team from the rain of paper. I negotiate with the bureaucrats to eliminate unnecessary stuff and to simplify the really important documentation. I also look for ways to spend my budget on sensible amounts of admin support to make sure the important paperwork is done on time and correctly. If I can transfer a few hours a week of form-filling and reporting from a highly paid sales rep to a more modestly paid administrative assistant then I'll do it: it's a bargain. This gives reps the chance to spend more time with customers, which is why I recruited them in the first place.

For example, in some companies, sales people are expected to credit-check their own clients. Even in today's automated age, thorough credit checking can be time consuming. Better to give the job to a specialist at a desk than divert a sales person from building relationships and closing deals. This also avoids offering sales people the temptation to skip some of the details... after all, if there's a big deal on the table, a little risk should be acceptable, shouldn't it? Maybe, but that shouldn't be a decision made by the sales person alone.

Too many staff meetings? I work with other departments to ensure that my team members only attend staff meetings where they can either obtain real value or contribute real value. Even then, I always question the need for everyone to attend. Often one or two people can provide enough useful input, rather than taking everyone off the road.

Here's a dramatic example of a boss stepping in to help people make meetings more productive and relevant. A friend of mine (founder and CEO of the company) mandated that meetings should be held in a conference room with no chairs. Penboards and flipcharts, but no chairs. In his company meetings started and ended on time – and people focused on addressing the real issues so they could get back to somewhere more comfortable. This might not work everywhere, but this manager came up with a novel way of protecting his people from time wasting meetings. They appreciated that, and responded well.

If the company comes up with a compensation formula that would lead to my team being assigned impossible budgets, then I use my umbrella to protect them from that: I negotiate with the company for realistic targets, and for compensation rules that will motivate the team to be successful (instead of motivating them to look somewhere else for a job with better carrots).

I use the oilcan to lubricate the machinery of the company for my team members. This means always looking for ways for the company to do things better in support of our sales efforts. I take an active interest in the way our products and services are marketed and advertised, and what sort of brochure-ware and demos are available to my team: all of this makes the path to a successful sale smoother and straighter. My oilcan approach extends to working with the delivery managers and their teams to make sure that implementation and post-sales support works well: if it doesn't, that inevitably means more effort and anxiety for my team.

Wielding an oilcan also needs me to be willing and able and available to step in to participate in a customer meeting or event when one of my team needs me. And lubricating the machinery extends to team members themselves: coaching my reps and making sure they get the right training.

Sounds obvious so far, doesn't it? Protect your people from a deluge of unnecessary corporate non-work. Oil the machinery so people can do the job better.

In reality, what needs to be done is often far from obvious. Many managers are so embedded in the company thought process that it is difficult for them to extract their thought processes from the mire. "Business as usual" is the way that most people do business, usually.

To make a real difference, you need to actively and consciously seek paths for improvement. One way of doing this is to regularly have team discussions and one-on-one discussions with your people that focus on these topics:

- What's getting in the way of you doing your job? If I can help to shelter you from unnecessary company bureaucracy, then I'll do it.

- What roadblocks and issues are stopping you closing deals? How are the company policies restricting you and taking time away from selling? If there's anything I can do to help you do your job better, then I'll do it.

Ask for suggestions. Your team will come up with some novel ideas. Be prepared to consider them all, even the silly ideas, like moving the chairs out of the conference rooms. Sometimes weird ideas work.

Pressure can be good. You need just the right amount of air pressure in your car tires: too little or too much and you lose control or risk a blowout.

Pressure cookers are used for cooking large quantities of food in the food processing industry.[68] By the application of a modest amount of steam pressure, food will cook more thoroughly and more quickly, while using less energy. But – apply too much pressure for too long, and you end up with mush.

There is a type of sales manager out there who understands that some pressure can be useful, but assumes that if a little is good then a lot must be better. As a result, this kind of klink can turn a good wholesome sales team into limp vegetables.

The message: keep your eye on the pressure gauge.

I can draw plenty of examples from my career in sales, but you may already be familiar with one of the best examples around: the character Blake played by Alec Baldwin in the classic movie Glengarry Glen Ross.[69] OK, so this is fiction, and something of an exaggeration, but not much.

Blake is brought in as a hotshot sales manager to stir an unsuccessful sales team into action. He starts off with an astonishing tirade, in which he insults and humiliates them all. He lets them know how much he despises them: "Put that coffee down. Coffee is for closers only." He tells them they are all fired, and they have just one

---

[68] I remember when pressure cookers used to be fashionable in homes, round about the time that everyone had fondue sets too.

[69] *Glengarry Glenross* (New Line Cinema, 1992). Screenplay by David Mamet, directed by James Foley. Starring Al Pacino, Jack Lemmon, Ed Harris, Alan Arkin, Kevin Spacey and Alec Baldwin. The 2002 DVD from Artisan Entertainment contains some thought-provoking extra features about real-life sales.

month to earn their jobs back. Then he tells them about the new rules for this month's sales contest. "First prize is a Cadillac Eldorado. Anybody want to see second prize? Second prize is a set of steak knives. Third prize is you're fired." Blake genuinely despises the people in his team because they are losers, and he finds many colorful and graphic ways of pointing that out to them. Blake's mantra is A.B.C. – Always Be Closing.

The problem with Blake is not that he doesn't know about selling – he is successful as a salesman in his own right, and ostentatiously boasts about his success. The problem is that he has no idea how much pressure on a team is enough to be effective, and where to stop to avoid the pressure becoming counterproductive.

Blake doesn't feel any need to take into account the quality of leads available, or whether the product (real estate) is actually sellable in any honest way. And clearly he doesn't care if there are casualties on the way, or the way in which deals are closed, as long as the deals are closed.

Blake's management style is one-dimensional, with psychological pressure the only real tool in his management toolbox.

In the movie the results of the unrelenting pressure are disastrous. In real life different types of pain and suffering may occur.

Sales people need to be robust characters. You shouldn't be in sales unless you can take some direct criticism and even some insults, from managers as well as clients. And some people may be impervious even to the ripe language and constant browbeating from a Blake-like character.

Applying constant excessive pressure is a pointless way of running a sales team. Some people will simply ignore tirades, and get on with their jobs as best they can. That's what I always tried to do when confronted by that sort of approach. ("Stu, don't just stand there - sell something.") I have seen others lose

> *Applying constant excessive pressure is a pointless way of running a sales team.*

confidence, panic, and fall into the trap of pushing for closure by misleading customers, thus demolishing any chance of building the sort of relationship on which ongoing future sales depend.

The best a high-pressure klink can hope for is that the team will be tough enough to keep going, despite the tirades and the petty rules. More likely, the wrong sort of pressure will only result in high turnover of sales reps and steadily declining sales.

What are the sort of things that we expect intelligent leader/managers to do, instead of browbeating employees and making threats? There's really just one thing: good managers will always look beneath the surface for the real reasons for poor performance, and then act intelligently and firmly to fix the problem.

The incompetence or lack of hard work of an individual sales rep may sometimes turn out to be the real problem, which can then be addressed. But often, poor performance is influenced by multiple other factors including, for example:

- Ineffective product marketing – no (or weak) demand creation programs;
- Unattractive sales material;
- A lead generation process that values quantity over quality;
- Flawed market penetration strategy, no special support for winning new customers;
- Inadequate training on products and services, or on product related selling techniques;
- Compensating people for selling the wrong things;
- Products and services that have acquired a poor reputation in the market place;
- Uncompetitive price/performance;
- Poor support and follow-up from other departments (late delivery, invoicing errors, poor technical support, and so on);
- Too few sales people trying to cover too many customers – or too many trying to sell to a non-existent customer base.

Football coaches are not noted for the delicacy of their language, or for restraint in pointing out defects in a player's performance. But a good coach doesn't just shout. A good coach coaches, by telling people exactly what they're doing wrong, helping players to improve their techniques, advising on exercise programs and diets, ensuring good equipment is available and schooling everyone in game plays. Good coaches also work very hard to create team spirit and a constant positive attitude that engenders success. When the team is dispirited a good coach finds some way to motivate the players again. They do all this on a platform of credibility because they know and love the game. A loudmouth bully will never be a really successful coach.

It's the same in sales. I once received an e-mail message from a manager (one with distinct klink leanings) that contained this pronouncement: "There are absolutely no excuses for missing the forecast by more than 10%. If this continues we will have to re-evaluate the size of our sales team. There is no room for failure and lack of discipline on our team!"

This is mild stuff compared with Blake – no swear words for example.

But this manager had no idea why we were failing to achieve our forecasts. If some people had simply not been trying hard enough, holding the sword of potential dismissal over our heads might have woken some people up. But in fact, there were underlying multiple problems, including: unrealistic forecasts that had not been based on an objective assessment of sales potential; too much effort directed to winning new accounts, not enough effort on building relationships with existing customers; and high staff turnover.

People don't like being threatened and hardly ever improve their performance just because they are scared. Not unless a leader can back up the loud noises with something helpful.

Pressure applied in the right way can be a tremendous motivator. Too bad that klinks know all about pressure, but nothing about the right way. Bill Parcells, head coach of the Dallas Cowboys had a reputation for forthright speaking. "The only way to change people is to tell them in the clearest possible terms what they're doing wrong. And if they don't want to listen, they don't belong on the team." Yes, that's pressure all right.

But Parcells also says "Holding frank, one-on-one conversations with every member of the organization is essential to success. It allows me to ask each player for his support in helping the team achieve its goals, and it allows me to explain exactly what I expect from him... In the end I've found that people like the direct approach. I have many players come back to me ten years later and thank me for putting the pressure on them. They say what they remember most about me is one line: 'I think you are better than you think you are.'" [70]

Sales people don't need managers just to tell them they're failing. They need managers to help them be successful. A bullying sales manager shouts about failure all the time, without providing any help to improve, and so inevitably drives the team into further declines in performance. These are the people who apply so much

> *Sales people don't need managers just to tell them they're failing. They need managers to help them be successful.*

pressure, they cause the team to burst at the seams. And these are the people who are always the last to understand that they are the cause of the blowout.

---

[70] Bill Parcells, *The Tough Work of Turning Around a Team,* Harvard Business Review, Nov/Dec 2000.

Predicting the Future

It sometimes seems that an essential tool for a sales manager, alongside the usual laptop, PDA and cell phone, should be a crystal ball. I'll buy one as soon as the technology is mature.

Sales managers seem to spend a lot of their time predicting the future. This is not easy. Yogi Berra put in nicely: "Predictions are hard, especially about the future."

The sequence starts when you have to work with the gurus in marketing and finance to build revenue forecasts for the next year or three. Then those forecasts are used to create targets for the sales teams and for individuals. Then as you work the deals, you and your team are expected to provide 'accurate' predictions of success for each prospect.

Annual forecasts are essential for the smooth operation of any company. The forecasting process is not there simply to keep those marketing people in a job and prevent you and your team hitting the streets to make some sales.

The real purpose of annual sales forecasting is quite simple. Forecasts are used to make an assessment of revenues and the associated cost streams so that the financial people can make sure the company is being run prudently, and has the financial resources to stay in business and grow. Forecasts are also used to make sure that delivery resources (products and people) are lined up to meet customers' expected demand.

Getting the forecast 'right' is something of a balancing act, in every business. In an ideal world, forecasts would be developed purely for the purpose of business planning. Realism, objectivity and accuracy should be paramount. In our less than ideal world there are incentives to tweak these figures for various reasons.

At the corporate level, revenue forecasts that are realistic but too low can depress the stock price, so there is a temptation to push them up. On the other hand a forecast that is high, but turns out not to be achieved, will probably have an even bigger impact on the stock price downstream.

When 'bottom up' figures are used to develop the annual forecasts, there are other conflicts that may reduce the integrity of the forecasts.

Some sales executives like to have inflated forecasts that will result in sales budgets being set that 'stretch' the sales teams. Stretching is

230

good, but if the forecasts are too inflated, the company could end up with products on the shelves and fulfillment people sitting around idle.

If executives insist on stretching too much, lower down the organization, when sales teams are asked to submit their 'realistic' forecasts for the year, then they will always provide a low estimate in and effort to compensate for the inflation that will take place higher up!

However if the figures remain too low, then the company may not fund the necessary resources to deliver. This can result in longer delivery lead times and maybe customer due dates missed. All of that makes it more difficult to sell!

What does all this mean for the sales manager? In my opinion, playing around with the numbers is self-defeating. Ultimately, the interest of the sales people, sales managers, executives and the company need to be aligned. And this means that everyone at all levels needs to start off by making annual revenue forecasts as realistically accurate as possible.

Sales targets are not forecasts. Targets are a separate management tool, used for a different purpose – the motivation and rewarding of the sales team.

To many people, targets and forecasts are interchangeable. This is a flawed approach, which can have negative impacts on both the business planning process (which needs realistic forecasts) and the sales compensation process (which needs stretching targets). The aim of forecasting is to achieve accuracy. The aim of targeting is to improve performance.

Once forecasts have been established, based on a realistic assessment, then the company can set sales targets (budgets)[71] based on the forecasts. But this is not just a simple exercise of adding a fixed percentage every time. The company needs to take into account how much production/delivery capability will be available. If the forecasts are achieved will there be a capacity shortfall or will there be unused capacity? This analysis, coupled with decisions on future investment, opportunities in new markets, and customers' expected spending patterns, may all influence the targets set for sales teams.

Then those targets need to be linked to compensation schemes that will drive sales of the right products to the right customers in the right amounts. The complexity of getting this balance right is challenging, and I can understand why compensation schemes are getting more complex. On the other hand, some compensation plans

---

[71] Depending on the company you work for, sales target = budget = quota = goal.

are definitely too clever for their own good, and can result in de-motivating sales people while failing to achieve the hoped-for revenue figures.[72]

Annual forecasts and sales budgets are not the end of the story. Our crystal ball is also needed for the reporting of prospects in the pipeline. The purpose of this exercise is principally to ensure that the short term planning for delivery resources and product manufacturing are finely tuned in the most economical way. Some executives also use these re-forecasts to encourage the sales teams to greater things: if they predict sales less than the original forecast, then they can't be trying hard enough; if sales look likely to be greater than the original forecast, then clearly their original projections were padded, which is always a good excuse for changing the commission structure yet again.

Once again, the only real defense is to predict the deals that are going to be closed as objectively as possible. It seems that it is difficult for sales reps to be objective, and so one of the jobs of the sales manager is to sanity-check success probabilities and revenue forecasts before they go into the corporate number machine.

The main thing to watch out for is unrealistically high assessment of the probability of success. For example, one of your sales people has just made a first visit to a new prospect. The customer said that they had already talked to four competitors and that they have no preference for any one supplier – yet. All the customer is prepared to say is that the money for the deal is in their budget and they are mandated to make a decision within six months. The sales rep seems to be feeling pretty good about the meeting: they smiled a lot and said complementary things about your product and your company.

In my experience, most sales reps would enthusiastically set the probability of success in this case at between 40% and 50%, for no obvious reason other than it feels good. A more realistic assessment would be around 20%, and you need to make sure some realism is injected into the prediction.

Suppose one of the competitors drops out. This would be really encouraging to most reps, who would likely give their prediction a boost. Right. The probability shoots all the way up to 25%.

Some companies ask their sales people to remove from the forecast all prospects with probabilities less than 30%. This is a realistically conservative approach, which helps to boost the likelihood of the consolidated forecast being exceeded. Companies do this because on balance, they would rather deal with the problem of

---

[72] See 'Financial Carrots' earlier in this Chapter.

having more business than expected, than deal with the problems of having less.

Yet some klinks interpret the "nothing less than 30%" rule to mean that any prospect below 30% should be marked up to at least 31%. (Otherwise you can't include it, can you?) This is a sure fire way of setting the sales team and the company up for failure. Don't do this.

Another thing to watch out for is the phasing of revenue forecasts for complex sales, using realistic lead times. Just because it's in the pipeline forecast, doesn't mean that all the revenue can be recognized next month. In fact revenues may be spread over several quarters. Forecasts should be linked to company revenue accounting rules to avoid misrepresentation, or possibly prison.

I really have only one over-riding recommendation to make concerning predicting the future. That is to recognize that ultimately it makes sense for the company and everyone in it to focus on reality and reasonable expectations and not to play games with the numbers.

Unfortunately some companies define the rules in such a way as to encourage executives and managers to deceive themselves and others. Rewarding people for fictional figures is no way to deliver long-term business success.

We have all seen this in action. Initial forecasts are too low for the company's purposes, so the people who build the forecasts are told to be more imaginative and bullish. Consequently the forecasts are inflated. Inflated forecasts lead to inflated targets. Actual revenues start to fall behind the forecasts. While earlier on the problem was poor forecasting, it's now seen as poor performance. The real problem is a lack of objectivity at all stages of the process.

As a manager in the middle of all this, you may not be able to change the fundamentals of your company, but at least you can attempt to inject some integrity and sanity into your part of it. It has to start somewhere.

The Danger of Attention Surfeit Syndrome

In business, attention to detail is very important, and someone must be paid to make sure things are done right at the detailed level. The 'big picture' is also important and most companies pay people to develop strategy and have big ideas. Most management jobs involve a balance of detail and big picture work, and a competent manager knows how to get the balance right.

This chapter is about a type of klink behavior that involves an obsessional focus on detail, coupled with an unwillingness to trust others to handle the details.

Most of you have probably heard of ADD - Attention Deficit Disorder. This is a problem for increasing numbers of children: they find it difficult to focus on any one thing, their attention is always wandering, they become passive and unproductive, and this impedes their ability to learn and become successful students.

Now I'd like to introduce you to Attention Surfeit Syndrome - ASS. This is a problem for increasing numbers of klinks in sales management: they find it essential to focus on the details of everything, their attentiveness to minor details is obsessive, they become proactive to the point of meddlesomeness, and this impedes their ability to manage a team and become successful leaders.

ASS is quite common. Some people use the term 'micro-management' for this syndrome. Other people call it 'getting in the way of people who are trying to accomplish something useful'.

The klink who exhibits Attention Surfeit Syndrome risks being a double failure: as a manager, the ASS klink gets in the way and stops sales people doing a good job; as a leader, the ASS klink fails to identify trends, set direction and create motivation.

How do we recognize a klink with an ASS problem? There are a number of symptoms to watch out for.

- An excessive need to be supplied with data.

- A need to know where everyone in the team is, and what they are doing all the time.

- A fear of allowing people to use their judgment, accompanied by the imposition of an ever-lengthening list of rules covering what to do in every imaginable situation.

- Is always fully informed about poor results, but knows nothing about the causes or possible solutions. .

Some of the favorite questions of this type of klink are: "Where are you?" "What are you doing?" "What have you been doing?" "What are you going to do next?" and "Why is your report late?"

Questions you will hardly ever hear are: "How can I help you close this deal?" "What do you think about…?"

I remember working (briefly) for a Sales VP who seemed to think he had been recruited as a babysitter, not as a team leader. He had never sold anything in his life (except maybe his soul). He saw his role in the business as simply to implement a range of controls and monitoring that someone else had decided must be good for the company. He didn't try to create a successful sales team – no attempt to lead, motivate, coach or provide active support. He decided that if he gathered the numbers the company was asking for, no one could accuse him of not doing his job.

As a result, everyone in the team had to monitor and revise forecasts every single week – even though sales cycles could last well over a year. We had to write up every visit, and log every contact and every detail of every conversation in the prospect database. Each rep had to clock up a minimum number of cold calls every week – no matter how fruitless they knew they were going to be. Our klink manager made it very clear that our judgment was less important than putting checks in the boxes.

His only attempt to motivate us was to repeat the formula: "You perform, we pay, otherwise you're out of here". You can imagine the reaction of the sales team, a group of well-seasoned reps: "Oh really? We have to *sell* something? We didn't realize that. Thanks for the helpful advice."

> *His only attempt to motivate us was to repeat the formula: "You perform, we pay, otherwise you're out of here.*

Don't get me wrong – filing reports, process discipline, standards and measurement are all important. What upsets and infuriates sales team is the waste of everyone's time and the unproductive stress caused by obsessive and excessive emphasis on data collection.

If a Sales VP doesn't really understand the business, it's not surprising that they'll do whatever the company says to make it look as if they're actually doing something useful. Demanding reports, compiling numbers and plotting charts can be useful. For the ASS klink it becomes displacement activity.

When they aren't chasing reps down for more and more reports, this sort of klink is usually checking up on your movements. This type of manager assumes everyone else is lazy, unmotivated, and can't be trusted.

This sort of behavior reminds me of an episode from the BBC comedy show *Fawlty Towers*[73] in which Basil has been ordered by his wife Sybil to mount a moose's head on the wall before she returns from her trip out of town. Basil tries very hard to get the job done, even though he has a lot of other things on his mind. Every time he is close to getting the moose in place, precariously balanced up a ladder with a large moose head and a hammer, the phone rings and he has to stop work. It is – of course – Sybil asking Basil if he's installed the moose's head yet.

Many years ago, I worked with a manager who would ask me, and everyone else in the team, *every day* what sales calls we planned to make. At the end of the day he would ask me how the calls went, what I was going to do next, and when I was going to move my butt and get it done. (And, by the way Stu, don't forget to send in your written report.)

One day, at the end of a really tough week, I finished my calls (and my reports) and left the office at 4pm on Friday afternoon to travel to pick up my kids at their grandparents' house, about ninety miles away.

About half way there my manager called and asked "Where are you now?" "I'm on Highway 175 half way to Athens, Texas." He exploded: "What are you doing there this time of day? You're cheating the company!"

I told him as calmly as I could that I was picking up my kids, I hadn't seen them in two weeks, and I was trying to beat the rush hour traffic.

I really thought I was going to be fired. I'm not the type to cheat the company, or anyone else. But of course he didn't know that, or couldn't believe it. (It turned out that he was just as worried as I was about being fired, and with good cause. Quite soon, he was moved on, and I wasn't.)

When a manager tells everyone in a sales team, in effect, that they must not exercise judgment, there is a real chance that people in the sales team will – guess what? – stop using their judgment. They

---

[73] *Fawlty Towers* (BBC, 1975). Written by John Cleese and Connie Booth. Sybil (played by Prunella Scales) is a something of a control freak, but Basil (played by John Cleese) is even more inept as a manager. Every episode contains a string of examples of clueless management, and some episodes have been used for illustration in management training courses.

will always have an excuse for poor results as long as they stick to the rules their boss has set. An atmosphere like this can be seriously de-motivating. A de-motivated team starts to perform less well. And the typical klink will respond to the drop in performance with even more of the wrong medicine, generating a further decline, or even a plummet.

Here is an example of that, an extract from an actual e-mail message sent out by an Attention Surfeit Syndrome klink, who was starting to panic as his team started to fall apart:

It has come to my attention that we are significantly below our forecast for the quarter. As of tomorrow I would like a daily status of the number of phone calls you are making, number of face to face meetings with a minimum of 10 per week with your clients, and a complete plan on how you plan to close each piece of business you have forecasted by this Friday.

Excessive micro-management gets in the way. But that's only half of the problem with this type of obsessive behavior.

While these people are spending time trying to control everything their team does, frantically issuing instructions and pulling strings as if as if they were in charge of a puppet show, they are failing to spend time performing their real duties as managers and leaders.

When a problem emerges, they don't work with the team to try to discover the underlying causes. They simply instruct people to make it better.

When a specific opportunity is lost to a competitor, or when a sales rep's performance is sub-standard, they don't try to take into account whether the rep has been properly trained, whether there are some underlying problems with leads or internal to accounts, whether some executive support will help. They assume that the rep is lazy or incompetent or both.

If the performance of a whole team is disappointing, they make no effort to assess what is going on in the light of the economic environment, industry changes, competitive activity or product marketing. They assume that the whole team has somehow become lazy or incompetent or both.

Managers have a wide range of responsibilities, and need a wide range of skills to do their job properly. A manager who behaves as if managing is about nothing other than checking up on indolent or untrustworthy employees is not managing effectively. Someone should check up on people like that.

Finale:
Setting a Good Example

An executive I know used to regularly remind his team of sales managers of the following: "Here's the good news, your team members actually notice what you do... Here's the bad news, your team members *really* notice what you do."

As a sales team manager, you are always on show for your team. People are often surprised that their actions can influence others - in positive ways and in negative ways.

Whether you realize it or not, your team members notice what you say and how you act. They observe your actions and attitudes, and learn something from them. You have a choice: you can 'walk your talk' and behave exactly in ways you expect your team members to behave. Or not. Unfortunately it seems that bad habits are easier to transfer than good habits.

> *Whether you realize it or not, your team members notice what you say and how you act.*

Throughout this book, we discuss many things that sales managers should do to build successful teams. If I had to choose just one instruction to pass on to sales mangers, out of all those in the book, here it is:

Set a good example.

Here is a short list of things you can regularly do to influence your team positively.

Have a positive attitude. If you want to motivate your team be motivated yourself. Work at being optimistic, persistent, enthusiastic, resilient and affable. If some days, you don't feel like it, act the part, and you'll find, amazingly that you'll feel better as you do it. The human mind is an amazing piece of work.

Continue to learn. Show your team that learning never ends. When you find out something interesting and new, tell everyone about it, and make them as enthusiastic as you are to acquire and build new skills. Become better informed about your industry, your products and your customers, and pass your new knowledge on. When someone in your team brings something new to your attention, say thanks!

Build great relationships. Work at relationships, just as much as you expect your team members to. Network, pass on contacts to your team, expect them to do the same. Nurture your relationships, and show your team the results.

Think things through, *then* **act.** Demonstrate the value of decisions based on rational thought and a consideration of all the angles. Show them that acting on intelligent decisions works better than either endless thought with no action, or immediate action uninformed by any thought process.

Manage effectively. A well-led team operates more effectively than a disorganized team, and is more successful. At the same time, you provide both structure and motivation for your team members, and they learn to like it.

Role models are *so* important. I have been very much influenced by some excellent leaders in my business life – for example Bobby Thomas and Don Jones, who are mentioned in earlier chapters. I have been truly fortunate to have been able to work with leaders of this caliber: people of integrity, energy and talent.

But the reality is that not every manager sets a good example. If the managers in a company have a contemptuous attitude towards customers, treating them as merely 'suckers' who provide a source of income, sales people will eventually lose respect for customers too. If managers try to rip off their customers by adding on hidden extras and shirking responsibility by inserting devious fine print in contract, sales people will pick up on that attitude and play that game too.

If managers consistently try to deceive stockholders by hiding or distorting the facts, or short-change employees by being unfair in their management practices and compensation plans, then sales people will quickly come to understand the true values of the company and will respond accordingly. Some people will say "I can't work here" and move on. But others will stay around and focus their efforts on getting as much out of the company as they can, for as little effort as possible.

In my view, every sales manager and executive in every company needs to bear in mind that their behavior influences the behavior of others in the company, including sales people. Poor performance usually starts at the top, and trickles down the company.

Equally, leaders with high standards of ethics, who value talent and intelligent behavior, and who strive for honest success, will sow the seeds of that attitude throughout the company.

It's been my experience over many years that customers always prefer to deal with people who they can trust. They feel happier and more confident when they do so. It is human nature to feel like that. It may seem to be a long slow process, but ultimately that indispensable element of human nature means that companies that consistently display integrity, competence and value, will grow and prosper.

As a sales manager, you must be part of that process. Generate trust, avoid klinkishness, be SMART, and become a role model for your team.

Long ago, when I was a clueless new sales person, my clueless manager sent me out to visit customers, with no preparation, no skills and no support. I soon realized that manager was a klink.

But you will be a different type of sales manager: a SMART sales manager. Your team will be skilled and motivated. They will have a good attitude to the job and to their customers. They will build relationships that lead to business success. And, thanks to you, they will apply some intelligent thought to the whole sales process. That means that if you ever feel it's necessary to say to your team *"Don't Just Stand There – Sell Something"*, they'll know exactly what to do.

The End

So you've made it to the end of the book! If you have any comments, criticisms or praise please feel free to get in touch. You can write to me c/o AuthorHouse, or contact me through my web sites at: http://competitive-excellence.com and http://dontjuststandthere.com.

Printed in the United States
30876LVS00004B/154-378

9 781418 496630